Summer *in a* Glass

The Coming of Age of Winemaking in the Finger Lakes

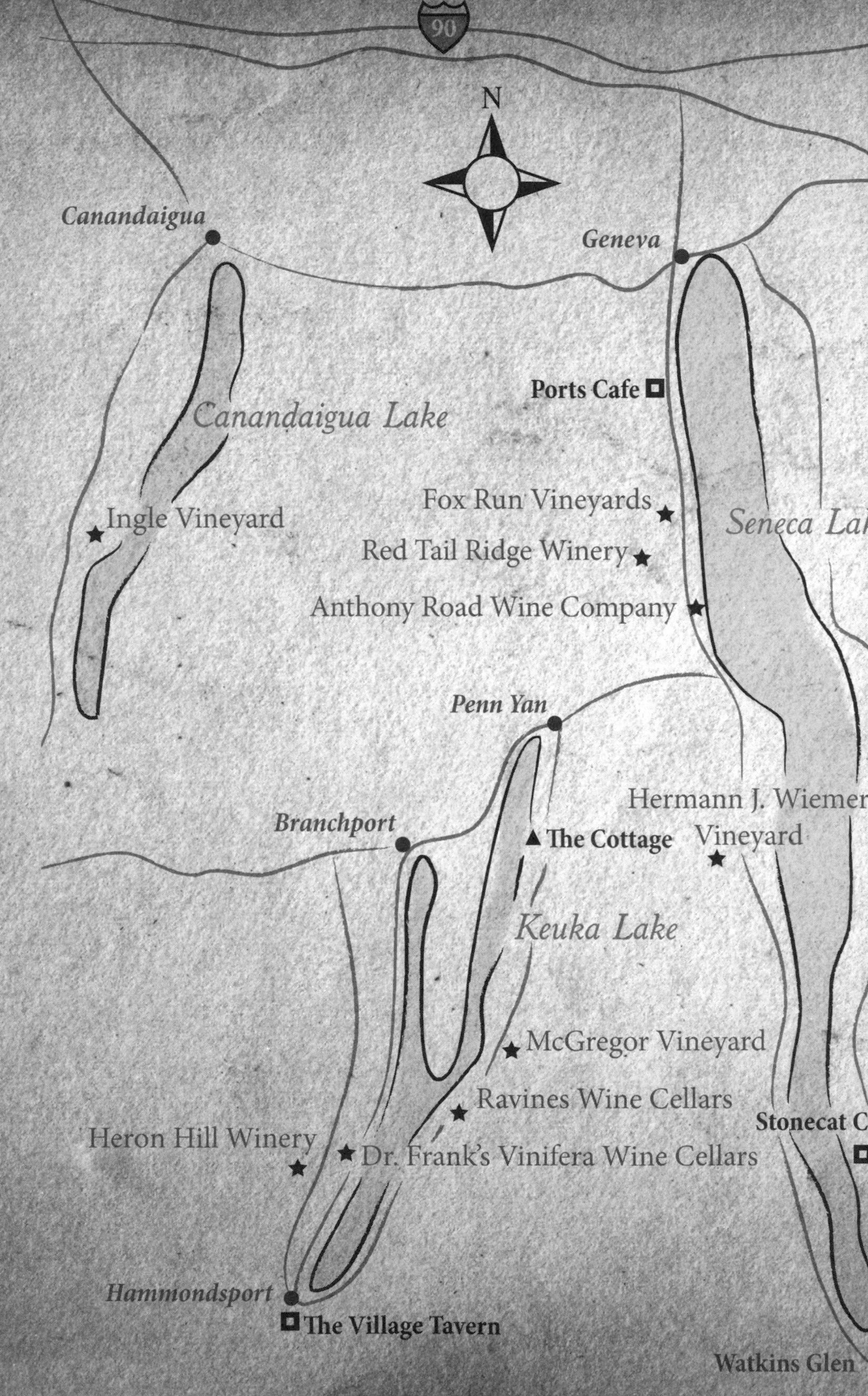
90
N
Canandaigua
Geneva
Ports Cafe
Canandaigua Lake
Fox Run Vineyards
Ingle Vineyard
Seneca Lak
Red Tail Ridge Winery
Anthony Road Wine Company
Penn Yan
Hermann J. Wiemer
Vineyard
Branchport
The Cottage
Keuka Lake
McGregor Vineyard
Ravines Wine Cellars
Stonecat C
Heron Hill Winery
Dr. Frank's Vinifera Wine Cellars
Hammondsport
The Village Tavern
Watkins Glen

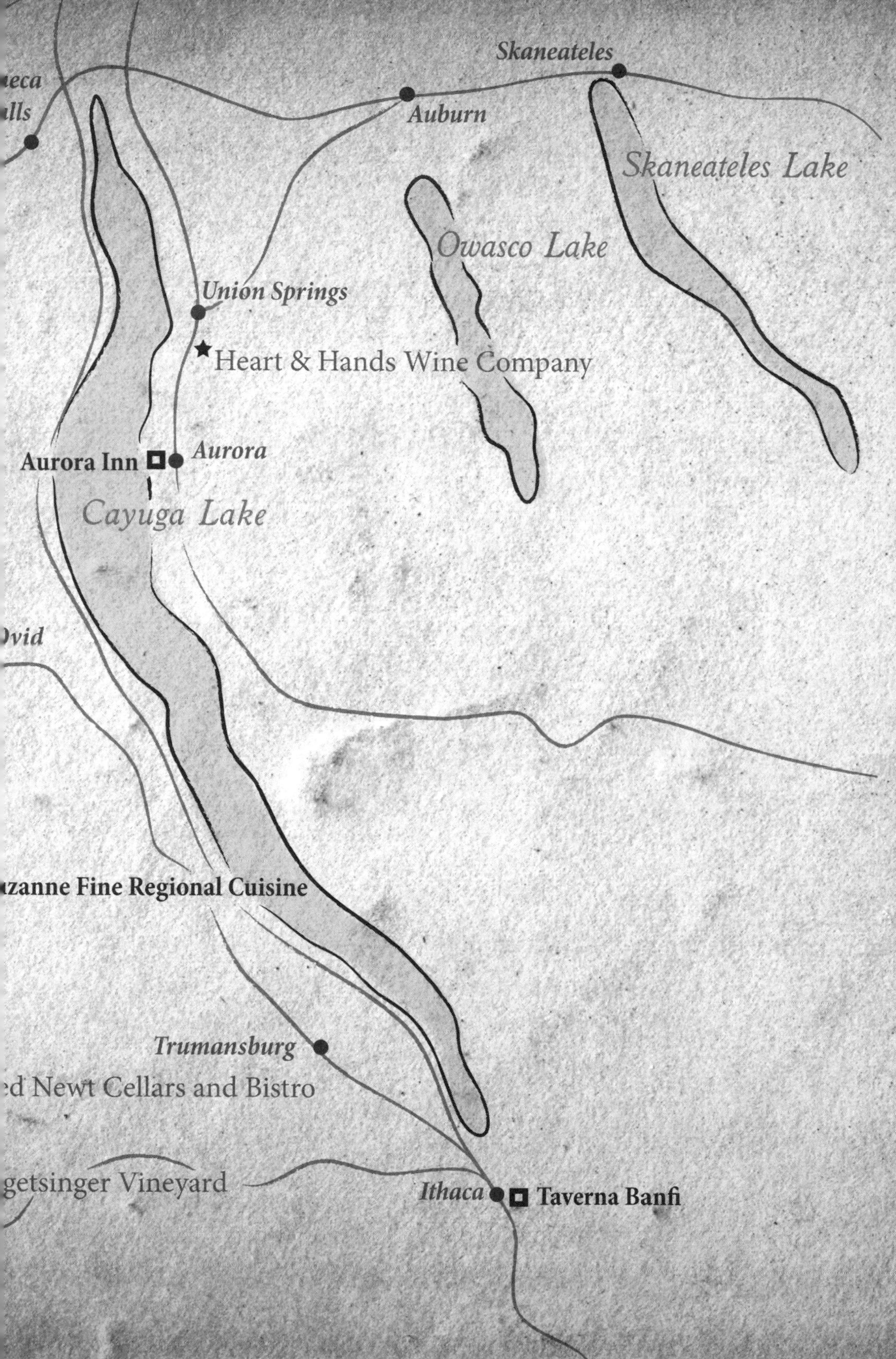
eca
lls
Skaneateles
Auburn
Skaneateles Lake
Owasco Lake
Union Springs
Heart & Hands Wine Company
Aurora Inn
Aurora
Cayuga Lake
Ovid
zanne Fine Regional Cuisine
Trumansburg
ed Newt Cellars and Bistro
getsinger Vineyard
Ithaca
Taverna Banfi

Summer *in a* Glass

THE COMING OF AGE OF WINEMAKING IN THE FINGER LAKES

by Evan Dawson

Foreword by James Molesworth

STERLING EPICURE
New York

For Sgt. Hall
Thanks for changing my life and setting
me on a path to the Finger Lakes.

An Imprint of Sterling Publishing
387 Park Avenue South
New York, NY 10016

STERLING EPICURE is a trademark of Sterling Publishing Co., Inc.
The distinctive Sterling logo is a registered trademark of Sterling Publishing Co., Inc.

ISBN 978-1-4027-7825-4 (hardcover)
ISBN 978-1-4027-8962-5 (ebook)
ISBN 978-1-4027-9710-1 (paperback)

Distributed in Canada by Sterling Publishing
c/o Canadian Manda Group, 165 Dufferin Street
Toronto, Ontario, Canada M6K 3H6
Distributed in the United Kingdom by GMC Distribution Services
Castle Place, 166 High Street, Lewes, East Sussex, England BN7 1XU
Distributed in Australia by Capricorn Link (Australia) Pty. Ltd.
P.O. Box 704, Windsor, NSW 2756, Australia

Endpaper map by Joanna Purdy
Chapter opening photos by Morgan Dawson Photography/
www.morgandawson.com

For information about custom editions, special sales, and premium and corporate purchases, please contact Sterling Special Sales at 800-805-5489 or specialsales@sterlingpublishing.com.

Manufactured in the United States of America

2 4 6 8 10 9 7 5 3 1

www.sterlingpublishing.com

Contents

Foreword

Wine writing can be easy. Many who call themselves "wine writers" are often offered press junkets to travel to well-known regions, during which time they easily coast along while penning positive prose. This, however, tends to do little to truly enlighten the reader about what is really happening on the ground or behind the scenes.

The hard work is when a writer takes his or her own time, fueled by a unique passion for a less-heralded region, to delve deep into the subject matter before presenting the reader with a story. And it's when that story successfully conveys the everyday drama and struggle that goes into growing grapes and getting a wine into the bottle that someone can really be called a "wine writer." It's an important distinction to be made, because the typical consumer doesn't see or even think of all that is entailed in getting grapes turned into wine when they grab a bottle off their retailer's shelf. It's up to the wine writers to convey this story—and only a few do it well.

Here, Evan Dawson gives you the back story of an emerging, still unheralded region—the Finger Lakes of upstate New York. Born of a volume-first, quality-second (if at all) industry that crashed and burned a generation ago, the Finger Lakes today is trying to retool itself so that it can compete on the world stage. A handful of winemakers are trying to change the region's image by changing the way they work, right down to changing the very grapes they grow. And they're doing all of this without the major outside investments that powered the growth and development of big-name wine regions like Napa Valley and Bordeaux.

But while the Finger Lakes wine industry is still a cottage industry, located in a cold and remote corner of New York State, it doesn't lack for warm and passionate people. From Sam Argetsinger, an Iroquois-speaking former lumberjack who was drawn out of the forest by the duty to keep his family's vineyard going, to transplanted European winemakers Morten Hallgren and Johannes Reinhardt, who were lured by the area's frontierlike feel, which offered an escape from the stifling rules of tradition, from the multigenerational history of the renowned Dr. Konstantin Frank winery to the tale of the young startup winery Heart & Hands of Tom and Susan Higgins, Dawson tells stories that will have you wondering, *Will they make it?* right through to the end.

Yes, Dawson prefers to tell the back story—detailing winemaker passions and back-room dramas that are as much a part of making the wine as the grapes themselves. But he tells these stories in a way that seasoned wine geeks and novices alike will appreciate. It's not too technical, with just the right amount of explanation when needed, while always staying focused on the personas rather than just the numbers. It's a sneak peek into a history that is being written right now by a cast of characters driven to put the Finger Lakes on everyone's wine map.

—James Molesworth

Introduction

THERE IS NO PRETENTIOUSNESS IN THE DIRT UNDER A WINE-maker's fingernails. Some people like to argue that wine is inherently pretentious, but that misses the point entirely. Wine's image suffers—particularly in the United States—from the stigma of pretense that emanates not from a glass of Merlot but from the braggart who announces that he keeps a case of '82 Petrus in his cellar—just so you know. But wine is not a trophy; it is an agricultural product.

I was finding all of this out on a day when I made the terrible mistake of forgetting to put on my long underwear.

Any notion of pretense melts away in the presence of a winemaker in the maelstrom of harvest. Or, I should say, that notion doesn't melt but rather freezes like my fingers had done on a miserable October day in the Finger Lakes. I had surrendered a week of my vacation to work harvest, thinking it would be easy. Every day for the preceding month had been seasonably warm and glorious. But my arrival at the Anthony Road Wine Company on Seneca Lake coincided with a plunge in temperatures and a soft, steady mist. I was there to learn, and my first lesson was that while wine might be romantic, making it is decidedly not.

And yet the harvest crew maintained a gregarious energy that made even the most menial tasks enjoyable. Every once in a while I'd feel the cold sting of a Riesling grape bouncing off my cheek. When I misjudged the amount of wine that I needed to transfer out of an old oak barrel—and it resulted in a geyser of juice spraying across the winery—I feared I would be chastised for being careless. Instead, all I could hear was side-splitting laughter. And every night during that long harvest week, when the rest of the crew had gone home, I'd stay late with the winemakers to chat. They were tired, but they loved to talk about what might become of those grapes. We would punch down the caps of red grape skins, our shoulders screaming but our spirits strong. By the end of the week I had worked at a handful of wineries on three different lakes—and I wasn't ready to stop.

This was only one week in what became a two-year odyssey. I had first considered writing a book after meeting many Finger Lakes winemakers through my job. Since 2003 I've been a news reporter and anchor for the ABC News affiliate in Rochester, which is just over an hour's drive from the heart of Finger Lakes wine country. I elbowed my way into covering most of the wine and tourism stories for my station, and that role introduced me to the industry. I also became the Finger Lakes wine editor for the *New York Cork Report*.

I found that much had changed over the past twenty-five years, and particularly the past decade, and that few people were aware of it.

If the Finger Lakes region was once known for producing candy wines, it had evolved to become something much bolder. The iconic image of the Finger Lakes is a summer's day, dotted with Adirondack chairs on the water's edge, a happy homeowner holding a glass of world-class cool-climate wine. And while no one can truly define what "world class" means, there is no doubt that the men and women who had been drawn to the Finger Lakes in recent years had come with a goal of achieving it.

The cliché is that wine captures its place in a glass. Most of the time, that's baloney. But the best winemakers in the most special places using the most perfectly suited grapes can do exactly that. In the Finger Lakes region, winemaking had become that elusive but invigorating search for a wine that captures the regional essence, a kind of summer-in-a-glass offering that can satisfy on a hot August day and conjure memories in the dead of winter.

When I committed to writing the book I also committed to working every job in a winery. The only way I could credibly understand and explain what goes on in a winery was to get my own hands dirty—and deeply stained with grape juice. I picked grapes, crushed grapes, sorted grapes, and cleaned tanks. I bottled wine and helped conduct taste tests. I learned the chemical components involved and discovered that yeast might make bread rise but it makes grape juice ferment. I poured wine in tasting rooms for discerning individuals—and for giggling bachelorette parties. I learned to pronounce words like *Brettanomyces*. I began to see grapevines in my sleep.

More important, these winemakers, winery owners, and grape growers welcomed me happily into their facilities and, often, into their homes. They invited me to observe and take part in secret tastings. They allowed me to witness some intensely personal and life-changing moments. They demonstrated why so many men and women in the wine industry want to come to this region.

The Finger Lakes region offers potentially the most fascinating tapestry of stories anywhere in the winemaking world. That's because the best winemakers have vastly disparate tales to tell. In old-world wine regions the winemakers so often come from a family line. That's wonderful, of course, and many families have stories to tell stretching back centuries. But in the Finger Lakes region, the dozen or so high-level winemakers have had to seek out this land and choose to stay when the prestige of so many other regions was calling. They have come from Europe, Australia, Canada, and California. Some grew up here and returned home to fulfill a dream that once seemed impossible in their hometown. They have battled oppressive bosses, governments, and occasionally even their own families.

To appreciate what is happening in the Finger Lakes region, it is not enough to meet the winemakers as they are now. The journey must start at the moments when these men and women started down their path to the Finger Lakes—a region many of them had never heard of before they arrived here.

Author's Note

Almost all quotations in the main chapters come from several hundred hours of digitally recorded conversations. I carried a digital recorder essentially everywhere during my research for this book, and whenever it was used, everyone present was aware the conversations were being recorded. Often the recorder sat in the breast pocket of my shirt or in my hand as I walked the steep vineyards with growers and winemakers. On other occasions it sat on the center of a dinner table or on a tasting room bar.

I am grateful that the subjects of this book were willing to allow all conversations to be recorded. I have cleaned up their comments only in the most gentle, unobtrusive manner, and never to change their meaning.

On rare occasions I have asked subjects to clarify remarks or restate their ideas during follow-up interviews. When the recorder ran out of space on one particularly long evening, I relied on handwritten notes to guide my descriptions.

The events in the back stories are true and are based on numerous interviews and many hours of research. My thanks to the subjects, their families, and friends for assistance in that regard.

ONE

The German in Springtime: Johannes Reinhardt

October 13, 1995
Neuses am Berg, Germany

Sitting on the edge of his bed, Johannes Reinhardt could barely move. Saturday was about to give way to Sunday and, just down the road, the lights in his family's German estate had long since gone dark. If he were going to do it, this was the opportunity. He would have at least twelve hours before anyone would realize he was gone.

But his six-foot, three-inch frame was nearly numb with the idea. Johannes knew that if he walked away tonight he might never speak to his family again. For this shy, courteous twenty-eight-year-old, the thought was nauseating. His mother and father had given him everything he had. They had raised him to continue the Reinhardt family tradition of classic German winemaking. They had taught him how to make the kind of mind-bending wines that inspire wine lovers around the world. If he left tonight, he would imperil the very survival of the family tradition—after all, Johannes was his generation's only possible successor to his father. Neither of his two sisters had the training. Neither lost sleep the way he did when harvest rains threatened a year's crop. More important, neither had his natural ability to guide grapes from the vine to the glass.

"Leave now," he said aloud, "and everything we've built for six hundred years could be gone."

And yet the thought of walking away from his family was instantly liberating. He had spent the past five years pleading with his father to allow him to try new ideas in the vineyard and in the winery, but the answer was always the same: "Tradition means not changing. Tradition means honoring the way our family has always made wine. Put those thoughts away."

Once, Johannes had considered suggesting a partnership with a neighboring winemaking family. He figured that if each family shared their best grapes and their techniques, they could make a wine together that would surpass what they could make individually. But he never made a formal proposal—he could already hear his father's words. "Germans don't collaborate. Germans honor tradition. Tradition means not changing."

The irony was that Johannes was very much a traditionalist—hardly a radical, like some of the New World winemakers working in places like California and Australia. He simply saw that some traditional ideas were hurting the wines. Vowing never to be as obstinate as his father, time after time Johannes summoned the courage to confront his family about what he thought needed to change. Every suggestion was dismissed as folly.

Tonight he remembered the words of a close friend who had urged Johannes to break away from the limitations of his family. "You worry about the price your parents will pay if you leave them," his friend had said. "But the price you will pay yourself is far greater if you stay."

A soft rain bounced off the apartment gutters, providing the only sound to compete with his thoughts. That afternoon, when the steady rain had started, Johannes felt that familiar nausea that accompanies weather problems during harvest. Now, for the first time, that consternation was gone. It was as if he had already left.

Still, he couldn't help but ask himself again if he could ever convince his parents to allow him to leave the winery. Of course, he knew the answer, but with the moment of departure finally upon him, he had to ask himself one more time.

Then, as he exhaled deeply, Johannes heard himself say one word: "No." They would not allow him to leave, and they would not allow him to change.

If he was going to create what he truly believed he could create, he would have to leave—because he could not do it here.

A peaceful calm washed over the tall German as he squeezed his eyes closed, opened them again, and looked at the clock. Midnight. It was time to go, time to wash the last ten years of asceticism away. Munich first, and then who knows? Perhaps somewhere else in Germany. France was a possibility—Alsace was intriguing. Johannes could even envision himself in the United States, acting on his energy and ideas, with no one to destroy his enthusiasm.

As he emerged onto the street, Johannes softened his step so as not to wake his neighbors. The town of Neuses am Berg was home to only a few hundred people, and the last thing he needed was for someone to notice him walking with an overstuffed travel bag. Even in the closed, private German villages, gossip spreads.

With one last glance down the road, Johannes could see that his family's estate was still dark. His car was parked nearby, and he started in that direction but then stopped. "I love you guys," he said quietly. "I know you won't understand that, but I love you. I do."

Then he turned and headed up the road, nervous excitement coursing through him.

JOHANNES REINHARDT WAS MARRYING ENTIRELY THE WRONG WOMAN. Since announcing his engagement three months earlier he had been besieged with requests to reconsider. Johannes's friends and coworkers offered their own ideas about whom he should marry—one man even offered his sister, promising Johannes she was intelligent and a good cook.

I had urged Johannes to consider it. We were talking about his well-being, his future. He told me he was not afraid.

It's not that there was something wrong with Johannes's fiancée. Just about everything about her was unequivocally delightful—she was tall (nearly six feet, just a few inches shorter than he was), thin, beautiful, elegant. At thirty-two years old she was nearly ten years younger than he, even though Johannes could still pass for his early thirties. She was always the smartest person in the room, and she was working toward a graduate's degree in flavor chemistry at Cornell University. And she had grown to love Johannes deeply.

The guys at work wondered how Johannes had ever landed such a gorgeous, driven woman. The girls knew. Though painfully shy and self-effacing with strangers, Johannes was gregarious and charming with those he knew well. Coupled with his accidental movie-star good looks—his dark, thick hair was only barely darker than his constant two-day-old beard, and his broad shoulders boasted of five days a week at the gym—Johannes was a perfectly attractive yet unthreatening man.

His fiancée had only one problem: Imelda was Indonesian and had no green card, no permanent status. If Johannes didn't marry an American, he would be at the mercy of the U.S. government, which could eventually deport him if he failed to get his own green card.

The very idea seemed absurd to everyone who worked with Johannes at the Anthony Road Wine Company on the west side of Seneca Lake. He had been the winemaker since arriving in 2000; how could the feds seek to send him away? Owners John and Anne Martini were furious about the possibility of losing the man who had elevated Anthony Road to new heights.

John had convinced Johannes to come back to the Finger Lakes and give it another shot. After leaving his family on October 13, 1995—the day Johannes now refers to as his "second birthday"—he worked in other parts of Germany for three years before taking a job at Dr. Konstantin Frank's Vinifera Wine Cellars on Keuka Lake. His tenure in America lasted one year, and he headed back to Germany to regroup.

Johannes had no intention of returning to the United States until John Martini tracked him down by phone. John had heard that this

German was a gifted winemaker and he lobbied Johannes to move to the Finger Lakes for a head winemaking position.

Just one month after Johannes had started at Anthony Road he declared, "This is the family I've searched for my entire life."

No one ever thought it would end in deportation. Johannes had racked up a cellar full of medals from wine competitions, but much more important, Anthony Road had enjoyed a meteoric rise in respect in the industry. Major publications like *Wine Spectator* were routinely pinning strong scores on Johannes's wines, especially his Riesling. The winery was making eighteen thousand cases a year, placing it firmly in the upper tier of producers (though such a total would rank much more modestly in California and many European regions). Most of the wines were sugary hybrids that were jokingly called "debt-paying wines." Johannes happily cranked them out because the Martini family provided the extra resources to make world-class dry and dessert wines.

But there was the matter of the German's green card, which had never been settled. The U.S. government had never agreed to give him permanent-worker status and now, with time running out, he was facing deportation. He could not afford the tens of thousands of dollars necessary to pay for more attorney bills and he couldn't appeal forever. He was going to run out of money if he didn't run out of appeals first. Of course, Johannes told me he would leave peacefully if the government ever moved to send him away.

It wasn't just the winery owner who was nervous about losing Johannes. The Finger Lakes had become a kind of brother- and sisterhood in winemaking, and Johannes had made many friends—even among his competitors. They had taken to writing long, detailed letters on Johannes's behalf, pleading with the government to let him stay. Privately, industry leaders knew they would suffer a tremendous embarrassment if Johannes were forced to leave the country. "Think of the headlines," a neighboring winery owner told me. "It would be like the New York Yankees giving Derek Jeter away to the Boston Red Sox for nothing."

Worse, Johannes had no easy or obvious place to go if he were deported. He was on speaking terms again with his parents, but he knew he could not go back to Neuses am Berg. It had taken eighteen months before he had summoned the courage to call his mother and father after leaving, and he had spent most of the conversation holding the phone a foot away from his ear so he could endure his father's screaming. "I don't blame you, Dad," Johannes had told him. "You deserve to be upset with me."

His relationship with his parents had gradually improved—to the point where he was able to take Imelda to Germany to meet them. While he still felt distance from his parents, they embraced his fiancée with the kind of warmth he could not have predicted. It was not a perfect relationship, and Johannes was thankful for the chance to improve it slowly, but he could not go home to make wine—not after leaving.

The standard for earning permanent-worker status seems rather simple. A foreign worker has to prove to the U.S. government that he or she is not taking a job away from a "minimally qualified U.S. citizen who is available to fill that position." Johannes had come to America with German winemaking training and he was focusing his efforts on Riesling, which flourishes in Germany. The Martinis told the bureaucrats that they would not choose anyone else—American or otherwise—over Johannes.

But what did it mean, exactly, for an American to be "minimally qualified" to do Johannes's job? Certainly an American with some basic training can crush grapes and turn them into wine, but that wasn't the job the Martinis had created. They had created a winemaking position that demanded a long list of qualifications and experience, and Johannes was the one applicant who could offer what they were seeking. John Martini often pointed out that he couldn't find an American to fill his qualifications—so he'd had to track Johannes down in Germany.

Adding to Johannes's case, the American government provides green cards to foreign workers of "extraordinary ability." The United

States sets an annual quota of forty thousand green cards for these exceptionally talented workers, and the Martini family sponsored Johannes's application with that idea in mind. "He's the definition of extraordinary," John Martini said about his winemaker. "He's growing our business, and that's creating jobs. He's helping improve the reputation of the entire region. I can't think of anyone more deserving."

The deciding committee was made up of three men in Lincoln, Nebraska. Their experience with wine was likely no more intimate than an occasional bottle of Yellow Tail or Kendall Jackson. Converting grapes into wine is easy, they figured—why not give an American the job? So every time Johannes applied for permanent status, the committee responded with a short, vague denial. They had ignored the job description created by the Martinis, instead assuming that any winemaking job requires the same minimal training. And they rejected the notion that Johannes was a worker of "extraordinary ability."

One of the rejection letters seemed to acknowledge Johannes's extraordinary skill and achievements, even before denying his request for permanent-worker status. The letter cited Johannes's "novel concept" of creating his own style of Riesling in the Finger Lakes. Then the committee recognized the stack of dozens of letters from winemaking colleagues, lawmakers, and industry leaders by writing, "Numerous testimonial letters from peers, colleagues, and professionals within the field attest to the beneficiary's talents and abilities as a winemaker." They also referred to Johannes's many awards—and the long list of publications that have written about his talents. Bizarrely, the committee then declared that, regarding the magazines and books in which Johannes's work had been reviewed, "It has not been established that all of the books and websites can be considered commensurate with major media." Johannes's application had cited his reviews in *USA Today*, *Wine Spectator*, *Better Homes and Gardens*, and more. To claim that those publications are not "major media" would be akin to denying that *Sports Illustrated* is a major sports publication.

At the conclusion of one particular rejection letter, the committee offered a breathtaking lesson in contradiction by writing of Johannes's many awards, "It is apparent that these awards are highly coveted in the industry," and then, "There is no evidence to establish what, if any, acclaim they may represent."

In the face of such intransigence, anyone might be inclined to give up. Johannes simply decided that he needed to offer ever more evidence to the U.S. Bureau of Citizenship and Immigration Services. The committee very clearly knew nothing about winemaking, and, to borrow their phrase, there is no evidence to establish what, if anything, they were doing to better understand winemaking.

And so his friends had implored Johannes, "Marry an American girl. Get your card. Then get divorced and marry Imelda." But it was no use; the tall European was determined to get his status "with integrity or not at all. If America doesn't think I deserve to stay, I'll find somewhere else to go."

* * *

Johannes and Imelda looked like a couple out of a fashion magazine, holding hands by the fingertips and doubling over with laughter as they entered the restaurant. It was an idyllic Finger Lakes spring evening—warm, still, comfortable—and my wife, Morgan, and I were meeting the couple for dinner at one of our favorite local spots. From the outside, the Ports Cafe lacked any kind of flash. Its casual atmosphere was a big draw for diners who wanted a relaxed setting in which to enjoy excellent local food. And local wine.

Because Ports sits on the northwestern side of Seneca Lake, we had a gorgeous view of the setting sun as Johannes and Imelda walked in. He was dressed in jeans, black boots, and a form-fitting white polo shirt. Imelda looked effortlessly graceful in a peach dress with a blue tank underneath, her long black hair spilling over her shoulder. Johannes, a serial hugger, greeted us with his customary hammerlock. Had I been able to breathe I would have told him that my chest felt like it was about to collapse.

I first met Johannes when he came to Rochester for a television interview. I am rather certain that he said fewer than a dozen words that day, allowing several of his colleagues to answer questions for him. It was a disappointment for my producers, who were positively swooning over his slightly high-pitched voice and his German accent. His accent is so stereotypical that he sounds like an American trying to imitate a German.

Despite his brevity we struck up a friendship after my wife and I visited the winery a few weeks later. Away from the garish lights of television, Johannes was magnanimous and animated. I found myself marveling at the quality of his wines, and the Rieslings in particular.

Riesling is the grape that is bringing worldwide recognition to the Finger Lakes, but it has a curious relationship with wine drinkers. A casual drinker tends to prefer sweeter wines—usually white—and Riesling fits the profile. But as they broaden their palate, a wine drinker tends to move to drier wines—choosing red more often—and they malign Riesling as a sugary wine for beginners. Only when they take the time to understand what gives wine potential for greatness do they come back to where they had started. It is the Cycle of Riesling.

The best wines can age for decades, and they need a strong acid backbone to do so. Riesling is blessed with electric natural acidity, giving it the quality to drink at a young age but also the potential to age and evolve in the bottle. In the past decade a handful of Finger Lakes winemakers had begun to make drier-style Rieslings, fermenting almost all of the sugar into alcohol, and highlighting the grape's sharp acidity. That shift in direction was disarming critics who had assumed the Finger Lakes region was home to little more than hybrid grapes and candy wines.

Johannes was helping lead the effort, as was only natural. Every grape has different needs, and so every grape has its own global sweet spots. Riesling finds ideal conditions in parts of Germany, and Johannes had grown up surrounded by aromatic white wines. He had discovered that the Finger Lakes region offers the right soils and topography, as well as the proximity to water, that cool-climate grapes like Riesling love.

In other words, Riesling is Clark Kent and the Finger Lakes region is a phone booth.

In the winter the lakes are warmer than the air and thus act as a heater for the vines. In the summer the lakes are cooler than the air and thus moderate the temperatures affecting the vines. Up-and-coming winemakers had spent long hours studying the effects of geography and, in particular, the Finger Lakes' effect on the grapes. Johannes already knew—it was in his ancestral blood.

Going over the menu at Ports, I suggested we order a bottle from the Hermann J. Wiemer winery, located about ten miles south of Anthony Road. Wiemer is another German winemaker with a penchant for Riesling. In fact, Wiemer had championed Riesling in the Finger Lakes back when it was out of fashion, and I asked Johannes if he ever thought about going to work for Wiemer. He shook his head.

"I love this man," Johannes said. "Hermann has been wonderful to me and he has done special things in the Finger Lakes. The only problem is that he's German!"

I pointed out that Johannes had earned a reputation for his own German precision. When asked by doctors to give his height, he liked to respond, "Six-two-point-five." When they would inevitably round up on health forms, Johannes would protest, "I am not six-three. I'm German. I'm precise. I'm six-two-point-five, or 189 centimeters."

"Yes, I'm German," he said with a laugh. "But Hermann is *too* German. It's not his fault. But it wouldn't make sense for me to leave Germany and then come to America and work for a German."

Wiemer was one of many local winemakers who had written letters to the federal government urging them to grant Johannes permanent-worker status. In the past several months even Senator Chuck Schumer had sent a letter. When I brought the subject up over appetizers it was Imelda who seemed eager to address it.

"We're trying not to think about it," she said. "We don't have any control over what the government decides. If we spend too much time worrying it makes us sad, so that's a waste."

It was not surprising to hear Imelda speak so firmly. She had grown up amid rioting and unrest in Indonesia, and her parents had asked their children to leave the country and find safety. Imelda and her siblings moved to the United States, where she earned a business degree and worked on her English. Like Johannes, she was also facing a long and difficult immigration process—with no guarantee of a green card.

"I wanted to stay in Indonesia, but I couldn't," she said. "I want to stay in America. We are not asking for very much. We want to work. But if Johannes has to leave I will eventually leave with him."

Her turbulent travels had convinced Imelda to be direct and honest in life, and she had challenged Johannes along those lines before their first date. When he called her, she had greeted him with a question: "How many girls have you dated in your lifetime?" After peeling his jaw off the floor, Johannes told the truth, offering any details she cared to learn. He had passed her most important test.

Over dinner Johannes and Imelda brightened as they told us about the J. Reinhardt Wine Company. A piece of property had become available for purchase not far from Anthony Road, and Johannes envisioned his own operation on the site. Imelda would help him make winemaking decisions with her education in flavor sciences. They would keep the production limited—just enough to cover the costs and keep a little money for themselves, as long as the wines sold. Johannes was not legally permitted to own a business without a green card, but he was well within his rights to purchase property, and that's what he had done. Of course, most people struggling to get a green card wait before acquiring property. Johannes and Imelda saw an opportunity and decided to take it.

"So, what do you think?" he said, beaming at us and putting his arm around his fiancée. "Is this nuts, or what?"

* * *

My wife and I pulled into the Anthony Road parking lot on an invitation from Johannes to tour his new property. It was a typical July day in the Finger Lakes: hot enough to smoke a rack of ribs on the sidewalk, humid enough to make you sweat just from turning your head. As we got out of the car the sky began to swirl from a vibrant blue to an ominous charcoal. We ducked inside to avoid what felt like an imminent summer storm.

Instinctively we headed for the tasting bar, and we heard the German's voice. "Perfect timing!" He emerged from a back room smiling, greeting both of us with a hug, his long arms nearly smashing us together in his grasp. I knew that Johannes was excited about his recent purchase, but his body language betrayed uncontainable joy. As he led us out the side door of the tasting room I thought he might bounce straight out of his tall work boots, which covered his jeans to the knee. Morgan and I were dressed much less appropriately for a hike—she in a khaki skirt, I in shorts and sandals—but the rain was drifting north of us and the sun had reemerged.

"We've had some rough weather this month," I said, looking skyward. "Does that make you worry about the grapes?"

"No," Johannes said plainly. "It's nature. Nature is a risky business. If you can't handle the challenge of nature you should find something else to do. The grapes tell me what kind of wine they can make each year. Once you accept that you can't control the weather, you stop worrying so much about it."

We made a brief stop upstairs in the lab, where Johannes had laid out ten potential label designs for his future wine bottles. He was, at a minimum, three years from having anything to fill those bottles, but the gears of his imagination were cranking at full throttle. The labels did not say his name, nor a variety of wine. They said only "Sonero."

"What does it mean?" I asked.

"It is the name for my entry-level wines," Johannes explained, his raised eyebrows pulling his mouth into a grin. "Sonero Red and Sonero White. *Sonero* is a term in salsa dancing. Imelda and I love music and we love to dance, and we thought it was a perfect word for my first wines." As he spoke, he seemed to be moving in some kind of almost-Latin style of dance. It was a little frightening.

Morgan had a different reaction. "You're a dancer!" she said, her eyes lighting up.

"Maybe, perhaps in one year we can decide? I am just starting lessons." Johannes's glance dropped shyly to the floor, but then his attention returned to the label. "Look at the symbol above the letters. Tell me what you see."

We studied the drawing, a simple curved line moving diagonally with rounded ends. Classy, certainly, but my eye clearly was not seeing what Johannes saw. After a long pause he continued. "It's okay. Most people won't pick up the same thing. But tell me: When you look at the line, does it look like a graceful woman, leaning back during a dance?" I had to admit that it did. In fact, I could envision Imelda's long, thin frame, being dipped by her husband. It was admirably, shamelessly romantic. Morgan and I were both nodding as Johannes smiled contentedly.

"But that's enough of that for now!" he declared. "That's not yet. Are you ready for a walk? Let's go!" He was bounding down the stairs before we could put the sketch down.

Several months earlier Johannes had finalized the purchase of twenty acres. That land was across Route 14 and up the hill—within site of Anthony Road winery, but a hike nonetheless. A gentle mist had begun to fall as the back end of the storm drifted across Seneca Lake. "Do you want to wait a few minutes?" Johannes asked. But the sun was still shining and we were infected with his enthusiasm. We started up Anthony Road toward the property.

As we approached Route 14 we could see that the twenty acres were covered by thigh-high wheat. I had expected to see vines growing already, because older vines are considered to make richer, more expressive wines. Johannes was going to have to start from bare earth.

"Once you can plant your vines, how long until you'll have wine ready to bottle?" I asked.

"Two years," Johannes said confidently. I stopped, and he could see I was surprised. "Everyone tells you four, right? Perhaps longer? It's another example of the problems of vineyard care in the Finger Lakes.

"Think about Pinot Noir. Most of our Pinot Noir in the Finger Lakes sucks. It is because those of us who grow it don't know how to care for it. We might not be Burgundy, but we can show the same kind of attention to the vines that they do in the classic regions. The problem is that most of us don't."

I recalled driving past countless vineyards in the Finger Lakes that seemed to have clusters out of control and exploding off the vine.

"Each grape is different," Johannes said, "and that's when you need to think about the individual clusters. A stressed vine is overrun with clusters. There is no balance and the wine has no character. But if we ask the vine to show us the proper amount of clusters, we can train it to make something special. We'll have to give up some clusters, some of the weight on the vine. Many people don't like to do that, because they think they are giving up cases of wine. They think about the money. When a man has staked his living on growing grapes, it's not easy to convince him to cut back on tons per acre or clusters per vine.

"To them it's just business. It's not about having a relationship with your grapes. What they don't realize is that each grape is trying to tell you something. Riesling requires a different amount of clusters than Pinot Noir, which has different needs than Cabernet Franc. And if you're not constantly learning and adjusting to what the wine tells you, you can bet the vines are getting stressed and the wine is not going to be good."

"That all makes sense," I said, "but what does that have to do with getting productive grapes in two years instead of four or more?"

"Ah, good question," Johannes said, smiling broadly. We had reached the bottom corner of his land and we had stopped walking. He was in a theatrical mood, using his hands to gesture as he continued.

"For years in this region, grape growers have made a fatal flaw when they planted the first vines. We knew that it would take some time for the grapes to provide the wine, so we let the vines run wild in the first year. We allowed the vines to decide how to grow. Vines can be trained to make lovely wines, but they need the training early. Otherwise they're like a child with no supervision and they go nuts! And this is what happened over and over again. When we wanted the grapes to give wine, we found they had lost control and it took several more years before anything happened. We battled the vines into something we could use, but there was no harmony. We were not helping the grapes, we were fighting the grapes."

With a little hop, Johannes stood on his right leg and dangled his left leg in the air, pretending to be on a tightrope. "Did I tell you it's about balance? Yes, Evan? Morgan? Balance! We have to balance natural farming with making sure we don't allow disease. We have to balance sunlight with shade. We have to balance acid with sugar. Balance!"

He started to walk toward his twenty acres before turning around quickly. "This does not mean we become . . ." He paused, searching for a word. "*Manipulative.* We don't want to be overinvolved during harvest, but during the first year of a vine's life it needs us. We guide it into rows, we prepare it for the life ahead. And instead of abandoning the vines in their youth, we establish that connection. In just one year we see the shape and direction, and in two years the grapes will surprise you with wine that tastes like it came from much more experienced vineyards."

Looking at Morgan, he asked, "You do not have kids?"

"Not yet," she said.

"We do! But not human children. The vines are like babies, then toddlers, then young children. The first six to seven years makes all the difference."

Then Johannes turned to look at the land that would someday hold his vines. "Guys," he said as he surveyed the fields rising before us, "this is it."

Since purchasing the property Johannes had made several trips a week to the site—sometimes to go over the details, sometimes just to dream. As we climbed the southern edge, the wheat crunching under our feet, the hum of traffic from Route 14 receded. Many wineries are built as close to a main road as possible to attract attention and travelers. Johannes described a starkly different vision. He would build the tasting room not at the front of his twenty acres, but all the way at the top, past the vineyards and away from the busiest roadways. Small trees and bushes would line the vineyard edges, providing a further barrier for noise. And his would be one of the only wineries in the state that would not allow limousines or tour buses.

"I don't mean to insult anyone who tours wineries in groups," Johannes explained almost apologetically. "But we're only going to make three thousand cases of wine a year. We won't need large groups who will run in and out. I want to attract people who will think about the wine and enjoy it slowly.

"We'll be open later than most, probably until seven at night. I can see people coming after work to have a small dark chocolate and a glass of red wine. Do not laugh, okay? I'd love to host people to have a glass of Riesling and a bite of food—what do you suggest?"

My wife's imagination had fully caught up to Johannes's: she spoke of boards brimming with local cheeses. They discussed appetizers and atmosphere. While I looked back on the lake, they talked about Johannes's love of music and his plan to bring out his friends who play classical instruments. It would be the ideal stop for a couple heading out for dinner or for friends who want to *understand* what was in the glass.

We continued toward the top of the property and started inward, where a lone tree had sprung up. It looked like an oasis in the wheat fields and served as Johannes's marker for the back edge of his land. From here we could see not just the lake, a sheet of glass after the storm, but also the Anthony Road tasting room and winery. And it occurred to me that Johannes would eventually be leaving the family who had convinced him to come back to the Finger Lakes—the family who had changed his mind and changed his life, while changing the very trajectory of local wine at the same time.

"What do the Martinis think about all of this?"

He shook his head and looked down. "I can almost not even believe it," he said. "They helped me with the purchase. They advised me. They told me to find my own way, and they have been more supportive than I could possibly describe."

Amazing. He had earned his status as one of the most skilled and expressive winemakers in this growing region, and the family who employed him had *encouraged* him to seek out his own vineyard. They were going to lose him and they knew it. And yet John and Anne Martini had given Johannes the gift that his own parents could not give him in Germany: his freedom.

Even with a green card, Johannes would not leave Anthony Road right away. In fact, he planned to launch his own company while still making the wine for his current employer. He figured that was the right thing to do.

Suddenly I realized that Johannes had begun to awkwardly sprint away from us. Then I heard the sound: the tintinnabulation of a fresh storm, roaring at us over the tree line, announcing its presence on the metal rooftops of distant sheds. Morgan and I took off behind Johannes toward the trees, which marked the northern edge of his land. Through the rush of the rain I could hear Johannes's high-pitched laugh. He skidded to a halt under the overhanging leaves and used his boots to carve out a space in the bushes for us to stand, partially covered.

"See, we embrace the weather anyway!" Johannes said, squeezing the water out of his shirt.

For several minutes we looked out at the storm. Seneca Lake, shining brilliantly only minutes before, was lost from view. The rain came down so fiercely that the canopy was quickly overrun. We could only laugh as the water soaked every inch of clothing and skin straight through. Morgan squeezed her eyes shut as the rain poured off her head. I later informed Johannes that his presence had ruined a moment ripe with romantic possibility, the kind usually reserved for movie trailers and summer camps.

After ten minutes or so the faucet finally shut off. Shaking out like shepherd dogs from Johannes's homeland, we began a gradual descent. He pointed out the site for his tasting room, and once again the lake came into view.

"Someday this very spot will be filled with people drinking your wine and gazing out the window at the water," I said.

Johannes seemed humbled by the thought. But I also knew that this dream could be delayed or crushed by the bureaucrats who continued to withhold Johannes's green card. A new ruling was due to arrive soon, and Johannes's friends sensed the gathering dread surrounding it.

He was thinking the same thing. "Tell me, guys," Johannes said, his smile fading for the first time today. "Did I buy my future winery? Or did I just buy the world's most expensive wheat field?"

* * *

Everyone in this room is undocumented, I said to myself on a fall day at the Anthony Road winery. It was a cynical reaction that turned out to be wrong; Anthony Road and many other wineries are showing more caution when hiring harvest crews. But that's not what had me fired up. I was frustrated to know that the twenty-five men on the sorting line were going to stay in this country as long as they pleased. Perhaps the feds had decided that they were workers of "extraordinary ability"—and the man making the wine was struggling to get his green card, only to face deportation.

Johannes was dealing with starkly different emotions that morning. He figured the ruling from the bureaucrats could arrive with that afternoon's mail, and he was light-headed with anxiety. But he was also feverishly excited about harvesting Riesling grapes for his first-ever Riesling Trockenbeerenauslese—better known as TBA, and translated from German to mean "dry selected berries."

Among the German wine classifications, TBAs are the sweetest and often the most desirable. They're also very difficult to make well and Riesling only rarely presents an opportunity to make TBA in the Finger Lakes. In eight harvests this was Johannes's first chance to make Riesling TBA. "It might never come around again," Johannes told me that morning, "so we have to get it right."

The weather all year long had been building to a kind of TBA crescendo in the Finger Lakes (though few winemakers had any idea how to make it and so only a few were even attempting it). Intense bursts of summer rains provided plenty of water, and while the grapes eventually shed their tumescence they retained the conditions ideal for rot. Strange as it sounds, rotting grapes can make some of the world's best wine.

But it's not easy. The winemaker has to first decide to allow bunches of grapes to hang past the time they would normally be harvested. Then the vineyard staff has to watch the grapes begin to rot, and they have to decide the ideal time to pick the grapes. And not all of the rot is welcome.

Johannes was looking for botrytis, which is a mold known in the wine world as "noble rot." Botrytis causes the grapes to dry out and shrivel, which in turn causes the sugars to concentrate and richen. But occasionally the grapes would become afflicted with "sour rot," which essentially turns them into vinegar.

The warning was clear: just a few sour-rotted grapes in a tank of TBA could drastically harm the flavor. The only way to prevent the rancid grapes from spoiling the TBA was to hire a large staff of sorters who would go through every bunch by hand. Our job—I had joined the sorting line after Johannes had practically pleaded for additional help—was to remove the Riesling grapes that had not been affected by botrytis, and we had to smell the bunches and pull out any grapes that had turned sour.

My twenty-five Mexican friends on the sorting line broke into laughter when I would occasionally sniff a bad bunch of grapes. "*Cuidado*!" they would yell. *Watch out!* Then, in heavily accented English: "Don't eat them!" I wasn't about to experiment. We had a heck of a lot of work and only a forty-eight-hour window to get it done.

Johannes had created that time frame based on his German experience with TBA. Once the grapes were harvested, he wanted them sorted and crushed within forty-eight hours to make sure the juice was as fresh and as concentrated as possible. Waiting too long to crush would lower the quality, "And that's unacceptable," he had said. "I don't care if I don't sleep for two days. We're getting this done." In the glass, many tasters find good TBA to be a symphony. What they do not realize is that at each previous step it is a two-hundred-piece orchestra with every instrument tuning simultaneously—and no time for a sound check.

As frantic as the pace was, we were having a hell of a good time. I dusted off my Spanish as I sorted alongside the Mexicans. We carefully attacked the work with the cheerful trumpets of mariachi bands playing over the loudspeakers.

The TBA harvest had come at a perfect time for Johannes. It forced him to focus on wine when he was increasingly anxious about the immigration letter. "Imelda and I feel like our whole lives are on hold, and until the American government says it's okay, we can't plan our lives," he had told me. "We can't own our own winery. We can't buy a house. We can only wait."

But he refused to let the government ruin his TBA. He was going to make sure it was made carefully, and that morning he had one more reason to be excited: 43 Brix.

Brix refers to the percentage of sugar in a grape. During harvest, most grapes are picked in the low to mid-20s Brix in the Finger Lakes. Late-harvest and TBA wines are often in the mid- to high 30s. But 43 was the highest Brix Johannes had ever seen, and that's the reading many of his Riesling grapes had given. During fermentation, much of the sugar will turn to alcohol, but starting with so high a level offered Johannes the chance to create something magical. Any other grape would be swamped by the sugar level, but Riesling's naturally high acid content offered the balance to make a rich, complex TBA.

The wine we were helping to make that day was destined to be one of the most expensive ever made in the Finger Lakes. It had to be if the Martini family wanted to offset the cost of all the labor required to make it. It was also sure to cost Johannes at least one pair of pants. He had to crush the small, shriveled grapes by foot, the old-fashioned way—and doing it bare-legged was no longer an option.

During Johannes's first harvest at Anthony Road he had been foot-crushing a batch of hybrid grapes, but the juice was splashing all over his pants, so he took them off. A woman working in the tasting room walked into the winery and thought Johannes was naked from the waist down, as his shirt was hanging down past his Speedo underwear. As he recalled the story for me, I interrupted him.

"Speedo underwear? Seriously?"

"I'm German, after all."

"But you're supposed to be an untraditional German!"

"Well, some traditions I choose to keep."

The woman had exited the winery screaming, and Johannes had promised to wear pants during all future foot-crushing sessions.

Some German TBAs sell at auction for thousands of dollars per bottle, and the bottles are small—half the size of standard wine bottles. Johannes figured his Riesling TBA would hit the tasting room at $100 per bottle, a huge total around here. We sorted all day, and once in a while I'd pop a raisined berry into my mouth, enjoying the concentrated sugar and texture. The Mexicans would shake a finger at me, reminding me in Spanish that I had just consumed several bucks' worth of juice.

Sorting grapes for hours on end might sound like a banal task, but we approached it with vigor. Everyone in the winery could feel Johannes's energy, and it translated into urgency and the desire to avoid mistakes. As the hours ticked on, my hands turned raw from the cold—the grapes are very cold when sorted, and it was not a warm day on Seneca Lake. But whenever I'd start to lose feeling in my fingers, my fellow sorters would belt out an effervescent Mexican tune and I'd sing along, forgetting about the numbness in my hands.

When I finally left for home that evening I knew that Johannes hadn't yet checked the mail. Perhaps he was so focused on finishing the TBA that he hadn't allowed himself the time. But I figured he was holding off on opening the letter until he felt ready.

We didn't speak of it when I departed. I thanked him for allowing me to experience the manic rush of TBA—which still required more sorting and then crushing—and he said only, "I'll call you."

* * *

I woke up the next morning sure that Johannes and Imelda were going to be fine. He hadn't called the night before, and by now—7 a.m.—he was undoubtedly sorting grapes like mad. Perhaps the letter had not come after all. Perhaps he had received it but decided to wait until after the forty-eight-hour TBA rush to open it. After all, a rejection letter would surely halt the momentum of the most important harvest of his life.

But I settled on another possibility: Johannes had finally been approved for permanent-worker status, and as soon as he finished stomping that evening he would call his friends and family. Given his generous nature, Johannes would probably invite everyone down for an impromptu celebration.

Still, I tried to imagine what I'd say if the news were bad. What, exactly, do you say to someone who has been rejected by the country he loves? How do you console someone who has just been told that he must get out, that he must abandon his dream? I knew that, legally, Johannes could make one more appeal. But he wasn't sure he could afford to appeal again, even if the government gave him one more legal chance to make his case. Each appeal cost him thousands of dollars.

If the government rejected his application this time around, Johannes would have to leave the country first and come back under a temporary permit—and that's if he decided to give it one last appeal. The very idea was insulting to someone who was trying to be as honest with the government as possible.

That afternoon I had gotten tired of waiting and I called Johannes. He didn't pick up. When he finally returned my call it was past 10 o'clock that night. He sounded exhausted.

"The grapes are crushed, and I kept my pants on," he said, laughing.

"Congratulations," I responded, hoping to move the conversation to the letter. "Do you have any other news?"

"Yes. There has been a decision." I couldn't sense any upward or downward movement in his voice.

"And?"

"And," he said, then paused. "And I am going back to Germany."

TWO

The German in Winter: Hermann Wiemer

December 24, 1981
Bernkastel, Germany

Getting fired is hard enough. Getting fired on Christmas Eve seems especially brutal. On Christmas Eve 1981, just as the first Champagne corks were popping in the Wiemer house in Bernkastel, Germany, a telegram arrived from the United States. The holiday celebration halted as Hermann, a thirty-nine-year-old winemaker, privately opened the terse note. It had come from the Finger Lakes, where Hermann had been employed for more than a decade by the iconic Bully Hill winery.

As Hermann paused to set down his glass a quiet buzz hung over the room. What could be so pressing as to merit a holiday telegram? Perhaps a promotion? Or perhaps Hermann's employer had written to declare that after years of arguments, he had been wrong and Hermann had been right. It would seem the perfect Christmas gift.

Before turning to his family, Hermann took a long breath and read over the telegram:

> Hermann,
> Due to financial problems, we have been forced to lay off employees. Unfortunately your employment is terminated as of December 29. If you are interested in negotiating

your position with us, please contact us at your earliest
convenience. Best wishes for the holiday thank you

Sincerely
Walter S. Taylor, Bully Hill Vineyards

The owner, Walter Taylor, was under such financial hardship that he had recently purchased his third airplane. Hermann particularly enjoyed the stunningly heartfelt "Best wishes for the holiday." Enjoy your Christmas: You're fired!

Hermann had returned home to Bernkastel to celebrate the holidays as he always had, but this year was different. After building the Bully Hill brand alongside Taylor, Hermann began to disagree with Taylor more often. Hermann argued passionately to convert the many Bully Hill vineyards from native and hybrid grapes (the varieties that can survive rough winters but don't often make great wine) to old-world, European vinifera grapes. He had urged Taylor to consider Riesling over Cayuga White, Pinot Noir over Concord, Cabernet Franc over Catawba. Taylor had grown impatient with Wiemer's proselytizing.

Even still, no one expected Taylor to fire his winemaker on Christmas Eve.

No one, that is, except Hermann. Traveling back to Germany several weeks earlier, he wondered if Taylor would deliver the blow on the holiday itself. Christmas Eve was close enough.

As he read over the firing once more—thirteen years washed away by forty-six words—he considered what his life might become without Bully Hill. He thought about returning to the United States without the stability of a steady paycheck. He wondered what might change as he neared his fortieth birthday.

Hermann turned to face his family. They leaned forward, waiting for the word.

"It has finally happened," Hermann said calmly, then broke into a wide smile. "Walter Taylor fired me!" Someone shouted, "Raise a glass!" A rousing cheer rocked the room as Hermann's family approached him with sincere congratulations.

Taylor must have had no idea that this was exactly what Hermann had hoped would happen. Having launched an eponymous winery in 1979, Hermann had quietly shifted his focus to his own vinifera wines. He laughed as he read the note aloud to his family.

"I'll return to America," the German said. "And I will never make a hybrid wine again!" Then, muttering to himself and shaking his head, he added, "Firing your winemaker on Christmas Eve. What a coward."

* * *

"Everything is dead." Barely twenty-four hours had passed since Hermann received that liberating telegram, but the celebration was now over. A call had come from the United States with an ominous message for the winemaker: "Everything is dead."

The caller from the Finger Lakes was referring to the grapevines. "How?" Hermann asked. "What happened?"

"They're already calling it the Christmas Massacre," came the response. "Yesterday it was 35 degrees. Today it is 10 below. Worse in some spots. The vinifera vines are dead. They will never survive the extreme change and the cold."

Then, in a cruel twist that made Hermann feel somehow worse, the caller said, "We think hybrid grapevines will be okay. They're better suited to deal with this."

"I know they are!" Hermann snapped. "Damn things could survive a nuclear meltdown!"

"Happy holidays," the caller offered before hanging up.

Typically stoic and unflappable, Hermann couldn't help but feel despair. If the reports were correct, the Christmas Massacre would mean more than a severe challenge for his winery. It could set the region back years in its slow march toward better-quality grape plantings. Few growers and winemakers cared to risk their operation on the more difficult old-world grapes. They felt comfortable growing the syrupy hybrids and labrusca varieties like Concords. The massacre would probably convince anyone who was considering vinifera to give it up and stick with the lower-quality, more durable grapes. If he still refused to grow hybrids, Hermann would be a pariah, dismissed as an obstinate fool.

He recalled a meeting from 1974 with the legendary California wine pioneer Robert Mondavi. Hermann and Walter Taylor had flown out to California for a series of meetings. Over lunch they met Mondavi, who urged the east coast winemakers to shift to dry, European varieties. Hermann was transfixed by the message. Taylor was unmoved.

"Dry wines won't work—at least not where we're from!" Taylor had said. "Mondavi's got it wrong." When Hermann pressed Mondavi's message, Taylor told him, "We have to stick with what's safe. We make hybrid wines."

On this disastrous Christmas, as Hermann arranged to fly back to the Finger Lakes to see the damage himself, his old boss's words echoed maddeningly in his head.

* * *

The massacre had wiped out most of Hermann's vinifera vines at his winery on Seneca Lake. He was crestfallen to find that the reports had been accurate.

Back in the Finger Lakes, Hermann spent the winter contemplating his future. He was determined to replant the lost vines, but it would take several years before they would be able to bear fruit suitable for winemaking. Having been fired from Bully Hill, where was the money going to come from?

One late-winter morning brought a rush of mild air to the region and Hermann decided to do one more inspection. He knew of a vinifera vineyard about ten miles north of his winery on Seneca Lake that served as an experimental site for the Taylor family. With the snows melting in the 45-degree weather, Hermann wondered what those Taylor vines would look like.

Walking up the hillside, the air felt warmer than it had down the lake at his winery. Hermann headed back to the car and tossed his coat on the passenger's seat.

When he reached the vineyard rows he could hardly believe what he was seeing. He dropped to his knees to get a closer look. There was almost no cracking. No splitting. The vines were alive. Stressed, yes, but *alive.*

He jumped up and headed for higher rows. They all looked the same. A cold snap can freeze a vine and cause the trunk to crack and split apart. The buds die and the grower is forced to replant from the bottom up. Only in the Finger Lakes will you find multiple trunks growing out from the same spot of soil, evidence of destructive winters past. But this vineyard was different. It would not require any replanting. It had withstood the very worst that western New York winter can bring.

But how? Standing there in only a button-down, long-sleeved shirt, Hermann began to wonder: Is the temperature higher in this spot? If this vineyard has its own mesoclimate, he figured other vineyards must have unique properties too. It would require careful exploration, but perhaps there were more superior vineyard sites, shielded for one reason or another from the harsh cold. And if vinifera vines could survive the worst in the Finger Lakes, they could surely thrive in most years.

The Christmas Massacre had not killed the dream of vinifera wine in the Finger Lakes—it had confirmed its very potential!

Eventually I will have this vineyard, Hermann thought. He wondered if anyone else would discover this secret, but he doubted it. The Christmas Massacre that had devastated so many other winery owners had given Hermann a gift, the perfect present. He only had to decide whether he wanted to share it with anyone else.

I had no idea what to expect as I made my way down to Ithaca on a fall day accented with crisp air and colors. Based on the descriptions I had heard of sixty-seven-year-old Hermann Wiemer, I was either on my way to meet a quiet genius or an obstreperous crank. I wondered how he'd respond if I asked an indelicate question, but there were so many questions. The debate over his legacy was quietly roiling in the Finger Lakes. Hermann had recently sold his winery and retired from the business, and simply getting a hold of him had been a difficult task.

But I knew I had to track him down. His legacy would help shape the future of this region, and he remained an enigma. I did the only thing I could think of: I called the other German winemaker in the Finger Lakes.

Before Johannes Reinhardt left for Berlin—where he would reapply, one more time, for a temporary work permit—he made contact with Hermann. Johannes was one of the few people who could expect Hermann to pick up the phone. The two Germans had deeply different personalities but they shared a mutual respect. After I had failed for several weeks to make contact with Hermann, Johannes placed a call on my behalf. Hermann agreed to meet for dinner just a mile from his home in Ithaca, where he spends his time when not traveling across Europe.

"The questions you have are fair," Johannes said, but warned, "He might not want to talk about everything. He's not a very open person. He is brilliant but he guards himself."

I appreciated the advice and wished Johannes well. He had decided to exercise what was likely his final legal appeal for permanent American status. His fiancée was still doing research and taking classes at Cornell, and she needed him to stay as long as he could. By law, Johannes had to return to Germany and reapply, which would take two weeks. After that, the U.S. government could take another year or so to process his application. It would buy Johannes a little more time—the holidays, and perhaps into the following summer—and then he would know if he had a future in this country.

But realistically, Johannes's situation had not changed. He understood that the recent ruling was likely to be repeated.

Unlike Johannes, Hermann Wiemer had never encountered any trouble getting permanent status decades ago, and he had become a giant in the Finger Lakes wine industry. In the 1970s and '80s, when Riesling enjoyed little favor in the wine world, Hermann doggedly kept planting it. It was not only the grape that shone so brightly in his hometown near Germany's Mosel river; it was the grape that he believed would thrive in the Finger Lakes. Slowly, Wiemer's drier Rieslings gained critical attention. His wines taught consumers that a bottle of Riesling could be dry and crackling just as well as it could be sweet and lush. When Riesling gained a loftier status around the world, Wiemer's wines became the standard for the Finger Lakes.

He had also stirred up plenty of controversy, and the wounds suffered by some of his colleagues remained fresh years later. Farmers in the Finger Lakes became winemakers, but many had little training—and they certainly had no experience with how to make world-class wines like Hermann did. But many of these farmers-turned-winemakers say that instead of reaching out to help them, Hermann closed his doors. The tension boiled into a *New York Times* piece about Wiemer in 1985. In it, Wiemer declared that most Finger Lakes wines were of "rubber hose quality." The writer also described the way other winemakers viewed Hermann: "A reverential gag around the west side of Seneca Lake is about the 'temple' of the winemaker Hermann J. Wiemer. The locals marvel at the winery built from a converted barn that includes a two-story apartment where, they jest, Mr. Wiemer sits on high contemplating the gleaming steel tanks below that hoard his highly regarded wines."

Hermann's "rubber hose" remark became so toxic that it inspired other professionals in the wine industry to write the *New York Times* and attack the German. Hermann offered a simple response: "Everything I said was true." Moreover, Hermann was frustrated that the rest of the article seemed to get little attention. The writer hailed him as a "wine innovator" and described his attention to detail in the vineyards. His "rubber hose" remark was aimed not at the winemaking talents of his colleagues, but of their decision to continue to make hybrid wines instead of old-world vinifera varieties. The Christmas Massacre had shaken their confidence in vinifera, but Hermann said it was a once-in-a-lifetime anomaly, and that there was no realistic threat of it happening again.

Hermann's animosity toward Bully Hill was made clear in the article, but he claimed it wasn't personal. "People want vinifera," he said simply, indicating that wineries like Bully Hill were stuck in the past. But he also told the writer that he had called a Rochester wine store and demanded they take his wines off the shelf—simply because they were placed next to Bully Hill wines.

Some of his colleagues were also upset that Hermann revealed to the *Times* that he would consider taking the words "Finger Lakes" off his labels. Legally he didn't have this option—wine labels must indicate where the product is from—but it was an indication that Hermann was not proud of the region. So had Hermann Wiemer elevated the status of Finger Lakes wines by making distinctive, world-class Rieslings, or had he held the region back by refusing to share his growing and winemaking skills with others?

As I pulled the car into the restaurant parking lot I wondered if I would have the guts to ask him this question.

* * *

Back before many people knew Hermann Wiemer's name, a man and his wife drove five hours from New York City to the Finger Lakes just to meet him.

The summer of 1982 was hot and dry and, tending to his vines one afternoon, Hermann found himself thinking back to the Christmas

Massacre. A bead of perspiration rolled lazily down his cheek. In the heat it was hard to believe he was working in a region that was ever threatened by extreme cold.

Hermann's tasting-room manager called out to inform the boss that someone had come all the way from New York City. Hermann's winery was not yet making a profit and, when you're constantly on the edge of financial ruin, you don't turn anyone away. So he dropped what he was doing and walked down to the small tasting room.

"How nice to meet you," the guest said, grabbing Hermann's hand in genuine excitement. "I tasted your wines at a party recently and they were some of the best I've ever had. I wanted to tell you that personally. And I would love to buy more!"

The winemaker was moved, and he uncharacteristically let his guard down. "That's wonderful of you to say. Are you a wine writer or in the industry, perhaps?" The guest was strikingly handsome, an athletically built black man probably in his mid-thirties, but Hermann did not recognize him. His wife was beautiful, and she smiled shyly.

"No, no," the man said. "I'm on Broadway, actually."

"Broadway!" Hermann was impressed. But with the economy in the tank, Hermann knew that most industries were suffering. "Must be hard to make a living on Broadway," he offered in a misguided attempt to show empathy.

"Well, I get by," the man responded sheepishly.

"I'm sure it's difficult," Hermann said.

"Well," the man's wife said, "he is a star, you know."

Hermann's tasting-room manager pulled him aside and whispered forcefully, "Don't you know who that is? That's Gregory Hines!"

"Oh," Hermann whispered back. He thought for a moment, then asked, "Who's Gregory Hines?"

After their awkward introduction, Hines and Wiemer became good friends until Hines's death in 2003. Hermann would bring a case of wine to New York City and the actor would leave him pairs of tickets to shows like *Sophisticated Ladies*. The significance of that first meeting never left Hermann: if someone was so inspired by his wines that they were willing to drive many hours just to buy more, he must be doing something well.

Tonight, in an Ithaca restaurant, the retired winemaker had become the star. I met him in the hallway leading into Taverna Banfi, a highly regarded restaurant run by the students of Cornell's hospitality school. As the hostess seated us, the general manager approached the table and commanded his staff to gather around.

"Mr. Wiemer is joining us tonight!" the general manager bellowed, and the staff broke into applause.

With more than a dozen uniformed workers cheering dutifully, Hermann hurriedly sent them off. "Please," he said. "That's very nice. You don't need to do that."

When they departed I leaned over and asked, "Do you always get that kind of reception?"

"No, no, of course not," he said with a wave of his hand. "I eat here once in a while and they've gotten to know me, I suppose." I gave him a smile as if to say, *C'mon*, but he just shrugged.

At sixty-seven years old, Hermann remained a strikingly handsome man. His wavy dark hair had allowed some gray to mix in and his sharp facial features showed the lines of age, but he wore his age with sophistication and vitality. He sported a simple button-down shirt with khaki pants covering a pair of long boots, and I recalled that in the old photos I had seen of Hermann he was always the best-dressed man in the room. A 1969 promotional photograph for Bully Hill's wines featured a smiling Hermann Wiemer kneeling beside a wine barrel, his floral shirt scandalously opened three buttons down. Later photos of Hermann meeting with governors and foreign leaders revealed a fashion sense consistent with European playboys, mock turtlenecks under sport coats often the choice.

Hermann grabbed the wine list and handed it to me. "Why don't you choose a bottle for the meal," he said, and slowly moved his eyes from the wine list to mine. I instantly felt intense pressure. His wines were featured prominently and I couldn't tell if he expected me to choose a bottle of Wiemer—or if this was a test of my wine savvy, given the international nature of the list. The possibilities of screwing this up were endless. I was hoping to earn enough of his trust to convince him to open up to me about his career, and I was faced with the possibility of eliminating my credibility in the first five minutes.

After reading through the list I set it down and tried to buy some time. I asked him if he had heard the news that a hybrid wine had won the Governor's Cup—an annual award given to the wine chosen by critics as the best in the state. Hermann's loathing of hybrid grapes had become legendary; he had even declared publicly that he would only sell his winery to someone who was allergic to hybrids. From the more than eight hundred individual wines submitted to a panel of judges, a Finger Lakes winery had recently won the award with a hybrid wine; when I brought it up, Hermann became animated.

"I can't believe it. I can't believe it!" he said, holding the long E of the second "believe" for three full seconds in heavily accented English. "This is ridiculous. Hybrids should not be judged with vinifera. It's a different category. Nobody wants to drink hybrids! The birds won't even eat the damn things!"

Once Hermann calmed down he asked about my connections to the Finger Lakes, and we began a comfortable discussion about local towns. He loved the culture in Ithaca but didn't care very much for other parts of the area. He asked about my wife's upbringing in Penn Yan on Keuka Lake. We became so wrapped up in the discussion that I forgot about the wine list entirely and was stunned to find that an hour had passed since we first sat down. But just when I thought that Hermann was truly enjoying the conversation he seemed to ice up.

"I don't understand why you even wanted to meet me," he said abruptly, crossing his arms and leaning forward.

"I want to understand why you did the things you did," I said carefully. "Finger Lakes Riesling would not be gaining world-class status without you. I'm curious to know why you wanted to make wine here and why you made the decisions you did."

He shrugged again and said, "I'm hardly that interesting. Why don't you choose a wine."

That sense of pressure returned. I stammered before offering, "I don't think we can go wrong with a bottle of Wiemer—"

He cut me off. "No, no, I've had enough of my wine." Then he smiled. "The theme here is Italian so let's drink an Italian wine." My wife and I had recently spent a week in Tuscany, so this was an easy choice: I selected a 2001 Brunello di Montalcino, one of my favorite reds in the world. Hermann offered his approval. I let out what felt like a day's worth of breath and leaned back in my chair.

* * *

When an American wine writer who calls himself "Dude" went to Germany, he discovered something unexpected. Joe Roberts, publisher of the popular website 1WineDude, spent a week in Mosel searching for the world's best Riesling. He met some of the most luminous names in the wine industry. To his surprise, the Mosel winemakers knew of only one winemaker in America who was producing anything worth discussing. They didn't spend much time speaking about their counterparts in the highly publicized Napa Valley, nor did they speak about the rise of cool-climate wines in America's Northwest. They were, however, quite familiar with the Finger Lakes.

"The name Hermann J. Wiemer came up many, many times in the Mosel," Roberts wrote upon his return. "They're quite proud of him. They consider him a hometown boy who is showing America how it's done."

Roberts didn't realize it when he wrote those words, but he had perfectly captured the image that many of Hermann's American counterparts had of him. They viewed him as the Outsider who never embraced the local scene. So during a break in our conversation, as we polished off the last of our butternut squash soup, I decided I had to ask the question.

The idea of helping a competitor might seem strange to many people, but a young wine region can benefit from collaboration. That's because the wine-buying public is often less interested in an individual producer and more interested in whether the region is capable of producing high quality. The sooner a wine region gains respect as a whole, the sooner the best individual producers in that region will break into new markets.

"I wonder," I said cautiously, slowly swirling the Brunello in my glass, "if you felt you did enough to help the other wineries when they were just starting out."

Hermann turned his head and squinted. "I don't understand."

"I just wonder if you agree with the idea that you didn't do enough to share your wisdom with the people who might have needed it most."

"Agree with who?" he said. I felt the oxygen leaving the room.

"There are winemakers and owners who point out that you never joined a wine trail," I said. "They say you kept your distance. They never felt they knew you. They talk about that *New York Times* article when you criticized local wines."

"Oh, the article," he said, seeming to smile. "The problem is you can't love everybody and you can't love everything that everybody produces. We should be focusing on the few people making great wine, not the masses of people making bad wine."

We sat silently for a moment. Finally I said, "But you didn't have to *love* everybody, right? You could have just decided to *work with* people who were making bad wine. That's what some people say privately—that you turned down a chance to make them better winemakers."

He shrugged abruptly and it occurred to me that this might be the first time Hermann had ever considered this possibility. If he had indeed built a wall between himself and his colleagues, he hadn't thought much about it.

"There was nobody. I was alone," he said after considering the question. We sat silently as his defiance seemed to hang over the table. He looked up and continued, "There was almost nobody. The Dr. Frank winery was here but you didn't see them reaching out. Besides that, it was just me, and there was nobody worth working with. I've told my assistant winemaker, who bought the winery from me, that you're basically alone here. You've got to maintain your integrity, make the best wines you can, and forget about the rest."

I focused on my risotto as Hermann took a breath and seemed to change his mind. I found myself dreading the thought of pressing it any further, and I hoped he would have something else to say without my prodding. He did.

"I did everything I could to improve the wines in the Finger Lakes. I met with the most prominent grape grower on Seneca Lake and I begged him to plant vinifera and get rid of this other crap. I told him it would work, but not very many people wanted to listen. I tried."

Suddenly he sat back and changed his mind again.

"But I was struggling. My first employer at Bully Hill didn't care about me. They fired me on Christmas! No one reached out to me in my time of need, so why was I going to reach out to them?"

I found the difference between Hermann and Johannes Reinhardt to be striking. Unlike Johannes, a German who had come to the United States seeking friendship and collaboration, Hermann brought a much more guarded personality. When his American employer fired him on Christmas Eve in 1981 it ensured that Hermann would never seek open work relationships. He had wanted to be fired, but he found his boss's timing to be almost impossibly rude, meant to deliver the maximum amount of pain.

And yet, after discussing the old wounds, Hermann seemed comfortable again. I wondered if I had misread him. The man who is viewed as an icy, hermetic genius by many of his peers didn't seem to struggle with his image. To him, everything was matter-of-fact: his colleagues were never in his league and probably never would be.

Clearly Hermann felt that no amount of his time or assistance would have ever changed that.

* * *

Once we had finally moved past the uncomfortable subject of Hermann's pariah status in the Finger Lakes community, the conversation took on a much easier, lighter tone. Over a meal of lamb and risotto, Hermann told humorous tales of his early days in the Finger Lakes. He recalled his former boss, Walter Taylor, crashing a wine industry meeting in Washington, D.C., to promote Bully Hill wines. "He was fearless," Hermann said with a laugh. "It was embarrassing as hell, but he was not scared of anything. He couldn't care less what you thought of him."

I wondered if Hermann might have just a little bit of Walter Taylor in him. After all, Hermann had made the rather bold—some might say fearless—decision to stay in America instead of going home and making wine in Germany. And he hadn't just chosen America; he had chosen a wine region that almost no one outside of upstate New York had ever heard of. So before I left that night I wanted to find out: Why the Finger Lakes?

"I could see the challenge in front of me," he said confidently. "There was this opportunity and no one else was taking advantage of it. I knew I could be the one to produce wines that would compete with European wines."

He leaned forward and smiled. "It's the soils! If you understand soil, you know that we have the same kinds of soils in the Finger Lakes that they have in Europe. Of course, every vineyard has different composition, but we have what they have. And I knew it from the start."

Hermann was very nearly gloating now, and I enjoyed seeing his more animated side. While it might have been a bit boastful, it was loose and easygoing. And it was clearly a side that very few of his colleagues had ever seen.

They certainly had no idea that Hermann had worked for the Vatican making wine. He had always touted—and understandably so—his training at some of the most respected institutions in Europe. But when Hermann first came to the United States it was to make sacramental wines. He might have been the only winemaker in the country aiming to make a 90-point Blood of Christ. Walter Taylor had met Hermann at a party and knew immediately that he had found someone of special ability.

"I could have gone home and fit in," Hermann said. "It would have been no problem to make wine in Germany. But I had started something here, and I felt the challenge."

These are stories I found myself wishing he had shared years ago. He could have ingratiated himself into the local winemaking community with stories of his commitment to the Finger Lakes, rather than hinting to the *New York Times* that he didn't care for the region. He could have shared the humbling story of having to sell his car to keep his own winery out of financial ruin.

"You know," he added, "they told me I was crazy to plant Riesling. I knew it had the potential for the Finger Lakes, but they said no one would ever buy it. So I planted it anyway, but I could have planted more. I considered planting only Riesling, and looking back, it would have worked."

"Why were you able to sell Riesling when others couldn't?" I asked.

"You have to know what people want," he said. "Riesling was not popular because everyone thought it was too sweet. So I decided to put the word 'Dry' on the label, because my wines were dry. Once people realized that, everything changed."

Then, almost defiantly, he added, "I was the first to use the word 'Dry' on the label, but everyone else followed me. It helped them." He was still focusing on the idea that he didn't do enough to help his colleagues. Approaching seventy years old, Hermann Wiemer's legacy had probably seemed secure to him: he moved the Finger Lakes past sweet hybrid wines and proved not only that vinifera could thrive but also that Riesling could be distinctive and superb. I wondered if he were only now considering that his legacy might also include his famously guarded personality—and his isolationist practices.

As we approached the end of our meal that was nearing five hours in length, I began to feel sorry for Hermann. His personality would never have allowed him to become the most collaborative winemaker in the Finger Lakes—he was never going to be Johannes Reinhardt—but I sensed that he never realized how much distance others felt from him. Perhaps the region would be farther along had Hermann been more gregarious, but no doubt it would be farther behind without his hardworking examples. He had offered help in the only way he knew how. And if some of his peers wanted to remember him as an outsider, he also deserved credit for his stellar wines.

More simply put, I just couldn't help but like the man. And if Hermann had given others the time he had given me at Taverna Banfi in Ithaca, I think they would have too.

* * *

In the charming village of Hammondsport, on the southern tip of Keuka Lake, there is a restaurant that attracts the region's true wine geeks. That's because the wine list at the Village Tavern is almost shocking in its selection of aged wines.

In Napa or Bordeaux or Rome this would hardly be so surprising. But in the Finger Lakes, consumers drink just about everything they buy within a few months of purchase. The concern is that the wine won't age gracefully.

And yet the Village Tavern eschews such concerns with flair, boasting the longest and oldest list of wines in the area. The Tavern can serve a mysterious McGregor Black Russian Red from the mid-'90s, or a selection of Cabernet Franc from the same period, or a flight of Finger Lakes Rieslings going back ten years. When my wife and I sat down for dinner on a sun-soaked fall evening we were intrigued by the list. The oldest local Riesling on the list was the 1994 Hermann J. Wiemer Dry Riesling.

Even with the respect we hold for Hermann, we had modest expectations. The world's best Rieslings can age for decades, but in order for this to be possible the winemaking must be meticulous. The grapes must come from ideal vineyard sites. Fifteen years old is quite an age for any wine, and few Finger Lakes wines had shown the stuff to keep improving for that long. Most were shot by that age, becoming little more than fruity salad dressing.

When the bottle finally arrived even the label looked tired, but the waitress assured us that the wine had been stored in the most careful conditions. The first indicator was a good one: this old Riesling was a gorgeous yellow in the glass, not the oxidized orange that afflicts so many of its ilk. My wife and I looked at each other curiously, swirled the wine, and buried our noses in its aroma. This was the real test.

The reaction from my wife was the same response from almost all wine lovers I know when they discover an old wine that is not only still alive, but thriving. After one long inhalation they look up in excitement and produce a kind of grunt that sounds like, "Ahh—Ohh!" No other words are necessary.

I felt the same. Hermann's Rieslings yield all kinds of interesting aromas and flavors, but in their youth they are nothing like this wine.

I found myself thinking of toffee, subtle petrol, and even tropical fruits that announced the wine's vitality. This wine wasn't barely hanging on. It was changing into brand new clothes to show off a different side.

"This seems . . . *young*," I said. "I can't believe it."

We were so excited that we insisted our waitress grab a glass and experience the wine with us. We laughed as she sniffed the wine and nearly shouted over the buzz of dining-room conversation. We wondered how we could somehow stretch out this bottle and share it with everyone in the restaurant.

That bottle lasted longer than most I can recall. We didn't want it to end. With the final sips resting in our glasses we chose to swirl and smell the wine long before we finally extinguished it. And when it was gone, I imagined Hermann's distinctive voice speaking through his ageless Riesling, reminding us that he might not have been a man of many words, but he helped his colleagues simply by doing what no one thought possible. That was enough for him, and for me.

THREE

The Local Boy: Dave Whiting

November 12, 1986
Watkins Glen, New York

There was no reason to hurry, which is convenient when the vehicle you're driving won't exceed fifty miles per hour. Dave Whiting was twenty-one years old and he was on his own schedule now. His freshly minted bachelor of science in biology from the State University of New York at Binghamton wasn't attracting any job offers and winter was just a few weeks away. Why not leave upstate New York for fairer weather—literally—and better prospects?

His plan was simple: he would drive south until it was warm and then he would turn right. He would stop when he felt it was time to stop.

But what seemed like a one-day journey turned into a full week when the sun refused to appear. The northeastern snow turned to pounding rain and, by the time Dave had reached Tennessee, he was sick of driving south. So he turned right.

The advantage to driving a 1971 Volkswagen Camper Bus was its roomy sleeping arrangements. The disadvantage was everything else. With the pedal to the floor, Dave's raggedy camper would cough along at forty-nine miles per hour, annoyed octogenarians speeding past him in adjoining lanes. Shaped like an oversized cinder block on wheels, it bore the undignified color of an Idaho potato, unpeeled and spotted with dirty bruises. This was not the vehicle that was going to convince young women to join him for a night out and, on occasion, disrobe in its back seat.

Dave was in no position to complain, however. He had no savings account, and his checking account could be described as containing hundreds, and not thousands, of dollars. Sure, the camper probably consumed a gallon and a half of gas just in starting the engine, but gas was cheap in 1986 and its poor mileage was more than balanced by the fact that it saved Dave hotel costs. He was able to cross the country for almost nothing, and by the time the sun returned to the sky he had driven all the way to California.

Staying with some family outside San Diego for a few weeks, Dave declared that he would become "a naturalist," whatever that meant. Or, if that didn't work out, he would drive to Sacramento and work for the California Department of Food and Agriculture. But before he could even apply for a job he found a new love: wine. And he could credit his aging camper for helping him discover it.

It happened on the banks of the Russian River in Sonoma County. Dave had traveled north to search for jobs and almost accidentally arrived in wine country. But unlike many tourists, Dave was not interested in the massive estates—"The buildings were more interesting than the wines," he would later say—and at first the industry didn't impress him. Then one afternoon he stopped into a small tasting room, bought a bottle of Zinfandel and wineglasses, and jumped back in his camper. That night, with no place to stay, Dave rolled his camper up close to the banks of the Russian River and made himself a classic bachelor's dinner. He built a fire, pulled up a folding chair, scarfed down some fast food, and opened the wine.

He was captivated by the wine and, he admitted to himself, by the romantic nature of the setting. It felt corny, but Dave thought it too perfect a moment to pass up the chance to pull out his banjo. Sitting there on the bank of the river, warm from the wine and fire, Dave plucked out a few jangly, upbeat tunes.

He spent the next week seeking out the smaller producers and low-watt estates. He found that those smaller wineries looked a lot like the wineries back home in the Finger Lakes. And while the Finger Lakes wine industry was not exactly booming, it was starting to grow. Dave resolved to head back east and break into the business, but he had one serious concern: everyone he met in the California wine industry—even the tasting-room staff, it seemed—had enology or viticulture degrees. He knew his lack of such a degree might be an impediment to higher-level winemaking jobs. He resolved to read every book ever published on wine. It would satiate his curiosity while preparing him for the Graduate Record Examination, or GRE, the following April. And he would take any jobs he could get, learning every part of the trade.

The GRE was offered only once a year, and after moving back east Dave signed up for the exam nearest his home in the central Finger Lakes. He figured the GRE would erase any doubts future employers might have about his education. He supplemented his book learning with a combination of vineyard and cellar jobs, learning how to pick and prune in the vineyard and how to operate the equipment in the winery. Over three months Dave read every book in the local library that had anything to do with wine, winemaking, wine drinking, and grapes. As April approached, he felt confident about the GRE, and he was making plans to follow a successful exam with an application to enology school. He would become a classically trained winemaker. No one would be able to doubt his credentials.

But on the morning of the exam his old camper once again altered his career path. Dave sat in the driver's seat on the top of the hill, trying to get the engine to turn over. It wouldn't. This was not necessarily a problem, as Dave had learned to get the camper rolling downhill and then jump in, starting it with the wheels already in motion. The vehicle was parked at the top of a long gravel driveway, so it was pointing downhill.

With sleet sticking to his glasses, Dave crouched low behind the back of the bus and shoved his weight into it. The wheels started to turn and he sprinted around to the front door. From the driver's seat Dave could see that the vehicle was pointed slightly off the shoulder of the road, and he tried to drag the steering wheel over enough to straighten it out. But the icy gravel would not cooperate, and soon the camper was rumbling downhill and picking up speed. Dave covered his face as the bus lurched off the road into a mud-filled ditch.

The camper's thud provided the final verdict: Dave was not going to make it to the GRE. He was not going to enology school. If he were to become a great winemaker, he was going to have to earn the industry's respect through a lot of arduous, backbreaking work.

And he was going to have to find the money for a new car.

I WAS GOING TO BE LATE, BUT DAMNED IF I WASN'T GOING TO TRY TO defy the laws of time and space. I had just turned south onto the main road that runs alongside Seneca Lake's northeastern side, and I was flying. Fortunately for me, there seems to be exactly the same number of cops in that area as there are old U.S. Army weapons storage facilities, which is to say: only one. I would take my chances and crank the speedometer.

Dave Whiting, the owner and head winemaker of Red Newt Cellars, had invited me to attend a rather exclusive dinner and wine tasting. Dave is a curious soul who loves to explore wine with people who share his enthusiasm for discovery. His curious nature is not only what led him to this career; it created opportunities to learn when he chose a path that did not include a winemaking degree.

Working his way through the winery food chain, Dave had worked for five different producers before launching his own winery in 1997, and he's never stopped asking questions. Every five weeks or so, Dave invites a group of fellow winemakers from the Finger Lakes along with other industry insiders to join him at his winery to talk wine. And taste a lot of it.

There are several secret society groups that convene in the Finger Lakes, and this is one of them.

Sharing wine is hardly the only attraction. Dave's wife, Deb, happens to be one of the finest chefs in upstate New York, and she prepares five courses to enjoy with the various bottles. It was Deb's cooking wizardry that convinced the couple that their winery needed an adjoining bistro. She also serves seasonal appetizers, and tonight that meant her highly sought fig biscuits. Everyone who attends is asked to bring one bottle of wine to fit the evening's theme, and every wine is tasted blind. This tends to spark all manner of debate over style, place of origin, and every fine detail that industry artists grow to appreciate. Only rarely do such debates lead to broken bones or broken friendships.

Though I had never been privileged enough to attend before, I had heard tales of towering conversation and philosophical conversion, of perspicacious winemakers boasting of their unparalleled palates, and others declaring some kind of spiritual epiphany. These were probably urban legends, but there was no doubting the depth of knowledge in which I'd be immersing myself. And trying, like mad, not to look and sound like a fool. I'm confident in my assessment of wines, and I've written about wine for various blogs and publications for quite some time. But in this case, on this night, everyone at the table would be either a winemaker or, at the very least, connected closely to the making of wine. Everyone except me. I hoped I could contribute to the conversation without making myself look too silly.

Of course, arriving late was not the ideal way to blend respectfully into my surroundings. I had left work in Rochester at precisely 5:59 p.m., fresh from the anchor desk and directly out the door at the conclusion of the five o'clock news. I hadn't even bothered to wash my face, which remained caked in two layers of makeup (foundation and bronzer, thanks for asking). That left me sixty-one minutes to travel seventy-five miles, one quarter of which were of the crumbling-path variety.

I could not have imagined a more glorious summer day to make such a furious drive. It was a windows-down, shades-on, carefree kind of evening. Even better, it came directly on the heels of three weeks of incessant deluge. The earth was saturated, the crops were pumped up and beautiful, and the crumpled landscape was a full Crayola box of colors.

I couldn't help but ease my foot off the gas just a touch; these moments are fleeting in wet summers, and I was trying to absorb the landscape while tearing through it. The road on Seneca Lake's northeast side is unusual—most lake roads hug the nearby body of water and provide the driver with stunning views. Here, though, a tight ridge of farmland separates the road from the lake, obscuring the view of the water but offering even more interesting vistas of soaring corn and sunflowers that seem to stretch to the sky. I was much more accustomed to wide, flat acres of corn. On this evening, out the right side of my Toyota, the corn hugged the rising land, bouncing the sun off the burnt orange tops.

I sped past roadside stands that provide local farmers a vital economic boost during these months. I smiled to see signs grow more jocular as I continued south: "Campfire wood." "Fresh vegetables—leave money in basket." "Hey Sunshine! Get your summer flowers!" "Sweeeeet corn." "Lemonade, only one dollar!!! Per cup." And, my favorite, "Make sure to stop at the Best Little Hair House In Hector!"

All shapes and sizes of wineries dotted the lakeside route—there are now more than a hundred in the Finger Lakes. I smiled as I passed the most visually interesting structure: Shalestone Vineyards, a tiny operation literally carved into the side of a hill. The large wooden door and front frame are half-covered with climbing plants, making it difficult to see that a manmade structure exists in the spot. Most peculiar of all is the sign proudly declaring, "Red is all we do." A Finger Lakes winemaker who chooses not to make Riesling is like an Irish pub owner who chooses not to carry Guinness. And yet owner and winemaker Rob Thomas had built a sustainable and thriving operation. I wondered if the fact that he doesn't stress about money helps him make outstanding wines. He's a quiet man, bearded and humble, and on my only previous visit I found myself engaged in thoughtful conversation for three hours. As Shalestone faded from my rearview mirror I made a mental note to schedule a return trip in the near future, and I wondered if I would see Rob at Red Newt.

I arrived at Red Newt at exactly fourteen minutes past seven o'clock, in time for the first pour. The cognoscenti made me feel instantly comfortable. Of the many compelling reasons to settle down in the Finger Lakes, winemakers often cite their joy over the gregarious disposition of the industry, the full panoply of which was on display when I arrived that night. Dave had saved a seat for me directly to his right and in the middle of the series of tables that had been pulled into a giant square to allow the guests to face one another. He had cleared the tasting-room floor to make room for his guests, so our tables were surrounded by two long tasting bars and several windows framing the setting sun. Many of the faces were new to me, but they extended the welcome of lifelong friends.

I delighted in the format and the theme for the evening, which was dry rosé from around the world. Rosé is usually dismissed as unserious wine, but a growing number of French producers had taken to making carefully crafted rosé at higher price points. The wider wine industry followed, and while prices have risen as a consequence rosé is still categorically a very good value for the price. We were all instructed to bring one bottle within the parameters of the theme. Dave explained that he wanted to give more attention to his own rosé bottlings, and he felt a rosés-of-the-world theme would be instructive for him. In the years since his first flirtations with wine on the banks of the Russian River, Dave has never extinguished his curiosity and willingness to learn. I have often felt that others in the industry would gain from taking such an approach.

There were twenty of us that night. Dave sends two bagged bottles around the table at a time, allowing each guest a short pour of the mystery pair. Only Dave knows what wine is inside each individual bag—and given the fact that he has to line up two dozen to pour, he tends to forget the order. While sampling the various culinary treasures composed by Deb, the guests banter over the possible origins of the wines, the styles and likely philosophies of the winemakers, and the varieties of grapes used.

We laughed as Morten Hallgren, the supremely talented winemaker at Ravines Wine Cellars, accurately guessed wine after wine's home region. Only a bizarre Chilean rosé halted his momentum. Then, when we agreed that one of the mystery wines was dreadful, Dave asked for my description. I confessed the wine smelled of unripe strawberries and unwashed socks. It turned out to be a Finger Lakes wine, and I exhaled when it was confirmed that the winemaker was not at the table.

Then the atmosphere shifted sharply from that of a wine-themed parlor game to the kind of purposeful self-analysis about which I'd heard so much. The jocularity softened when I asked if the winemakers viewed rosé as a nice summer wine or something more. As he often does, a man named Bob Madill delivered the critique that many of his colleagues didn't enjoy hearing—and he took the occasion to move far beyond my question about the status of rosé wines.

"Sometimes we have to ask ourselves, 'What the hell are we doing?'" he said. Bob is the part-owner and winegrower at Sheldrake Point on Cayuga Lake. A short, thin Canadian with thinning gray hair and a mustache, Bob was a ubiquitous presence at Finger Lakes wine events. He was generally acerbic and never shy to tell someone they were wrong, but he also commanded the respect of the industry. He declared that too many of his colleagues—including some of those in attendance that night—did not have the proper focus to survive long-term in the Finger Lakes.

"Our focus needs to be *aromatic white wines*," he said, adding an emphatic staccato to the last three words. "We want to connect to the gatekeepers of the industry, right? Then can someone explain why we're making so much Merlot? We have to focus on our strength and show how we do it differently. If we don't focus on aromatic white wines, we're bound to fail. We don't have to like the game, but we have to play it."

The ensuing gap of silence provided me the opportunity to probe deeper. "But Bob, the wider industry doesn't view aromatic white wines as wines that can age—not from here, at least."

"And they're wrong," he said, raising a finger. "They think those ridiculous high-alcohol California wines can age fifteen years, but they want everyone to drink Finger Lakes wine now? It's laughable! Now, most of our consumers have no intention of aging their wines, and as a consequence very few of us even keep a library. But people would be *shocked* to find out what a Finger Lakes Riesling can do in ten years. It's our responsibility to focus on that potential."

Bob was speaking to the hundred or more wineries that had sprung up in the past two decades only to make inconsistent, mediocre wine. The Finger Lakes wine industry was doomed to failure if it continued to imitate warm-weather regions like Napa. But positioned as the cool-climate alternative with world-class Riesling and, on occasion, other world-class offerings, there was reason to believe that the Finger Lakes could see its profile rise and its profitability grow.

Eventually the light-hearted games resumed, and everyone sat back in their chairs. I left the Newt that night with a bounce in my step, fueled by the thought of ever-improving local wines. There was so much left to be discovered, but at least the pioneers of our region were seeking the answers. The only question I had was whether those answers would be found in my lifetime.

* * *

Every great wine region has its culinary treasures, and the Finger Lakes can now claim the same. The jewel—at least for those who have discovered it—is Suzanne Fine Regional Cuisine on the southeastern side of Seneca Lake (the restaurant strangely declines a possessive in its name). Two weeks after I attended the wine cognoscenti's party at Red Newt, I convinced Dave and Deb Whiting to join my wife and me for dinner at Suzanne. It was a chance for Dave to continue his study of rosé wine.

Suzanne was not my first suggestion. Deb Whiting's talent impresses diners at the Red Newt Bistro every day and night, and I left the dinner plans open to her. I have found that dining with winemakers and chefs can be a delicate matter at times; should I suggest that the chef make the meal? Would a chef find it insulting if my first choice were somewhere other than his or her own kitchen? Similarly, should I order a bottle of the winemaker's wine for the meal? Would most prefer to try other wines, or would they be offended if I didn't ask for their own creations? The nightmarish start to my dinner with Hermann Wiemer had embedded a small scar on my brain that tingled every time I sat down with a winemaker.

But Deb had removed all discomfort from the scenario. When I broached the subject of dinner, Deb immediately parried any thought of eating at the bistro.

Suzanne is a trove of Finger Lakes bounty. The chef and owner, Suzanne Stack, combines the salubrious with the sumptuous and has crafted an impressive list of older regional wines. The restaurant is a house built in 1903 that has hardly changed a bit since then. It borders Suzanne's impressive organic garden, which is the source for many of the chef's ingredients. Having dined at Suzanne previously, my wife and I arrived with the ebullience of young sports fans walking into the ballpark.

Dave was dressed as formally as I've ever seen him—black mock turtleneck and a suit coat. Deb was wearing a simple summer dress and wore a permanent but genuine smile that betrayed her excitement over the meal. I rarely trust thin chefs, but Deb is an exception; she carries the figure of a woman unaffected by caloric intake whatsoever. Her short hair matches the same soft brown color of her husband's, but while Deb's hair is always neat, Dave's bushy mop seems never to be combed the same way twice. Even his mustache seems to be a different length on each new visit to his winery. He is not blessed with his wife's immunity to weight gain, but he carries only the expected softness around the edges of a man at middle age.

As we sized up the menu, Dave explained that his Volkswagen bus was long gone, but it had left an indelible mark on his relationship with Deb.

"He made me push that thing on our first date," Deb said, wincing at the memory.

Dave smiled proudly. "That's true. I came home from work, got to the end of the road that led to my house, and there's Deb. She was very early and very nervous. I didn't know how long she'd been there, but she was pacing back and forth. So I stopped the camper and got out to say hello. We got back in the camper and it wouldn't start. I said, 'Not to worry, I'm used to this.' So I got out and started pushing it down the hill. That's when I heard Deb say, 'Is there anything I can do?'"

My wife dropped her face to her hands. "Oh, no," she said.

Dave smiled more broadly. "Yep. I said, 'Well, you can help push if you want!' And so she hopped out and did!"

"I should have known," Deb said. "When I met him at a party he told me he was a cellar master. I thought that meant that he kept rats. He was not your everyday guy."

Dave asked me to order wine for the meal, but I insisted he take the lead. He wanted to wait until we selected the food for the evening first. That turned out to be nearly impossible. It's impractical to order everything on a restaurant's menu, but we felt nearly compelled to try. We finally settled on a wondrous compilation of local foods: salads fresh from the garden out back (with the most delicious heirloom tomatoes I've ever had, including one that nearly robbed me of my sight thanks to its packed juices); warm asparagus soup with local goat cheese; a stack of duck confit; and a main course of filet mignon from grass-fed cows that were raised just a few miles to the north.

For the first course Dave ordered a bottle of 2007 Ravines Dry Rosé. He wanted to extend the theme from two weeks before, and he thought it would pair nicely with the food. He was right. But it was the second bottle that left an impression on me that remains pure and vivid to this day.

The idea of Finger Lakes Pinot Noir is a good one. The practice of it is another thing entirely. Unlike many of the popular red wine grapes of the world, Pinot Noir does not need a scorching climate. In fact, Pinot wilts and retreats if the temperature gets too hot. The Finger Lakes provides the kind of warm days and cool nights on which Pinot thrives in its native Burgundy. But Finger Lakes grape growers have rarely been willing to cut down the cropload and give the grape a chance to shine, and if it's overcropped, it makes thin, simple wine unworthy of anyone's time or cash.

I harbored some optimism when Dave ordered the 2005 Ravines Pinot Noir, however. Winemaker Morten Hallgren had stunned me with his 2005 Meritage blend, and I was anxious to see if he could turn such a trick with the fickle Pinot Noir. Given its track record in the Finger Lakes, I was doubtful.

The wine simply overwhelmed us. Not with power, but with subtlety and grace. Reviewers love to use the term *elegant* to describe a wine, but it's often difficult to discern what that means. The 2005 Ravines Pinot defined the word. It was finesse and silk, and for a wine that many drinkers would describe as being light in body, it had a mile-long finish. I could hardly believe it, but I contained my enthusiasm long enough to ask Dave for his thoughts on the bottle in front of us.

"This is really something," he said. "Really complex. That's rare. Really rich cherries, a cedar box element, and a lot of earthy flavors."

I was relieved to know I wasn't nuts. My wife was burying her nose in her glass a second and third time to unwrap the wine completely. This Pinot was far better than almost every Pinot I've had from America's West Coast (with a few happy exceptions). It sold out not long after release—Morten doesn't make very many cases—but I sought it out aggressively in the weeks following that dinner. It was, for me, a kind of Grail Wine, a wine that proves that distinctive, complex, special red wines are possible in the Finger Lakes. I was eager to find more.

Like Morten Hallgren, Dave Whiting gets the bulk of his grapes from other growers. He has had the chance to evaluate varying Finger Lakes sites over the years, and I asked him his thoughts about the concept of *terroir*—the impact of the location where wine is grown and made.

"It's a really neat concept," he said slowly and carefully. "It's a really loaded word, and I try to shy away from using it. The problem is that it's overused, so we can never be sure what someone means by it. I prefer to talk about wine's sense of place. I've seen things that amaze me. You can definitely see the sense of place every day."

"Give me an example," I said.

"You see it in individual vineyard blocks. One of the vineyard blocks I've become very familiar with over the years has been the vineyard that is now Atwater just a few miles from here. It used to be a very small winery that would sell most of its fruit. The various places I worked during the 1990s bought fruit from that farm and I got to know it well. There were, I think, seven different Riesling plantings on that farm. They all had slightly different soil, different topography, and different clones. And every one of those Rieslings was distinctly different. You could literally throw a stone fifty yards from one planting of Riesling to the next, and those two plantings would be remarkably different in expression. I was just fascinated—and still am!—to see such variability in such close proximity."

Deb nearly jumped out of her chair after her husband's story. "Evan and Morgan, you simply must come to our Gewürztraminer dinner that we're having soon. You'll see exactly what Dave is talking about."

They explained that Dave had decided to bottle his Gewürztraminer without blending different vineyard crops together. The result, they thought, would be several wines from the same stretch of land but with wildly different personalities. Most winemakers—in the Finger Lakes and elsewhere—blend different lots of wine together; the better lots can mask some of the weaker lots' deficiencies.

We finished the meal with lemon pudding cakes. Dave said he would let me know when Red Newt was prepared to host the Gewürztraminer dinner. "Find a way to clear your schedule for it," he said with a mysterious smile. "I think this could really change things for me."

* * *

Three months to the day after I made that initial, furious drive down to Red Newt, I found myself making the same sprint under starkly different conditions. Gone was the summer green. The crops had left the ground weeks ago. The leaves had all turned and fallen. All of which would have made for a much drearier setting for a drive, had I been able to see any of it through the snow.

The first major snowfall of the year always seems to come at the most inopportune time, and that was certainly the case on this occasion. I arrived late for the Red Newt Gewürztraminer tasting, but fortunately, so did everyone else.

Deb Whiting greeted me with a hug, and the winemaker emerged from the cellar with a gaggle of bottles under each arm. He resembled a happy hunter, boastful of his marksmanship. Setting the bottles out on the bistro bar, he smiled at me and said, "Get your eyes off these bottles or you'll ruin the tasting for yourself!"

No winemaker in the Finger Lakes exposes himself and his wines to the unmerciful condemnation of colleagues more than Dave Whiting. At the blind tasting parties like the one I had attended in August, where guests tend to be viciously honest, Dave loved to pour his own wines. He welcomes the criticism. That is not by any means the norm when it comes to his ilk.

But tonight he was undertaking a particularly risky experiment—one that could hurt him financially and injure the reputation of the wine he pronounced to be the "best he had ever made." When a winery has a special wine, the easy thing to do is slap a marked-up price on it, withhold supply, and try to drive the market artificially. Dave had resolved to do the exact opposite. He had invited fifteen friends and colleagues to the bistro for a private tasting. He would pour a dozen wines blind, and somewhere in that group would be his two new single-vineyard Gewürztraminers. Guests would take as much time as they needed to consider the aromas, the taste, and the finish. Each wine would receive a score of 0, 1, 2, or 3, and each would be totaled and discussed before Dave would reveal what had been tasted.

His goal was to see where his prized wine—the Curry Creek Vineyard Gewürztraminer—would rank against some of the best Gewürztraminer on the world market. But not every bottle was an expensive one, and not every wine was a high-end one. Dave and Deb Whiting had chosen carefully. The bottles ranged in price from $12 to more than $70, and they came from the most respected region for Gewürztraminer —Alsace—as well as Germany, California, and even South America.

Dave thought he had found the Finger Lakes version of the great Côte d'Or vineyards in Burgundy, at least when it came to Finger Lakes Gewürztraminer. But he wanted to be sure.

"What happens if your Curry Creek Gewürztraminer ranks last?" one of the guests asked as we took our seats.

"Well, I guess that means it's not nearly as good as I think it is," Dave responded with a shrug, and then, "And it probably means I'm not as good as I hope I am."

Before we began I thought of a column written by Lettie Teague in *Food & Wine*. She had visited the Finger Lakes to do a story on outstanding Riesling, which she found. But she had been so impressed with Finger Lakes Gewürztraminer that she convinced her editors to allow her to shift the focus of the piece. Teague wrote:

> Like a character in a Jane Austen novel, I ended up falling in love with another: Gewürztraminer. . . . I'd met three producers who made great Gewürztraminer, a wine that is incredibly hard to grow, that virtually no one (outside of Alsace) makes properly. . . . It occurred to me that Finger Lakes winemakers took Gewürztraminer for granted the way I did New York [wine]. I only hoped it wouldn't take them two decades to figure out that what they had in Gewürztraminer was greatness enough.

One of the three producers that Teague had referred to was Whiting. The other two were Standing Stone, where Dave had previously made wine, and Hermann Wiemer.

The bistro staff had pulled several long tables together for the tasting, and we would need the space. Each guest was presented with a dozen wineglasses, a glass jar for dumping and spitting, a water glass, and a bread plate for the various palate cleansers Deb had prepared.

Gewürztraminer is very much like a rock band that will perform only if the concert organizers can deliver on a long list of silly demands. Remember the rock group that demanded all brown M&M candies in their hotel room? That's Gewürztraminer. Warm weather but not hot; stressed soils, but only if they don't contain chalk; late picking to allow the grapes to develop complex aromatics, but not so late that the acids drop away. Oh, and a little rain but not too much, because Gewürz is easily afflicted with disease. It is a recalcitrant grape that thwarts many of its most careful, respectful suitors.

But when its demands are met, Gewürztraminer can become rock and roll in a glass. The best Gewürz smells like an exotic party. It has a wide variety of spices, flowery aromas, and plenty of tropical fruit. For an encore Gewürz often provides a long finishing note of lychee, an Asian tree fruit.

"No holding back," Dave instructed as he began to pass sealed brown-bagged bottles around the table, each bag labeled only with a number. "Be thorough." If Finger Lakes wines really could stand up to the world's best, we were about to find out.

* * *

This was hardly the Judgment of Paris—the famous 1976 tasting in which a handful of California wineries beat their French counterparts—but it was plenty significant to Dave Whiting's career. And, if the expressions on the faces of his guests were any indication, they too were hoping his Curry Creek Gewürztraminer would perform well. Finger Lakes winemakers are constantly itching for opportunities to compare their wines to wines from other, more highly publicized regions. When one local winemaker stands out, the entire region stands to benefit.

We had tasted through the entire flight in near total silence, swirling, sniffing, and sipping the dozen wines. Only the occasional clink of a glass or swishing in a taster's mouth dented the quiet. While I hoped to be able to identify Dave's wine, I knew that would be difficult. So I focused on each wine individually, and when it was over I was surprised at the variety of Gewürztraminer in front of us. Some were spellbinding. Others were standard, solid wines that wouldn't stand out in a crowd.

But two of the wines were undrinkable. I could only hope that the Curry Creek Gewürz was not one of them.

I was seated next to Brandon Seager, Dave's stylish young assistant winemaker who had a brilliant nose and palate for wine. As he stood up to stretch I peeked at his notes. They were opened to the second wine, which I had scored zero points. I had found the wine to be "hot, boring, too sweet." Brandon's notes revealed a more articulate take: "For 50 cents I can get a real creamsicle and not pay a ton for this garbage."

It was not, thankfully, the Curry Creek.

A curious scenario unfolded as we revealed our scores and analyses: most of the wines earned wildly inconsistent scores, while two wines were roundly panned and one split the judges in half. The polarizing Gewürztraminer caught our attention as we read off the scores for this wine aloud: 1, 1, 1, 1, 3, 3, 3, 3, 2, 1, 1, 1, 3, 3, 3.

The thin majority that had given the wine three points (myself included) wanted to know what the others found lacking. Paul Brock, a highly talented young intellectual, and the winemaker at the very well regarded Lamoreaux Landing on Seneca Lake, provided the opening salvo in what would become a deluge of debate. "It's a nicely made wine, but I'm worried that this is all there is to it."

The bistro dining room reverberated for the next half-hour with the sounds of lively discussion about the potential and character of Gewürztraminer. Peter Bell, winemaker at Fox Run Vineyards across the lake, explained that he finds that most Gewürztraminers need at least twelve to eighteen months in the bottle before they begin to peak. "That's if the wine is well made," Peter added. "If it's poorly made, then it will always be crap."

This wine seemed to have its own personality. It was fascinating without being obviously European. Not everyone was convinced this was a good thing. Then, Bob Madill—the omnipresent Canadian—put forth an idea that had every one of us nodding in agreement.

"We're not in France, folks," he said with a shrug. "If Alsace is your model for what Gewürztraminer should be, there's not a whole lot of room there. It either is or it isn't. But we're on Seneca Lake, which means we're not looking for one narrow definition. We're looking for the best wine. That's it."

As the coterie continued its critique, I sat back and listened, thinking of what I might say about this wine. Straw-colored, it boasted the kind of crisp acidity that the best Finger Lakes Rieslings offer, but it also had a kind of luscious exotic fruit as well. My notes read simply, "Love the nose / passionfruit / a little tight? Tremendous balance, acidity."

More than anything, I was nervous. If this were Dave's wine, would he be pleased with the polarized discussion?

Before Dave pulled the bottle out of the bag, he asked for a final opinion. The guests agreed that if the wine was more than two years old, it was a nice wine with nowhere to go but down. If it was still an infant, it had enormous potential.

The label was familiar and we applauded as Dave revealed that the wine in question was his Curry Creek. He had listened to the debate with a kind of insouciance—which should have been a dead giveaway that he was feeling exactly the opposite, no doubt taking in every critical word. Dave offered to pass his wine around and what followed was the strange palpation that occurs when a group of wine lovers discover a special bottle.

I caught him grinning with satisfied relief, and as we continued our analysis of the other wines, I couldn't help but feel a great sense of pride in what Dave was accomplishing.

* * *

Just a few months later, one of the most important wine publications in the world noted Dave's achievement. *Wine Spectator* gave Dave Whiting's wine 90 points, the first Finger Lakes Gewürztraminer ever to land that high a score—and it wasn't even Dave's Curry Creek bottling. Dave's 2007 Sawmill Creek single-vineyard bottling earned the 90-point score; Dave's Curry Creek snagged an impressive 89 points. Reviewer James Molesworth had written that Dave's wines were "very tight still," and it was clear that he saw the same aging potential that we saw on that November night at the bistro.

Dave likes to say that magazine scores are for the masses, and I agree. But they are powerful nonetheless, and *Wine Spectator*'s reviewer had taken the time to come to the Finger Lakes and visit with Dave for a private tasting. He discovered that Dave Whiting's curiosity has not been even slightly extinguished since he fell in love with wine on the banks of the Russian River. Dave is still learning with each passing vintage, and reaching the 90-point mark is a high honor indeed for the man who had started out with little more than an old VW bus—and a plan to drive south and turn right—a quarter-century ago.

FOUR

The Great Dane: Morten Hallgren

Summer, 1978
Provence, France

It was just a short drive south to the Mediterranean Sea, but fifteen-year-old Morten Hallgren was more interested in the skeletons. And the Knights Templar. And the old Roman coins. The sea was fun, sure, but there was so much to discover in his family's new estate.

The Hallgren family had just made a bold, exciting change: moving from their native Denmark to Provence in the south of France, the Hallgrens were going to make wine. Coming from a real-estate background, the Hallgrens had no experience making wine—but they were going to learn quickly. Many old-world European wineries are handed down from generation to generation, and the Hallgrens impressed upon their kids their hope that this winemaking enterprise would become a Hallgren family tradition. Morten, the oldest of four children, was willing to consider a future in the business, to the extent that any fifteen-year-old can think so far ahead. At that moment he was happier to pass his hours exploring.

His family had purchased 270 acres comprising the estate known as Domaine de Castel Roubine, and more than half those acres were planted with vineyards. The remaining hundred acres swelled with history and mystery. The property's first grapevines were planted by the Knights Templar in 1307. When they weren't fighting in the Crusades and—depending on what you believe—guarding the deepest secrets in human history, the knights were cultivating farmlands across Europe. Morten liked to imagine them, gallant in chain mail and on horseback, patrolling the estate grounds.

But long before the Knights Templar arrived, the Romans made their own lasting mark at Roubine. As the Roman Empire expanded, gladiatorial combat ascended as a form of entertainment. The Romans built a dungeon and stable in the nearby hilltop town of Lorgues to house the animals in preparation for the brutal games. Soldiers would march the beasts to the Roman arena in the town of Frejus, traveling from the menagerie in Lorgues along a winding road that cut through the fields that eventually became the vineyards of Roubine. The museum in Lorgues commemorates such events with all manner of Roman artifacts, but Morten took more delight in hunting for mementos on his family's new estate. Hidden under layers of earth were rare coins made of bronze and brass, silver and gold. And somewhere below the structure of the Roubine home, the bones of Roman women took their well-deserved rest—Morten would find out years later that the house was built on top of an old Roman bordello.

The stunning three-story stone estate, remodeled with high windows and balconies, opened to a tiered grass courtyard, replete with fountains, statues, and a coat of arms on the wall that stood over the gently rolling countryside below. Past the vines, Morten and his siblings reveled among the trees that bore an array of fruit: fig, apricot, cherry, pear, and apple. Weaving through the trees were wild berry bushes and herbs that would season the family meals. Morten could not have known it then, but he was training his palate to recognize the dozens of nuanced flavors that would emerge in his wines.

It was truly an Elysian life for a young boy, but Morten would not return to his family's estate as an adult until many years later.

After graduating high school in 1983, he began nearly nine years of college in the United States. In that decade, Morten piled up degrees and certificates on his way to becoming an astrophysicist. When his family and friends would ask what he was studying, Morten would respond dryly, "I build models of the universe. I'm learning the structure of the cosmos."

The more he tried to explain the structure of the universe, the more he found himself thinking about something far simpler—the structure of the grapes hanging in his family's vineyards. He contemplated how much more useful a life in winemaking could be. "There's not a whole lot of practical application in cosmology," he conceded to friends.

So in 1992, at the age of twenty-nine, Morten quit his pursuit of astrophysics and went home to his Danish family in southern France. He found himself back in the cellar, relearning the wine trade. His siblings had come home too. Everything was in place for the next generation of Hallgren children to turn Domaine de Castel Roubine into a world-class winery, just as their parents hoped they would. Morten's wife, Lisa, a smart, cheerful Texan, had a background in marketing and would take care of sales. His sister had an MBA and a specialization in finance, so she would run the business end of things. His brother-in-law was training to become the vineyard manager. Morten began several years of winemaking school and internships, which led him to Cos d'Estournel in Bordeaux, a revered chateau that produces some of the most aggressively sought wines on the international market. There, Morten learned the importance of balance in wine—he found that the best wines have some muscle but also plenty of grace and, when made well, can age for decades. The staff at Cos occasionally opened bottles from the early 1900s, which were still drinking beautifully. Morten was inspired.

Back at Roubine, Morten's parents were enjoying the work and rewards of the wine life. They produced wines from a range of grapes: Mourvèdre, Grenache, Cabernet Sauvignon, Carignan, Cinsault, Ugni Blanc, Sémillon, and Clairette. It was a constant learning experience, and they expected that when Morten was ready to assume winemaking duties at Roubine, the quality would rise. As their children's career paths converged in 1994, the couple prepared to slowly hand over responsibilities. They transferred the title of the estate to their children's names. Then, the Hallgren family saw an opportunity to expand the wine operation. A large building bordering their estate was for sale and they decided to purchase the building and turn it into their brand-new winery. The Hallgrens made plans to secure the necessary financing for it. Morten had completed winemaking school and, at the age of thirty, was nearly ready to take the top job at his family's operation.

With the approval of local agencies, the Hallgrens began to build what would become one of Provence's first new wineries in more than forty years. The complicated financing appeared to be in place, with the family working with a French bank.

On the morning that the Hallgren family was set to finally close the deal, everything came apart.

* * *

Most people have probably never heard of the French mafia, but for the Hallgren family, it was easy to wonder if the mafia was targeting their property. Instead of closing the deal to finance the new building—their new winery—they learned that the bank representative who had facilitated the deal had been fired. The bank informed the Hallgrens that the building would now be sold via an auction. This was a curious turn of events, but Morten and his siblings resolved to place a strong enough bid to win the auction and obtain the building.

Several days later, they received notice that the bank was not simply auctioning the building that they intended to convert into a new winery. The bank was auctioning *all of Domaine de Castel Roubine*. The vineyards, the buildings, the house. Everything was going to be sold out from under the Hallgren family.

"This is ridiculous," Morten said with a shrug. "Of course we're not selling the estate. We're adding to it. There's been a mistake."

"They have documents," his sister explained, the blood draining from her face. "Stacks of documents. They have our signatures on the documents."

The room began to spin vertiginously as Morten attempted to grasp what was going on. "We never signed anything. We never signed!"

"I know," his sister said. "But I don't think it matters."

After a frantic but futile effort to stop the auction, Domaine de Castel Roubine was sold to an unknown buyer. The estate was appraised at $15 million, but the winning bidder spent just a tiny fraction of that price, and by the time the bureaucrats had taken their cut, Morten's family didn't have much. Everything had happened so quickly.

The Hallgren family began contacting the authorities that should have been in position to help them, but every effort was stymied. The notary public in charge denied that the signatures were forged. The judge presiding over the auction declined to investigate whether any papers had been falsified and claimed to have no time to hear the Hallgren family complaint. France has an agency that oversees the sale and purchase of agricultural property, but representatives sent a curt reply indicating their assessment that the sale of the Roubine estate was fair.

Morten tracked down a handful of lawyers in Lourges and the surrounding area, but no one was willing to get involved.

That week the Hallgren family sat quietly together at dinner. "We're going to lose the estate," Morten said. "No one will help us." His siblings wondered if the entire court system had been bought off, but even if that were the case, what could they do? A judge would have to decide to hear their case, which could take months or years to play out.

Morten was determined to try. The court that conducted the auction instructed the Hallgren family to vacate Domaine de Castel Roubine within just a few weeks, and in that time Morten and his parents compiled evidence for a lawsuit. Amid the chaos of packing to leave their home, the Hallgrens constructed their case, finally filing a lawsuit claiming they had never consented to the sale of Castel Roubine.

Some family members suggested looking into other means to get the estate back. They floated the idea of contacting courts in other parts of France, and they debated the idea of making a more public protest in the nearby town. But those ideas ultimately went unexplored when some in the family admitted they were scared. While it might have been difficult for outsiders to believe a family's entire 270-acre estate could be essentially stolen, this was a part of France dominated by loose deals and even looser laws. Some in the Hallgren family wondered what might happen if they pressed their protest too fiercely.

They decided to go forward with a criminal court lawsuit, hoping a judge would be sympathetic.

While they waited, Morten took a winemaking job in west Texas, not far from his wife's home. It offered Morten the chance to escape the tumult back in Provence while his family's case slowly moved through the criminal court system. His parents had moved out of Castel Roubine into a small apartment just a mile or so up the road. They were left with nearly nothing, and lived without electricity and a working phone for a short while. Morten was in constant contact with his siblings, who were waiting for the judge to hear their case.

But nothing was happening. After two harvests in Texas, Morten and Lisa moved to North Carolina, where Morten landed a winemaking job at the massive Biltmore Estate. The huge property was reminiscent in some ways of Roubine, boasting a 250-room estate, farm, gardens, fountains, and vineyards. Lisa, a culinary dynamo, appreciated the surroundings but continued to push her husband to stay in touch with his siblings. The problem was that there wasn't much news. Until the judge in France decided to hear their case, there was little to say.

By 1998, four years after the Hallgren family lost Castel Roubine, Morten and Lisa had to make a decision. Morten had become a budding star in American winemaking, and a handful of offers had come in from across the country to steal him away from Biltmore. The most attractive offer came from a winery in upstate New York that promised to make Morten the head winemaker for an operation with a strong reputation. But he and Lisa didn't want to start over again unless they were going to stay. This would essentially mean the end of the dream of going back to Roubine.

After a short conversation with his parents and siblings, Morten felt that they had given up. The judge had shown no interest in hearing their case.

It was nearly impossible to get any information at all. And so, after aiming to build a life in the south of France, Morten and Lisa Hallgren packed all of their things into a small truck and drove north to a region about which they knew almost nothing: the Finger Lakes of New York.

And the Hallgren family stopped speaking of Castel Roubine entirely.

TAKING RISKS IS EASY WHEN YOU'VE ALREADY LOST EVERYTHING once. At age forty-five, Morten Hallgren's immunity to risk could be traced to the loss of Castel Roubine. He had become one of the best winemakers in the eastern United States thanks largely to his willingness to confront the kinds of challenges that carry enormous downside. Most winemakers simply choose to avoid such perils altogether.

Morten and his wife, Lisa, had invited my wife and me to their Penn Yan home for a dinner party on a rain-drenched July evening.

I was eager to learn more about Morten's approach to making wine in a region that never seems to see the same weather patterns twice. Morgan and I looked forward to Lisa's highly regarded culinary offerings, and we knew there would be exciting wines opened over the course of the night. As I have met and dined with dozens of Finger Lakes winemakers, I confess to being amazed at how few are truly enamored with wine. Some winemakers have never sampled a Loire Valley Cabernet Franc; some seem to have no interest whatsoever in trying any wine not made in the Finger Lakes. This is not about eschewing snobbery in wine—it is about lacking the passion requisite to understanding wine and all its complexities. The Finger Lakes is undoubtedly a unique winemaking puzzle, and no one should expect to be able to duplicate the flavors and styles of other regions around the world. But the best winemakers I know routinely seek out wines from all over the world—sometimes to learn, but often to simply enjoy the individuality of a wine's sense of place. Wine is a story, and there are endlcss fascinating tales to discover.

Morten Hallgren suffered no such lack of interest in wine.

When we arrived for dinner, the Hallgren home was its typical maelstrom. A high-ceilinged house from the 1800s, it brimmed with potential, yet it must have been a jarring contrast to the majesty of Castel Roubine. This house was in dire need of repair and renovation. Lisa Hallgren, a fair-skinned woman with a youthful face and soft voice, was racing around the tight quarters of the kitchen, which lacked even a finished floor and doors on some of the cupboards.

Morten had just walked in with reinforcements for Lisa's dinner menu. His short-sleeve flannel shirt was half-untucked from his jeans, and his thick, wavy dark hair betrayed the frantic pace of the day. The extra pounds he had added since coming to the Finger Lakes could be blamed directly on his wife's cooking and his lack of sleep. The Hallgrens had hired no full-time employees since opening Ravines Wine Cellars on Keuka Lake in 2002. With three school-age kids, a house in its never-quite-finished state of remodeling, and the burgeoning winery that produces 7,500 cases a year, rest was a luxury rarely enjoyed.

While we waited for other guests to arrive, Lisa sent Morten, Morgan, and me out to the long, covered front porch. The percussion of the deluge offered a nice backdrop as we opened the first wine of the evening, a dry rosé from southern France. Lisa had picked it up for $35 in a New York City wine shop, and she had spent the next week enduring her husband's incessant ribbing for spending so much on a rosé. Lisa countered that the wine was made just a few miles away from Castel Roubine in Provence, and that region would always have a piece of her heart. It helped that the wine was a classic Provençal rosé—extremely floral and well made, and perfect for a summer evening. We sipped the wine while enjoying Lisa's stylish red pepper spread on toasted baguette.

"This is going to be a heck of an interesting year if the rain continues," Morten said. Hoping to prod him into speaking more about Castel Roubine, I asked him what separated the Finger Lakes from other wine regions—such as Provence. "This," he said, pointing to the sky. "Not because the weather is bad, but because the weather is never the same. There will never be a model from which to work. If you try to grow grapes and make wine the same way every year, you're going to get buried. Making wine here requires an extremely open mind and a willingness to adapt."

As we finished the bottle of rosé, the other guests arrived, including Bob Madill, the general manager and winegrower at Sheldrake Point on Cayuga Lake. I recalled Bob's stirring pontifications at Red Newt Wine Cellars and I wondered what I might learn from him tonight. Bob shook Morten's hand violently and immediately barked, "Here, decant this." He handed Morten a 2005 Pouilly-Fumé Pur Sang, which was a famous Sauvignon Blanc from the Loire Valley in France. I figured the bottle cost about $100, and deservedly so; winemaker Didier Dagueneau had shown an independent streak in crafting wines that spoke deeply of their origins. This was my first bottle of his wine, and I fear it may be the last—Dagueneau died in a plane crash later that summer.

Lisa finally joined us with the Pur Sang and I watched with amusement as Bob examined the wine. He poured it carefully into his glass, then cupped his hand over the top and shook it like a bartender making a margarita. As drops of wine splashed about, Bob quickly dropped his nose into the glass and inhaled. "Strange," he said slowly. "I'm not convinced there's nothing wrong here. I'm worried this wine is corked."

"It's not corked," Morten concluded, "it's just not typical. It's fascinating."

The rain subsided, but Bob's histrionics did not. There are few spectator activities in the Finger Lakes as enjoyable as watching Bob

Madill joust with a winemaker over the merits of a particular wine. It is exactly why so many people are put off by Bob, and it's also exactly why I find him so endearing. The Finger Lakes would benefit as a wine region if more winemakers shared Bob's studiousness and fervor for wine. Morten was an ideal match for him. This was going to be a fun evening.

* * *

It is easy to see why Morten Hallgren once wanted to be an astrophysicist. His pleasant, even-keel nature rarely reveals emotion. He approaches questions in a straightforward manner that values fact over supposition, and he is not afraid to concede error and search for different solutions. If you ask, he'll discuss the chemistry of winemaking or the science of the cosmos for hours.

And yet when drinking wine, Morten resorts to visceral, gut-level reactions. This is an important distinction. Some winemakers come from backgrounds heavily steeped in science, but they cannot relate to the raw pleasure of wine. Morten displays the necessary balance as a winemaker.

This removes any intimidation his guests might have when they drink with him. As dinner moved inside to the dining room—a sparse but spacious room with a long table and creaking old floorboards—a lineup of alluring wines engendered intense discussion, but Morgan and I never felt the need to shrink from sharing an opinion. We enjoyed a crisp white Burgundy, then compared a pair of Pinots.

Morten poured a highly touted 2002 Côte de Nuits alongside the first Pinot Noir he had ever made in the Finger Lakes, the 1999 Dr. Konstantin Frank Pinot Noir. Most critics would never waste their time opening a decade-old Finger Lakes red wine, but most critics are not aware of Morten Hallgren's approach to winemaking. His 1999

Pinot was still drinking nicely. The bright fruit of youth had mellowed, pushing forward the loamy, leathery notes along with a scent of violets. It did not offer a particularly long finish, but it was certainly a strong interpretation of Finger Lakes Pinot Noir. The big-ticket Burgundy, on the other hand, was a muddled, confused wine. I was glad I was not the one who dropped $65 on that bottle.

The Dr. Frank winery on Keuka Lake was Morten's first head winemaking job, and he had held the position from 1999 to 2005. He and Lisa opened Ravines three years into his stint at Dr. Frank, and he served as the winemaker for both operations for three years. Dr. Frank is probably the most prestigious, highly acclaimed winery in the eastern United States, so I was curious to learn more about Morten's time there. To my surprise, he was not eager to share much.

Lisa recognized the tension and helped steer the conversation into more pleasant waters by snatching an empty bottle off the dining room buffet. "Have you seen my '66 Haut-Brion?" she asked. I was learning that Morten Hallgren was a thoughtful winemaker, but he does not give away much of his own emotion.

* * *

The thought of getting older does not sadden or concern Morten Hallgren. Rather, he claims to feel invigorated by the thought of prospering not only from the wisdom of his mistakes but also from what he learned in France. "Each passing year softens my rougher edges," he said. "It allows me to show some grace—when I might previously have made a fool of myself."

He could just as easily have been talking about wine. The best wines enjoy the same opportunity to improve with age, and few winemakers whom I've met appreciate that more than Morten. Dinner concluded with a wine that sparked our collective curiosity—we enjoyed grilled steaks with a twenty-year-old Finger Lakes wine. It was a 1988 Dr. Frank Cabernet Sauvignon, and more than most wines I've opened, this was a mystery. Twenty years is a long time for almost any wine to survive and thrive, let alone the oft-maligned red wines of the Finger Lakes. No one was under any illusion that Cabernet Sauvignon was ever going to assume a place in the constellation of Finger Lakes varieties—it simply needs a longer, hotter ripening season.

Still dense with brown edges in the glass, this wine did not impress us with its quality—but it was *alive*. Far from vinegar or oxidized grape juice, the 1988 Dr. Frank Cabernet Sauvignon was eminently drinkable with the beef. It led me to wonder what Morten's best reds will taste like with twenty years of age. Someday my cellar will offer me the chance to find out.

Lisa punctuated the meal with a dessert of fresh local cherries cooked in a cassis liqueur. Morten poured a fascinating wine that was slightly oxidized by design: the 2002 Savagnin from Stephane Tissot of France. It was a full-bodied white wine that evoked butter cream and almonds, and I asked Morten why a winemaker would intentionally take his wine to the edge of ruin. "With this variety, you have to take a chance," he said. "Too much oxidation would make this wine over-the-top and undrinkable, but it's worth the risk to get it exactly right."

As the guests leaned back to digest the wonderful meal, Lisa retired to the kitchen and I stepped surreptitiously out of the dining room to chat with her. I wanted to know if she and her husband ever wondered what was going on back at Castel Roubine.

"*I* certainly do," she said almost sheepishly. "It's hard not to wonder. It was such a beautiful place. But Morten's family acts like it was all a dream. It's so strange—they talk about everything in such detail. They'll talk for hours, but they just do not talk about Castel Roubine."

"Does Morten talk about it with you?" I asked.

"Not often. But I think he wants to build our life here and make great wines as a kind of tribute to his parents. He was so hurt to see them lose the estate." She stopped washing a dinner plate and looked up. "He doesn't specifically say that his winemaking is a tribute to his parents, or a way to make up for what we lost in France. But that's a fair observation. His parents are always so proud of his work. They were proud of Castel Roubine."

I was surprised to learn that Morten's parents had chosen to stay in Provence. They had opened a real-estate business designed to make sure others did not suffer the same pitfalls that eventually led to their loss of Castel Roubine. They catered to out-of-towners who were building or buying in Provence for the first time. Morten's parents had carved out a modest life for themselves, but they devoted a lot of their attention to their children's careers, and it was easy to see why they took such pride in Morten's work. His wines challenged assumptions, and I wanted to learn more about what separated his wines from most other Finger Lakes producers. I made plans to work the fall harvest for half a dozen winemakers, concluding with Morten.

* * *

"The impact of our decisions will echo for generations," Morten told me on a cold, drizzly October morning. Harvest was in full throttle throughout the Finger Lakes, but Morten was only beginning to ask his growers to bring in grapes. I was heavily layered and ready for a wet, sloshy workday. While his own small, six-acre vineyard and tasting room are situated on the east side of Keuka Lake, Morten shares a production facility with Shaw Vineyard on the west side of Seneca Lake. "Today I'm going to show you some of the special places I've found in the Finger Lakes," he said. "Winemakers here have decisions to make. We can decide to continue our search for the very best vineyards and the very best places to grow grapes, or we can stop searching and make mediocre wine. I didn't come here to make boring wine."

He didn't come here knowing what to expect, either. Morten only expected, of course, to be back home at Castel Roubine by now, improving upon his parents' legacy. When that dream died, he came to the Finger Lakes in 1999 to figure out how he could make world-class wine in a place that most of the wine world ignored. California wine never interested Morten—too much hype, too expensive, he thought—and his wife's home in Texas was too extreme a climate to produce world-class wine. After losing Castel Roubine, Morten had quietly decided to find the place that made his family happiest. If they ended up far away from Roubine, all the better—proximity might have been painful, anyway.

At Roubine, Morten had been prepared to inherit a glorious wine estate—along with excellent weather for his grapes. In upstate New York, "I inherited a mess," he said with a laugh. "Dr. Frank had a bunch of problems, and the region was suffering from underachieving wines. The weather was occasionally an enemy. And there was almost no discussion about where the best sites were for growing grapes." He spoke in laconic, matter-of-fact terms. Some winemakers in the Finger Lakes might find his assessment to be arrogant, but it was hard to argue the veracity.

When he and Lisa decided to open their own winery in 2002, Morten chose not to plant a huge new vineyard to supply the grapes. Instead, he began experimenting with grape growers from across the Finger Lakes. He wanted to find the ideal site to grow each individual variety. He had witnessed dozens of winemakers make the same mistake: they grew complacent with their own vineyard site or the small number of growers with whom they worked. They stopped searching for the best sites. To Morten, this was a serious error.

"The great wine regions of the world have had centuries to define their *terroir*, so to speak," he said as we opened the workday by punching down the caps in his first lots of Pinot Noir. (Red wine ferments in contact with the skins in large, chest-high containers, and twice a day the winemaker needs to push the "caps" of grape skins and seeds down into the juice to extract more color and add structure to the wine.) I watched as he used a special tool, imported from France, to shove the heavy caps down. "Think about Bordeaux. They needed decades upon decades to learn what varieties work there, what style of wine to make, how to grow the grapes that make the wine. We've had, what, thirty years? So we're the ones defining it in the Finger Lakes, but it only matters if we're open to searching for the best locations."

He explained that when he started work for Dr. Frank in 1999, he began keeping a mental database of vineyard sites. In the Finger Lakes there are hundreds of sites, but many have obvious flaws—poor location or, by far the most common problem, massive overcropping of grapes.

When he opened Ravines, Morten began paring down the list of acceptable growers. Then he began experimenting with different varieties, purchasing a spectrum of grapes from a wide range of sites. When he noticed a consistent lack of quality, he eliminated that site for that particular grape. When he was pleased with the quality, he spent time in that particular vineyard, trying to understand what made the site superior.

As we moved among the eight bins of freshly pressed Pinot Noir, I asked if he thought he was getting closer to having a mental map of the very best vineyards in the Finger Lakes.

"I'm not there yet," he said with a smile, thrusting the punching tool down into yet another bin. The juice hissed and bubbled. "I don't know why the Riesling from one vineyard block has certain properties that are totally different compared to a vineyard on another lake or even a mile down the road. In Riesling, I'm looking for floral and mineral qualities, and the best way to find the answers is to do it empirically. I notice something—an aroma will stand out year to year, and I just record it as specifically as I can. I'm not creating some perfect map. I'm using experience and memory to chart it all out."

He paused from punching caps and wiped his forehead. "Down the road, as we get to know our *terroir*, we'll start to know why things are the way they are, just as they do in Bordeaux and Burgundy. For now, we only know *what*, but we're just starting to learn *why*."

Then he smiled again slowly. "This is the time to pay close attention. The *terroir* of the Finger Lakes is revealing itself, but only to those who are paying attention."

We stepped outside to find a sliver of sun parting the clouds, though it wouldn't last. September had delivered spectacular weather, the kind that can salvage a rough season preceding harvest. But October had opened with a dive in temperature and a steady drip for three days. This shift had provoked many winemakers to start picking most varieties—even the ones that need the longest hang time to ripen. Morten had only brought in one lot of Pinot Noir, and only because it had ripened at a frighteningly fast pace. "Something strange is happening over there, and we're going to go try to figure out what that is," he said. He packed a bag and we hopped in his truck, bound for Chris Verrill's vineyard on the other side of Seneca Lake.

* * *

Morten Hallgren is a risk taker, not a thrill seeker. He likes to say he is a risk taker not by choice, but by necessity. This gives his accountants nightmares.

The idea is simple. The longer the grapes hang on the vine, the more they concentrate with sugar, and the more they develop what winemakers call "phenolics," which refers to aromatics and flavors. But the longer grapes hang, the more they are exposed to the risk of inclement weather, rot, disease, and even over-ripening. Most winemakers in the Finger Lakes region make the safe call to pick grapes before those ruinous factors can strike. Morten tends to bring his grapes in a full two weeks after most of his peers, and the final days before picking can be gut-wrenching for him and his wife. One mistake can cost the Hallgrens half of their income for the year.

As we made our way north on the eastern side of Seneca Lake, rain fell in heavy sheets. "Doesn't this bother you?" I asked. "September was dry and perfect."

"This doesn't bother me yet," Morten said. "We're still taking the long view. We don't have to pick most varieties for a while yet. Other growers might panic and pick now to prevent the grapes from getting even more diluted from the rain, but that's a mistake." With more sun and dry weather, the grapes would have a chance to reconcentrate and keep developing. But continuous rain could make Morten look like a fool for not picking now.

"That's always possible," he said. "You have to be willing to be the fool."

Straining through the waves pelting the windshield, Morten ran a hand through his hair. "We're talking about the difference between good and great. You have to take risks if you want to make great wine in the Finger Lakes. This is a cool climate, like Germany or Burgundy. We need the entire season to maximize the ripeness of the grapes. We can't just say, 'We always pick the first week of October so we're going to pick now.' We can't willingly pick the grapes when they could hang for another week or ten days."

He laughed. "Of course, it can be a dangerous game. You walk the vines, and you see this beautiful fruit, and it's ripe enough to make very nice wines. You can pick the grapes now and you know you'll have income. In some cases you can have some extremely high quality wines. But you have to ask yourself, Do you want to find out the full potential of your vines? If you do, and if the weather isn't going to blow the grapes to the ground, you have to embrace risk."

"It can be pretty nerve-wracking, can't it?"

"It literally comes down to one day. Pick one day too early and you'll have basic, enjoyable wines—but you miss the chance to have something special. Pick one day too late and you can lose half your crop or more."

"Has that happened to you?"

Morten's lips curled slowly upward. "It has. One time. It was my best vineyard, and we had to decide whether to pick on a day when I didn't think the grapes were ready, or wait a full week later because the pickers were all contracted to be elsewhere. I didn't think we had any choice but to let the grapes hang for several more days and it backfired. The grapes rotted." He shook his head. "I had to take complete responsibility, but I didn't want ordinary wine. We could have picked when it was safe, but I knew it wasn't going to be what I wanted it to be."

He was laughing, but I thought about the impact of losing half my income for a year, and it didn't seem all that funny. Of the roughly one hundred wineries in the Finger Lakes, a large number are struggling financially. Accountants and winemakers are not natural friends. The passion to make world-class wine can pave a fast track to financial ruin.

"At least you didn't have to answer to a boss when the grapes rotted," I observed.

"That's a real factor for so many other winemakers," he said. "I understand that. If you have an owner who is nervous, you're a lot less likely to risk it all. You want to keep your job! And if your owner wants to have all the grapes off the vine, what are you going to say? But I tend to think that I have a *greater* risk, because if I make a mistake, I'm the one who pays for it!" The rain stopped in nearly an instant as we turned down a gravel drive. "We just don't have the luxury of time in this climate," Morten said. "Not if we want to show the world what our wines can be. We have to stomach the risk and go to the very end."

Sticking with the theme, Morten was meeting with his grower to discuss picking Riesling earlier than they had ever picked it. The grower, Chris Verrill, had called the previous day to warn Morten about the acids in the grapes. Chris worried the acids were starting to drop because the sugars had rocketed up. Morten was incredulous, but wanted to taste the grapes and find out for himself.

We got out of his truck and walked toward the high end of the vineyards. The vines were cared for meticulously. It wasn't Castel Roubine, but it was beautiful in its own right.

The grower was a pleasant, fit man wearing blue jeans, a beat-up gray sweatshirt, and a baseball cap. He greeted us with his dog, a Husky, galloping playfully by his side. Every vineyard needs a dog—not just to provide companionship to the grower, but to control pests. In the late 1990s, when his vineyard was in its nascent stage, Verrill lost thousands of pounds of grapes to deer. Only when he adopted two Alaskan Huskies from a dog adoption agency did the deer problem cease. The dogs also keep turkeys, raccoons, and rodents away from the vines. Best of all, they continue to work for nothing more than two cans of food per day.

After conferring with his grower, Morten led us on a walk through the vineyards. I lagged behind them a bit, which allowed me to occasionally steal and taste a few grapes. We had reached the Riesling block on Verrill's land, and I popped a couple into my mouth. They were tight as a drum, even after the day's rain, and the grapes were exploding with acidity. If the acids were dropping the way Verrill had said they were, it was difficult to notice.

And yet Morten noticed immediately. We had stopped walking so Morten could select a sample of Riesling grapes, and as he chewed the berries his eyebrows shot up. "What a difference," he said. I reminded myself that Morten visits with his growers quite often during the growing season, which gives him the chance to observe how the grapes are evolving. He was surprised. "I'll be honest, Chris," he said. "I came here today to tell you to hold off on picking. We've never picked Riesling so early. But something is going on here."

Their rapport was impressive and I was enjoying watching them interact.

Just a few days before, Verrill's vineyard had produced some of the ripest Pinot Noir grapes that the region has seen in several years—and Morten felt the need to pick them instead of letting them hang and become raisins. Now he was considering picking Riesling earlier than ever. It seemed to go against everything he had told me, and I asked him about it.

"I've never seen a year like this," he said, with Verrill nodding alongside him. "I can't imagine picking this early again, but it's not just about getting the sugar up. You have to also watch for flavor development, and these grapes are almost there. And you can't allow the grapes to lose their natural acid. That's what makes our wines so distinctive."

We walked farther, heading down a long row of Riesling and making our way to the Cabernet Franc. "They're going to be amazing," Verrill told Morten, "but I don't know if anything will be better than the Riesling."

They agreed that 2008 was shaping up to be a historically good year for Riesling and Pinot Noir in the Finger Lakes, but it was too early to tell with the other varieties. Cabernet Franc, which is one of the last varieties picked, was coming along nicely. When I tasted the berries I would have guessed them ready to go, but Morten said they needed a lot more time. He made his assessments by chewing on the skins of the grapes, looking at the seeds, and tasting for acid and sugar. It was the kind of decision-making that required experience.

Morten had convinced Verrill to lower the yields by almost half, which leads to a smaller cropload—and much more concentrated, complex wines. Growers in the Finger Lakes get paid by the ton, so naturally they want to grow as many tons per acre as possible. Heavy crops lead to more diluted, simple wines, but it's hard to blame growers who seek to maximize their income.

In France, where Morten had seen the importance of low crop yields, there are laws against cropping too heavily. As I stood there sneaking mouthfuls of the beautiful Cabernet Franc, I asked, "How did you convince Chris to lower the yields? That's unheard of around here."

Morten smiled. "I don't pay him by the ton. I pay him by the acre."

I thought I understood what he was saying, but I wanted the Dane to clarify the meaning—because no one pays for grapes by the acre in the Finger Lakes. There are nearly three hundred vineyards, and state agencies are not aware of growers who contract by acre.

"But if you pay him by the acre," I said, "and he's growing half as many grapes as most growers, he's losing a big chunk of money."

Chris laughed and said, "I'm not the one losing money. Morten is!"

They explained that Morten agrees to pay his growers for the same cropload that they would normally provide to other winemakers. That meant Morten was paying the cost of four or five tons of grapes per acre when Chris was only growing two—or less—with some varieties. Winemakers in other regions structure their agreements this way, but as far as I knew, this idea was new to the Finger Lakes.

It was an enormous financial risk to willingly give up thousands of cases of wine each year.

"The Pinot Noir that my growers pick for me is by far the most expensive Pinot Noir in the Finger Lakes," Morten said, not referring to the cost per bottle to his customers, but to the cost he incurs for wanting lower yields. "And that's okay. That's my choice. If I want Chris to leave the grapes on the vine for a long time, and we lose some grapes, I'm the one at risk. I'm still paying him by the acre even if we get nothing. It's more fair to him, and it's also the only way to make great wine."

It was no coincidence that the Ravines Pinot Noir I had recently drunk was the only noteworthy Pinot I'd ever had from the Finger

Lakes. Some had come from Verrill's vineyards, some from other growers. "I love a well-made Pinot," Verrill said. "If I didn't love it, and if Morten didn't make it so well, I'd take a damn bulldozer to those vines tomorrow. 'Cause they are a pain in my ass."

I asked Verrill how he felt about Morten's willingness to assume the risk of hanging grapes late into the season. "I was a little hesitant at first," he said, "because it's just not done that way here. But Morten is serious as a heart attack about getting his wines right. A lot of growers still think it's about tonnage, but they're not working with guys like Morten. I think things will start to change, but other winemakers have to want to make better wine too. It's not just the growers holding things up. It comes down to priorities," he said.

Then Verrill offered an aphorism that I'd like to see adopted by the entire Finger Lakes wine industry: "Do you want every last dollar, or do you want the best bottle of wine you can make?"

Verrill confessed that he had learned a lot about growing techniques from Morten, who was willing to be pleasantly blunt when things went wrong and effusively cheery when the wines approached his stratospheric expectations. As we trudged back down the hill toward the road, the skies began to flicker to the west once again. Morten told his grower that they would pick in three days' time as long as the weather improved as the forecasters said it would. I went home that night impressed with the partnership that Morten had cultivated with his growers—due largely to his insistence on taking risk away from the growers and putting it on his own back.

* * *

When I met Morten's father, I felt my heart break. He would never have known that, and it was only a brief meeting. Six weeks after harvest I had agreed to pour wine at a local charity event for Morten and Lisa, who were entertaining Morten's parents. They were paying a short visit to the United States. I didn't expect to see them at the Hallgren house when I stopped by to pick up the wines.

When I stopped inside the dining room, Lisa handed me some supplies for the charity tasting, and I noticed that a man who had to be Morten's father was having a cup of coffee at the table. He waved at me pleasantly, so I took the opportunity to sit down for a moment at Lisa's invitation.

Mr. Hallgren looks very much like his son, with the inevitable wear of age and stress. His wavy hair had partially succumbed to gray, and the years had added long folds to the center of his cheeks. He spoke an accented but clear English, and for a couple of minutes we chatted about his visit to the Finger Lakes. I was hesitant to bring up Castel Roubine, given that Morten told me his family had long since stopped talking about it. I decided to approach it broadly and vaguely.

"Given what your family has been through, does it surprise you to see how successful Morten has been here in the states?"

He smiled and shook his head slowly. "Not at all. He has so much talent." Morten's father paused and leaned back in his chair, perhaps searching for words. I sensed his mood changing. "We knew that wherever he went, he would be fine."

For a moment the dining room was silent. I decided not to press the subject any further, though I remained deeply curious about the family's reaction to losing Castel Roubine. Morten has laid out, in intricate detail, exactly what happened. I have corroborated parts of the story through sources in France; I know that the Hallgren family lawsuit has never been heard by a judge. But Morten does not speak about the events with much emotion—Lisa says he has tried to move past the pain. Looking in his father's eyes, I saw a man who is proud of his son, but I wondered how much happier he would be if the family were still together, working the land of southern France, picking grapes in unison, pouring wine for one another during long, lazy dinners.

The Hallgrens had moved on with a quiet acceptance that I found difficult to comprehend.

Before leaving, Morten's father mentioned how much he enjoys the Ravines Meritage blend. There was no doubting the source of his son's outstanding palate.

* * *

Wine snobs struggle with the idea that Finger Lakes wines might be worth their time. Morten Hallgren's wines tend to disarm the doubters.

A good friend of mine is decidedly not a wine snob, but is vastly knowledgeable about the world of wine. A professor at the University of Rochester, he enjoys the chance to travel across Europe on occasion for work purposes—which inevitably become wine explorations. When I poured the 2005 Ravines Meritage for him—Morten's blend that is led by Cabernet Franc—I asked what he thought. "Tastes very much like a French wine," he said, and then, "It's fantastic. Rich without being a monster, like great wine used to be, you know?" When I told him the wine was made not in France but in the Finger Lakes, he was thrilled. He later sent me an email with this undeniably hyperbolic praise: "When I think of wines that are memorably outstanding and varietally indicative of great Cabernet Franc, the Ravines 2005 Meritage is in the conversation with the 1990 Cheval Blanc."

The Cheval now sells for around $1,000 per bottle, and it's one of the most prestigious wines in the world. Even Morten would quell any comparison of his Meritage to the renowned French chateau, but clearly his wines were making an impact.

When I met him for lunch in the Ravines tasting room that winter he wanted to pour his 2006 Dry Riesling, which I thought was among the best Riesling I'd ever had. We sat in the tasting room looking out at the icy Keuka Lake. It had not frozen over, which meant the waters still provided an insulating blanket to the lakeside vineyards. This was hardly the season that most wine drinkers enjoy Riesling, and yet the wine was captivating, a mélange of lime peel, lemon curd, and wet stone. I asked him if this was the future of Riesling in the Finger Lakes.

His eyes lit up. "To me, this is sort of the reference," he said. "This is what I associate with Finger Lakes Riesling now. It's that firm acidic backbone. It's taking a *long* time to open up. There are other fruit components in there but they're just starting to show up. This is a wine that's going to age very well, and it's only revealing itself slowly."

He laughed as he swirled the glass. "My various distributors have always thought I was crazy to *only* make this kind of Riesling. They love to ask me, 'Where's your other Riesling? You know, your sweet one?'"

Morten and Lisa have grappled over the idea of producing at least one sugary wine—a "debt-paying wine," as many winemakers refer to simple, sweet wines. But Morten had always refused.

"You've gotten a feel for what winemaking is all about out here," he said. "Seven days a week, twelve hours a day, sometimes more. If you don't wake up with a sense of excitement every day—if you're not making the kind of wine you truly want to make—what's going to happen? It's human nature. You're simply not going to put in all the effort and time that it takes. So I've just decided that I'm going to make the wines that I feel strongly about, and if it can't provide for my family, I'll have to do something else."

"And so far?" I asked.

He raised his eyebrows and flashed a wide smile. "I've never been afraid to answer my accountant's calls."

Morten's cell phone rang, but it wasn't his accountant—it was his son, Max. As his children approach high-school age, Morten admits he's thinking about the future of Ravines Wine Cellars. He's decades away from retiring, but he already knows the sting of losing a family winemaking business. His problem is not unique to the Finger Lakes; the best winemakers will have a challenge in convincing their children to take over the operations down the line. What is a natural succession in Europe is not so simple in the United States.

"I'll never force my kids to make wine," he explained. "But I hope to trick them into wanting to do it! I'll have to be subtle."

Morten's kids don't know the full story of what happened at Castel Roubine. Perhaps one day he'll tell them. For now, he's content to keep working on his artisan wines in a place he would never have imagined years ago.

"Castel Roubine was special," he said. "But I think about it a little less every year."

* * *

The next summer, before harvest, I was surprised to see Morten's name on my caller I.D. on a Saturday afternoon. We didn't have any appointments or trips to the vineyard scheduled for several weeks.

"Have you been over to see Sam Argetsinger yet?" he asked.

I only knew that Sam Argetsinger was one of Morten's growers. "I have not," I said. "Never met him. I just know the name is on one of your bottles of Riesling."

"Oh, I'm sorry," he said, and then added with a strange kind of urgency, "Listen, you'll really want to do this. You've got to do it now. It's time for you to meet Sam Argetsinger."

FIVE

The Iroquois: Sam Argetsinger

"What do you think you're doing?"

I turned to see a shortish man emerging from the vines. His long brown and red hair sprouted wildly from underneath a dirty white bandana. His skin bore the deep red that comes from long hours of outdoor work, and his weathered hands were as dirty as his jeans. I couldn't tell if he was forty or sixty-five.

I had just pulled down a winding dirt drive on the southeastern side of Seneca Lake that led past an old farmhouse and around a dilapidated red barn. Acres of vines rose above and dipped below toward the water. Three big, grinning dogs had offered a friendly greeting as I got out of the car, but I was stopped by a distinctly unfriendly shout.

I turned to face the man who was walking toward me. "Hi—are you Sam Argetsinger?" I asked, hoping he wasn't.

"Why?" he asked, rather threateningly.

"I'm supposed to meet him here and—"

He interrupted me with an unintelligible series of belligerent shouts that convinced me he was drunk. I stood there for thirty seconds or so, grimacing as he hurled what sounded like insults my way. Finally, mercifully, he stopped. We stared at each other for a long moment.

His face broke into a wide smile.

"How'd you like that Iroquois greeting, brother?" He was laughing now, and he clearly knew how frightened I had been. "I'm Sam Argetsinger. You must be Evan."

"Jesus!" I said, releasing several minutes of breath and shaking his hand. "That was Iroquois?"

"Yes, sir! I told you that it was an honor to meet a good and curious soul. I welcomed you to this land."

"Yeah, well, that's not what it sounded like."

"You look like a scared rabbit!"

I shook my head and laughed as Sam wrapped an arm around my shoulder and squeezed several times. I had no idea what to expect from this man. Morten Hallgren had told me only that Sam's vineyard produced some of the best wines he had ever tasted, but he didn't want to tell me much about the grower, preferring to allow me to discover Sam's personality for myself. Other local winemakers—the ones who had heard of Sam Argetsinger, at least—had colorful stories to tell. A Google search had turned up nothing about him.

Looking around his land I was instantly curious. The vineyards looked like none I had seen in the Finger Lakes. They were more feral.

"So what are you here for?" Sam asked pleasantly.

"I don't know exactly," I said. "I mean, I think I know. Morten Hallgren told me I simply had to meet you. He didn't say why. But I trust Morten and so I figured I would know when I met you."

"Morten's a great soul," Sam said, smiling. "Let's take a walk. You want a beer?"

He ducked into the barn while I continued to survey the property. The land was steeper than any other local vineyard I had seen, which is a tremendous asset for grapes—it allows for more direct exposure to the moderating effects of the lake. Some of the most stunning vineyards in the world seem to teeter on breathtakingly steep land overlooking rivers in Germany, Portugal, and France.

But this land was home to much more than grapevines. A small plot of sweet corn stood just a few feet from us, which bordered a patch of potatoes. Peach and apple trees dotted the perimeter of the rows of vines above us, while various trees and plants were interspersed with the vines that sprawled below.

"What do you think?" Sam asked excitedly as he emerged from the barn and flipped me a can of beer.

"It's steep," I said clumsily. "I don't think I've seen another site like this around here."

"You haven't," Sam said. His narrow, intense eyes—surrounded by a day's worth of dirt—lit up as he looked toward the top of his forty acres. "I'm going to take you right to the best. Let's go see our Riesling."

It occurred to me that I couldn't tell if Sam was simply American—a hybrid of many nationalities like most people in the United States—or if he was, in fact, Native American. His name conveyed old-world European but everything else screamed Iroquois, and he sprinkled his sentences with Iroquois words.

We started the climb and Sam's dogs circled us, barking playfully. Occasionally one would notice an intruding critter somewhere in the distance and barrel off. As we walked I tried to get a stronger sense of this man and his vineyards—I couldn't help but feel a strangely numinous quality to the land.

"Morten says you're the genuine article," I said as we passed rows of vines that presented dark, gorgeous grapes. "You speak Iroquois. But what do you consider yourself?"

This question clearly amused him. His wide smile shoved his dark orange mustache under his nose and the lines of age finally appeared at the corners of his eyes. "I'm an American. Proud to be an American, brother. Just like you."

We walked on in silence for a minute or so before he continued. "I speak to schools and libraries and anybody who wants to know about our heritage. I always start my talks by saying, 'First of all, I'm not an Indian. I'm just a logger and a grape grower, and everything I'm about to tell you I learned in the woods.'"

Sam's Dutch-American family had produced lawyers and judges

and playwrights and businessmen. He explained that he had chosen a different path after hearing about the Iroquois tribes as a young boy.

"I asked my mother how I could find out more about the Indians, and she said, 'Why don't you go meet them?' I first met the Onandagans and the Senecans up by Syracuse when I was a young man. Must have been forty years ago. And they said, 'We'd like to talk to you, but you should speak our language.' And they were right, of course. It's always polite to speak someone's language. So that's how I got to learn it. I listened and I spoke.

"There are so many myths and half-truths from our side about them, and I found that it doesn't really bother them. I always felt it bothered me more than it bothered them. I grew up a farmer, a peacekeeper. I come from a tradition of using legal strategies to resolve conflict. And it's so crazy that we don't really know the Indians' true story. Instead, we rely on stereotypes and we tend toward war."

He paused again, distracted by one of the clusters on the Pinot Noir vines. The grapes in Sam's vineyard were more densely bunched, deeper in color, and I wanted to grab a cluster to taste them. The fruit offered a distinct balance with the rest of the vineyard: the vineyard was wild and the grapes were orderly. There were all manner of grasses and, occasionally, weeds growing freely in all directions, but the grapes seemed focused and controlled. After plucking a light-colored berry from one of the bunches, Sam turned his focus back to the American Indians. He was remarkably detailed in describing Iroquois culture, and I did not for a moment find him to be a contrived character. I found myself wrapped up in what he was saying.

"This land draws, brother. This land loans gifts to Man, and it draws the best from far away. That's how we got Morten here. This land just brought him here. How else could we get that guy here? The land did it 'cause She needs him. And we need to get to this next evolution where the farmer and the grower and this beautiful land remove barriers and work together. Eliminate conflict. If She wants Morten here, and She wants me to work with Morten, who am I to make other demands? We all listen to *neh gawanutneh*."

"We listen to what?" I asked. Now Sam was starting to sound, well, a little out there.

"*Neh gawanutneh*. It's 'the voice that rises.' All living things speak this language. We're all so happy to be alive, and we just say, 'Wow!' And we speak in unison. *Neh gawanutneh*. We speak in the voice that rises. But you must remember that the land takes in all that is around Her. The grapes, the apples, the corn—it's not just speaking, it's listening."

Sam obviously loved telling this story. He was smiling wide enough to nearly obscure his eyes as he raised his arm, glanced around, and said, "Look out and tell me what you see."

I looked down across the soaring stalks of corn and up at the dense trees in the distance. "I guess I see corn. Corn and trees."

Sam turned and pointed to climbing rows of vines. "And here?"

"Grapes?" I offered, searching in vain to say something profound.

"Well, shit, sure. Grapes. Corn. Trees," he replied, taking on the air of a professor admonishing a student. "But what you really see are the Standing People. They stand among us, and they absorb everything that's going on in that spot. They absorb the season. They absorb the rains and the drought. And they absorb our energy. Everything you say, everything you feel when you're working in that field, is absorbed by the Standing People. They expect you to give your best, and why shouldn't you? Only a man misled by his own priorities would fail to give his best, and I mean his *best*. His best work, his best effort, and his best spirit.

"When it comes to making wine, my role is to work with the land to give our best. When I give the grapes to Morten, it's in his hands. And when he turns those grapes into wine, and that wine ends up in your glass, you're hearing *neh gawanutneh*. That voice doesn't just come from Morten and it doesn't just come from me. It comes from all of us."

The land grew steeper as we climbed onward. We crossed a long path separating the Pinot from a plot of Chardonnay and made our way for the corner of his property. I was tempted to stop and devour the grapes straight from the vine—I have a voracious love of wine grapes that borders on addiction—but I was busy laughing to myself as I enjoyed Sam's stories. His enthusiasm was unimpeachably sincere, and it never felt like he was lecturing. But I still had to wonder—did this Iroquois approach truly change the quality of the vines?

I asked him how grapes came to his family's land.

"The greatest agricultural tradition of this land where we now grow grapes—and we have for, what, 150 years now? We're young. We're just infants," he said. One of his dogs—an aging black lab—dashed happily in front of our feet, nearly knocking me over. Sam didn't seem to notice, and I realized that he was just as caught up in his stories as I was.

"The tradition tells us that this was the land of *deohako*, the three sisters of agriculture: corn, beans, and squash. I'll tell you, brother, the Iroquois knew their agriculture. And they knew early on that corn, beans, and squash had a great relationship. Corn has so much goodness for us, but it's a heavy feeder. It needs a lot of nitrogen. Beans just need something to grow up on, and they *give* nitrogen. So you plant the beans in there with the corn, and the corn gives the beans somewhere to go, and the beans give the corn nitrogen. The squash then grows all over the floor of that field and it keeps the weeds down. It holds moisture in. So the *deohako* is about a very symbiotic planting, and that's what sustained the Iroquois for so many years. Our three sisters support our life.

"And there's all kinds of symbolic stuff here too!" he said, smiling knowingly. "Corn represents the balance in our lives: male and female, giving and taking. The beans represent gratitude. We need to give credit to the land, just as the beans give nutrients to the corn for providing a place to grow. Squash represents humility, keeping down the weeds of our ego.

"This land was warm when we got here, brother. It had been cleared for thousands of years! Think about where most of our vineyards are now.

Where are they? They're all along old Indian villages. They changed our world before we even knew it was happening!" Sam was laughing again.

"So if we've gained wisdom and understanding from the Iroquois," I said, "why do you think there are so many people who live here who don't know these stories? Or don't care?"

"There's no good answer, but that's changing," Sam said, his eyes narrowing again and the smile receding. "What I hear so often on the reservation is positive things about us. Think about that! They call us their younger brothers. One day I said, 'I never hear you guys talk about the white man. You never run us down. You've suffered so much.' And they looked me in the eye and said, 'Your people came to this land with a lot of problems. It hurt us. It really hurt us tragically. And it hurt the land—you were so cruel to the land. You spent all your anger and rage by destroying so much of the land. You made the water dirty, and you started to wipe out the animals and wipe out the forest. But the land has assimilated you and healed you. You're becoming more and more *American* every year.'

"Well, they were right. We're becoming more and more like the land. Travel around this area and you'll see. You meet these farmers who have grown up on the land and they are so in tune with what's going on. They're just hooked up. And now, the land loves them. The land loves our families and blesses us like it blessed the Iroquois."

Sam stopped walking. We had reached the Riesling vineyard and were nearing the top. I could feel how wounded he was when he talked about the way the Iroquois had been treated.

"The land forgives, if you let it. It changes you," he said. "It's changed our culture and our people, and it's healed us. At different times in our lives I think all of us are strangers to the land. I guess we're in a hurry to get somewhere else, you know? But in the end, we're right here, and we're starting to realize that."

I began to feel deeply moved by what Sam was saying. There was a part of me that found the whole idea kind of hokey—*neh gawanutneh*, *deyonhaithco*, the healing power of the land. But I was drawn to Sam's openness and perspective, and I wondered if this was how Morten Hallgren had felt when he met Sam ten years ago.

"I don't question what you're saying," I said, "but you talk about your Iroquois brothers and sisters as if they're incredibly understanding people."

"It's easy to assume they'd be angry, and I'm sure on many days they are angry," he said. "But when you hold anger and allow it to control you, the land absorbs it and your entire community suffers. Eventually, there is no *neh gawanutneh*. There's just thousands of loud, angry screams."

Sam's words hung in the air, and we stood silent, casting gazes around the impressive countryside. I thought of my drive down, when I had been stuck behind a loaded pickup truck at a red light for what seemed like hours. I had cursed and shouted at the truck to move. It was a needless moment of anger, one of countless such occasions that made me feel, in retrospect, like one of the many hurried and distracted people that Sam was just talking about.

He gave me a gentle nudge in the ribs, grinning. "Shit, don't get all sentimental on me. Save it—you haven't even tasted the grapes yet!"

* * *

Grapes do not taste like wine, so it's always difficult for amateurs to discern just what kind of quality wine the grapes are going to make when you taste them on the vine. But wine grapes—vinifera grapes—do not taste like the table grapes most people grow up eating. Wine grapes are smaller and more explosive, usually packed tightly with flavor. Deer and birds love them, which is why wineries must spend lots of money on fencing and other protective measures.

I was about to find out that Sam Argetsinger's grapes tasted unlike any other wine grapes in the Finger Lakes. He spoke of them like they were his children, and he couldn't understand why most growers douse their vineyards with chemical sprays and fertilizers. "Think about that," he said as he picked a bunch of Riesling grapes. "We're killing five or ten things to make one thing grow. You think that's balance? That's not balance—that's crazy. And if you think the land doesn't feel that destruction, that's crazy too."

Sam was not, it should be said, a biodynamic grower. Not technically, anyway. On extreme occasions he was willing to use some kinds of sprays, but only after consulting with Morten. And Morten knew that Sam preferred to keep chemicals to a minimum.

He handed me a bunch of Riesling grapes and, smiling, said, "Try 'em out!" It was the first week of September, well over a month before these grapes would be ready for harvest. The berries were small, soft yellow in color, and speckled with brown spots. I popped a couple into my mouth. The juice burst onto my tongue and the first thing I noticed was the acidity, intense and vibrant. My mouth began to water as I chewed the grapes and tasted the sugar, still young and developing. It was hard to believe that a small berry could pack such strong and complex flavors.

"Wow," I said, reaching for another bunch. "There's so much spark that my eyes are almost watering."

This obviously delighted Sam. "Embrace it, brother! We don't need to add no acid to this wine. It's all there."

His Riesling vines were nearly four decades old, some of the oldest in the Finger Lakes, and in addition to his Iroquois growing techniques Sam had another ally: limestone. While the glaciers that formed the Finger Lakes deposited a wide variety of soils well suited for grape growing, there wasn't very much limestone in the Finger Lakes. Winemakers love limestone. Grapes grown on limestone-based soils tend to show more structure, which means they can age gracefully. Some winemakers believe limestone imparts unique conditions that lead to more interesting flavors.

"Can we check out your Pinot?" I asked Sam. He smiled. "You have good taste," he said, starting back down the hillside.

Sam was preparing to plant new Pinot Noir vines, but it was clear that he treated the existing vines like newborn children as well. I tried to imagine what Morten Hallgren could do with Sam's Pinot Noir years down the line, when the newer, better clones had matured. From Sam's Iroquois growing techniques, to the limestone soil, to the meticulously low yields, to Morten's skilled hand in the winery—it all worked together to produce *neh gawanutneh*, Sam would say. It had spoken to me before I had the chance to realize what it was saying, before I had even tasted the wine. Yes, I was buying into Sam's ideas. I was becoming a believer.

"Pinot Noir is a bitch," Sam declared, breaking my reverie. "But it's the kind of bitch you just have to love. It's like a poet. It's expressive." He rolled his eyes theatrically. "It's easily offended and moody, but you know what? The land is moody!"

He plucked another green berry and mumbled, "Pinot, you bitchy little poet."

When Morten Hallgren learned of the unique limestone outcropping fueling Sam's soil, he didn't push Sam to adopt every tenet of the Burgundian growing tradition. Morten simply saw an opportunity to learn from the great Burgundy winemakers who spoke about the benefits of limestone—but he would also respect Sam's growing style. No one had any idea what the full expression of Pinot Noir could be in the Finger Lakes because it had never been achieved. The grape had always been overcropped and the wine had always been made the exact same way other reds are made.

Morten and Sam worked to keep yields down on Sam's older vines. After seeing so many vineyards in the Finger Lakes that seemed to be flooded with grapes, it was refreshing to see vines with a clearly lighter load. In order to keep yields down, growers like Sam have to cut off grapes throughout the growing season—they call it "dropping fruit."

"I've talked to winemakers and growers who hate dropping fruit," I said as we inspected more of his vines. "They feel like dropping fruit is dropping money. They think it's a waste, even if keeping the fruit means making weak wines."

"It's not a waste!" Sam said eagerly. "When we drop grapes, the land drinks it or the critters get to eat. And the remaining grapes get stronger. That's not a waste—that's the land at Her best!"

Occasionally Sam would regale wine distributors with stories of his land's geology, and he loved to talk about the limestone. "You think it's an accident that we have limestone below us?" he would ask with a wry smile. "The land brought the vines here, man. We're just listening to what she wants!"

He and I admired the undisturbed blue sky. "Days like today inspire us, but then tomorrow maybe the weather and the land will challenge us. Fascinating! And that's Pinot. You'd better be patient and you'd better be willing to work with the land, because she's going to really challenge you with Pinot. You can't push Pinot around, 'cause she will shut down on you." I told Sam about the 2005 Ravines Pinot Noir that had changed my view of the grape in the Finger Lakes. "We embrace the challenge and the land rewards us," he said.

* * *

I wanted my wife to meet Sam, and we made an appointment to see him two weeks after I first toured his vineyards. I use the word *appointment* loosely; Sam prefers to tell visitors when he'll be working, and he invites anyone to come say hello. He claims to own a phone but does not know its number. I wasn't terribly surprised to find his truck missing when we pulled into his farm.

We decided to visit several nearby wineries to pass some time. The Finger Lakes wine trails are unique in the wine world, more open than even California wineries. In Europe, visitors must make appointments to taste wines, and the appointments often require a tour of the winemaking facility or vineyards. At the conclusion of the visit there is pressure to buy, and not just one bottle. West Coast tasting rooms tend to be imbued with the mellow feeling that is so common in that part of the country, but tastings can be expensive—$30 or more per person in some places. Most Finger Lakes tasting rooms will pour wine all day for no more than $5 a head, and often it's free. My wife and I drove just a few miles north to the Damiani winery, a relatively new producer.

There we learned that everyone on the east side of Seneca Lake seems to know Sam Argetsinger. Even tasting-room staff have stories to tell about Sam's exploits, his Iroquois demonstrations, and the quality of his grapes. And Sam's influence seems to impact nearby vineyards, whose growers improve their craft like a music student who lives next door to Johann Sebastian Bach and listens carefully to each evening practice. At Damiani Vineyard, grape grower Phil Davis is Sam Argetsinger all the way down to the long hair, weathered hands, and diminutive stature. It turns out that Phil and Sam had become close friends, and Morgan and I found that Damiani was a kind of southeast Seneca Lake secret—the small-town diner that the locals love and only begrudgingly reveal to visitors. And while Phil did some things differently in the vineyard, it was becoming clear that there are many ways to grow excellent fruit. The one prerequisite is a respect for the land.

When we returned to Sam's farm several hours later I was very curious to see what my wife would think of the grower. Morgan is a very good judge of character, and I wanted to see if she found Sam as authentically charming as I did. We arrived to see him smiling and standing just off the road. Apart from a green shirt this time, Sam was dressed exactly the same as when I first met him. He greeted my wife with a hug and a rather offbeat question, even for Sam:

"Morgan, your husband has told me such delightful things of you. Welcome to my farm. I've been dying to know: What do you think about crows?"

As if being pulled by a string my wife's eyebrows touched the top of her forehead. She looked at me, totally bewildered. "I . . . don't think I've ever thought about crows," she replied searchingly.

"Evan tells me you're a forensic chemist," Sam explained. "The crow is nature's forensic chemist. The crow will move a dead animal off the road and take it apart. It's an important duty. I thought you might feel a closeness with crows—we've got plenty around here!"

We all laughed, and I tried to remember when I had mentioned my wife's profession to Sam. I couldn't recall it coming up in our first meeting, and in fact my wife had recently left the crime lab to start a photography business. I figured I must have dropped it into our conversation two weeks ago.

This time Sam wanted to show off the lower parcels of his property, and we walked down a path and through some waist-high grasses into a block of vines. The clusters of Cabernet Franc were nearly black in color and, with a month or more left on the vine, they looked to be coming along gorgeously. After the violently wet midsummer, the season was ending on a warm, dry streak that seemed custom-ordered for winemakers. Sam pulled a device out of his pocket that resembled a tube with an angled glass cap at one end. It was a refractometer, he explained, and he invited us to help him check the sugar levels on the Cab Franc.

"What?" he said, smiling playfully. "You think this grower doesn't understand science?" He asked Morgan to grab a bunch of grapes from the vine. The refractometer is a simple tool that measures the weight of the sugar in a liquid, providing a rough estimate of a grape's Brix, or sugar content. My wife squeezed some juice from the Cab Franc berries onto the open end of the refractometer, and then followed Sam's instructions to flip the face closed. "Now look in one end and hold it up to the sun," Sam said. The device reminded me of a kaleidoscope.

My wife held up the refractometer and peered in. "What do you see?" Sam asked. "There should be a numerical scale." My wife squinted for a moment and then said, "Twenty-one."

"That's funny," Sam said incredulously. "What does it really say? It should be something like sixteen or seventeen, right?"

"No, really. Twenty-one."

Now it was Sam who grew wide-eyed as he asked to see for himself. After confirming the number, Sam grabbed several bunches of grapes and began plucking berries seemingly at random. "We've got to do this again," he said. "I've never gotten a reading this high this early in the season. The sugars should be much lower."

"Is this a problem?" my wife asked.

Sam stopped and turned to her, shaking his head and grinning. "Not at all, my lady! This would be unprecedented. We could see the ripest Cabernet Franc ever produced in this region if this reading is accurate!"

He took a fresh sample and squinted into the open end. "Twenty and a half. I'll be damned." He turned to us and said, "You're bringing wonderful energy to this land. We might not allow you to leave!"

* * *

I was pretty sure we had a perfect opportunity to go skinny dipping. Sam had led us on a long, invigorating tour of his land, and we had crossed over the main road on the northernmost side. There we had descended a rather steep ledge of shale and dirt that led to a crystal-clear stream. After hiking down the stream and back, Sam had vanished. I was certain it was a courtesy to his guests.

Earlier, when we had started the hike Sam had pointed out a large swimming hole, easily six feet deep. The water drifted down in a tight stream until it emptied into the hole. Further down the trail, the stream picked up pace again and wound around a series of rock outcroppings. Several trees seemed to hang in mid-air off the side of the gorge wall, the erosion of time having carved out the earth underneath. As we hopped from stone to stone and along the edge of the stream, Sam pointed back to the swimming hole. "My girlfriend Joanie and I go skinny dipping there all the time," he said happily. Morgan smiled at me and stopped for a moment.

"He's so connected to his property," she whispered.

"What does skinny dipping have to do with it?" I asked.

"He's just so . . . joyful. Most people who have property around the lakes take it for granted. They stop appreciating it. That's not a problem for him!"

When we headed back up the stream, Sam and his dogs got out ahead of us and disappeared. My wife and I got back to the swimming hole and I realized it was Sam's way of offering us a chance to enjoy nature by doing what comes naturally. No doubt he and his dogs were already back at the farmhouse. But late on that September day, the air had plunged to sharply crisp temperatures and as I dropped my cupped hand into the stream I knew it was cold enough to make me pass out. We agreed to sneak back on a warmer day.

Back at the farm we found Sam digging in the dirt with his hands, unearthing red-skinned potatoes. "For you!" he said excitedly. He had already grabbed several ears of sweet corn and a basket of grapes. "I want you to go home and enjoy the gifts of our land. This land loves you, brother. I can already sense it."

"We'll open a bottle of the 2007 Argetsinger Riesling," I said, noting the fact that Morten Hallgren had recently decided to separate the wine that comes from Sam's vineyard and bottle it under a single-vineyard label. It's a high compliment to a grower, and a signal from the winemaker to the consumer that something about that particular vineyard is special.

Sam dropped his head and sighed. When he raised his head again I could see that there were tears in his eyes. "When Morten put my name on the bottle, I did not know what to say. It's the ultimate honor, brother. That man can get his grapes from anywhere he pleases. He chooses this vineyard."

But why, I thought, looking around his land—why would Morten choose anywhere else?

* * *

As special as 2007 was for red wine in the Finger Lakes, it was a much more challenging year for Riesling. The drought had robbed the grapes of much of their acid, and some Finger Lakes Rieslings were off balance, not crisp, kind of fat. And that's what made the 2007 Argetsinger Riesling so inspiring.

My wife and I opened a bottle of the Argetsinger in our Keuka Lake cottage on a splendid fall afternoon. As I poured her a glass I asked, "How would you describe Sam to a stranger?"

"I'd say to go meet him in person," she said. "He's worth the time. I'd say you might never meet anyone like him again." Then she laughed and shook her head. "I want to spend more time with him myself. He has so much to say!"

"Do you think some people would think he's a little crazy?"

"I think Sam might think he's a little crazy, but he's so genuine. It doesn't take long to buy into his ideas."

We considered the wine. The vibrant yellow liquid gave such a powerful bouquet that the room was filled with it. Finger Lakes Riesling often tastes like wet stone, and sometimes critics use a more general description of "minerality" in the wine. I no longer had to wonder what that meant. Burying my nose in the glass, the wine smelled like the clear, crisp waters racing over the stones on the edge of Sam's farm. Then it evolved into the ubiquitous fennel, before turning over to a scent of peach. I took a sip and felt the electric acidity that was supposed to be missing from this vintage. The wine evoked an image of his land so clear that I felt I was back on Sam's property.

Swirling the wine and taking in its aromas, my wife confessed that she had considered actually applauding Sam several times that day on his farm. She was so moved by his connection to the land that she felt the only response was to clap. This did not surprise me. Morten Hallgren recently took a distributor from Winebow to meet Sam, and Morten said the wine rep went back to New York City, passed a bottle of the Argetsinger around the office, and placed an order. He was converted.

There's a bottle of the 2007 Argetsinger Riesling in my cellar, and I have written instructions to myself not to touch it until at least 2020. Morten has told me that 2008 will be much better, but tasting the 2007, I found that hard to believe. I want to know how the wine will evolve and what it will say when it's left alone for some time. I can already hear the stream, I can see the steep vines rising over the lake. I can hear, with such beautiful clarity, *neh gawanutneh*, the voice that rises.

SIX

The Canadian: Peter Bell

February 12, 1986
Ontario, Canada

He was going to scream if the phone rang one more time. They didn't want the house. They didn't like the neighborhood. They didn't have the money.

More than anything, Peter Bell and his wife, Joanna, didn't want to give up their hopes of working in the wine industry.

But the phone was going to ring. Their Realtor had already called twice today, and she had promised to "keep checking in." She wanted Peter and Joanna to commit to the house and during her last call she had offered to loan them the money to make the down payment. She knew that a couple in their twenties needed a prod to buy their first house, and she was going to keep the pressure coming.

"Maybe this *is* the right time to buy," Joanna said, staring at the phone in the kitchen. "The market is going crazy. Prices aren't coming down." She paused before adding, "She has been terribly aggressive."

"If she's any more aggressive I'm going to suffocate," Peter said.

As much as they didn't want the house, Peter and Joanna could feel themselves giving in. With the Realtor's help making the down payment, at least they could afford the mortgage for a while. It was cheap. They were tired of throwing money into rent, and Peter's efforts to break into the wine industry hadn't amounted to anything tangible. He had picked up a job making beer in Toronto, but his thirst was for producing wine.

He had been on track to get a winemaking degree until the rules changed. After spending time in Australia with friends, Peter applied to a prestigious winemaking college. The school had accepted Peter the previous February, eleven months earlier. But instead of starting classes right away, Peter asked for and received a one-year deferment. That's because he felt that he and Joanna needed time to get their lives organized. She had just delivered their first child, and Peter would have had to start school in less than two weeks. He was relieved that the college was willing to give him an extra year before he had to start classes.

Then, in early January, just as Peter and Joanna were finalizing plans for the move to Australia, the Aussie government sent a letter. Peter was out. They had changed the rules for foreign students and he had missed the window to start classes.

It was a tremendous disappointment, and one that forced Peter and Joanna to consider new plans. They were realists who knew that getting into the wine industry without the aid of nepotism or illustrious credentials was extremely difficult—and expensive. American programs required suitcases full of cash that they didn't have, and without the Australia opportunity, Peter had little choice. So they decided he should keep making beer and they would settle near their home of Toronto, even if it didn't excite them.

The house would make it permanent. They might have acquiesced sooner if not for their feeling that the house brought a sense of finality. But they were worn down, and Peter knew they were close to breaking. If they were going to stay in Toronto, they were going to buy a house, and their Realtor knew it too.

There was compelling reason to believe that it was time to settle down. They had spent a peripatetic year that would make even the most experienced backpackers envious. Travel came naturally to Peter. As a child he had moved with his family to Amsterdam, then to Berkeley, California. He and his cousin, both barely fourteen, had bummed around Europe in the summer of 1970. He spent a year after high school living on a sailboat in Spain, working odd jobs painting, teaching English, and bartending.

A few years later he bought a used Citroën 2CV car—the low-rent version of a Volkswagen bus—and driven all over Europe and then down across a large swath of the Sahara.

After trying to come back to Canada and settle down, Peter and Joanna felt themselves being pulled back to a life free of a permanent address. They began another year on the road, picking grapes at Château d'Angludet in Bordeaux. Peter's itch to make wine was starting to erupt into a full-blown spiritual sore, driving him to make the journey to Australia, where the world-class winemaking schools were more welcome to foreign students.

Or so he thought. But now it was about to be over, a dreary, gray-toned end to a lifestyle that had been packed with color and adventure.

For a few minutes they sat in the kitchen and said nothing. Joanna wondered what she would tell her family about their new house. She had always envisioned a scene filled with excitement after signing for their first home. There would be no celebratory glass of Champagne this time, but at least they wouldn't have to be there forever. Someday they would be able to afford something with more space, in a better neighborhood.

The phone rang.

Squeezing his eyes shut, Peter silently walked over to pick up the receiver. He drew it slowly to his ear and finally barked, "*What?*"

For a moment there was nothing on the other end, and then a familiar voice. It was not the Realtor's.

"Peter! It's Ross, calling from Australia. Listen, you're in."

Peter cocked his head and squinted, recalling the voice of his friend. "What? Wait, Ross, how?"

"Yeah, mate, my member of Parliament made this happen. I hope that's okay with you." Ross explained that when Peter called to say he had been shut out of the winemaking school, Ross contacted his member of Parliament to protest. He didn't expect to hear back, but the government decided its new rules were unfair. Peter was one of a small handful of foreign students who had regained their eligibility.

"I guess they kind of called in a favor for me," Ross said, laughing.

Peter's eyes flew open wide and Joanna knew something was up.

"You're in the program, Pete," Ross said. "Can you get here in two weeks?"

"We'll be there," Peter said. "We . . . will . . . be there."

"Good. Pack your bags."

As Peter hung up the phone he collapsed onto the dingy linoleum floor of their apartment kitchen. Joanna stood over him and said, "What happened?"

"We're in," Peter said, convulsing with laughter. "I'm calling the Realtor. I'm going to tell her to sell that dump to someone else."

DON'T LOOK DOWN. FOR SOMEONE ONLY MILDLY BOTHERED BY heights, I was surprised to find myself dizzied by the sight of the cold cement floor below. Focusing on the task at hand, I reminded myself: *don't look down.*

Unfortunately, I had to look down to finish this job. I was standing on a narrow metal catwalk above the massive stainless-steel tanks inside the winery of Fox Run Vineyards on Seneca Lake. On the invitation of winemaker Peter Bell, I had joined the crew for harvest. After helping with the crushing of Riesling grapes, and transferring wine into and out of oak barrels, Peter had called me in to keep watch over one of the tanks. He was filling it with fresh juice and he asked me to make sure it didn't overflow. There's no simple way to see inside the thing, so I climbed up to the catwalk and then vaulted over to the top of the tank. Leaning out with one foot on the sloped top, I peered inside the small opening, trying not to think about the distance to the floor.

"Uh, isn't wine supposed to be relaxing and romantic?" I called out to no one in particular, keeping my eyes inside the tank.

"Are you implying that this is less romantic than a hunk of cheese, two glasses and a picnic basket?" Peter responded. For a man that had recently turned fifty he was almost two-dimensionally thin with comfortably disheveled short hair, glasses, and a constant stubble. When he laughed it looked like he might snap in half.

We had been laughing all day despite the intense pressure of harvest aggravated by some awful weather—the kind where you can stand outside and not realize it's raining until your face is covered with freezing mist. None of that affected the crew at Fox Run. It was a day rife with examples of Peter's harvest philosophy: winemaking should be fun.

I didn't find the tank measuring job much fun but I made it down safely and caught my breath. Outside the winery there was the intermittent laughter of a half-dozen crew members. Inside the winery there was music. The sounds of upbeat acoustic guitar bounced off the tanks. I imagined the juice, roiling inside, fermenting to the tunes, the acidity brightening, the sugars mellowing and retreating. Perhaps the secret to great wine is a combination of careful work in the vineyards and Crosby, Stills, and Nash in the tank.

But for Peter, music is about more than a good guitar hook or a catchy chorus. I started to remark on the song but he grabbed my forearm, almost involuntarily, and said, "Wait! Listen for the Hammond. Here it comes."

Then, in a soaring burst of jazz organ, the Hammond B-3 rose above the other instruments. Peter looked up, taking in the sound, satisfied. A boyish grin lightened his face.

"It's just a perfect layer, perfect for that spot," he explained, and I realized he could have just as easily been talking about wine.

"I once spoke at a conference with four hundred people in the audience, and I invoked Ringo Starr to explain the effect of oak in wine," he said. I gave him a look begging for an explanation.

"Okay, there I was, and I figured that the audience had seen enough pie charts and graphs by that point, so I pulled out a CD player. I told them, 'You've all heard this Beatles song before, but I want you to listen for the drum fills. Just listen. You don't notice them unless you listen, but they're exquisite. They're essential. And if the drummer were some showboat, the song would not be as brilliant.' Well, that's oak in wine. Most of the time you don't notice it, and you shouldn't. But remove it and you lose a key component. So Ringo Starr is the perfect metaphor for oak in wine, though I doubt he'd describe himself in those terms!"

The best winemakers have that sensibility. They appreciate art, or food, or wine, or music, taken as a whole—but they intuitively break down its brilliance into discrete parts. My nose might dive into a glass of Cabernet and detect dark berry fruit and pepper, but a winemaker peels back the layers like they're instruments creating a song. Plum and blackberry fruit supported by a bass line of leather and portobello mushrooms. Similarly, I might enjoy a song for its melody, but winemakers are drawn to the layers of sound that work together. They hear each slide on the guitar, each hi-hat from the drum kit, and they celebrate the moment that the bass kicks in and pulses through the sternum. Winemakers like Peter can practically drink James Taylor's guitar riffs while bottles of their Cabernet Franc play "Steamroller Blues."

I was impressed with Peter's technical knowledge and his ability to solve problems very quickly. He knew each wine so intimately that he could rattle off exactly what it needed in its early life—what kind of grape handling and crushing, what kind of yeast for fermentation, what kind of aging program. Working harvest with him was like taking a crash course in wine science. And when something would go wrong—whether it was a lack of tank space or a key material running out—Peter knew the most efficient solution. It was no surprise that he was in heavy demand as a winemaking consultant.

But even more impressive was Peter's constant invocation of a simple but often forgotten phrase: "I don't know." While his peers and his employees looked at him as a kind of oracle, he loved to remind people that when you stop learning, your mind stops expanding. He has no patience for poseurs. As much as Peter loved to talk about wine and laugh during the workday, he shuts down when he encounters a know-it-all.

Critics might argue that Peter is overly technical when making wine; after all, there is a popular movement that champions the idea of making wine in as natural a way as possible. That harvest day I found that the Canadian wasn't buying it.

"Do you know what the most natural outcome is for grapes?" he asked as I prepared yeast at his instruction. "They rot on the vine or they become raisins. The very act of picking grapes is the start of a cascade of human actions. Crushing grapes is not natural. Everything we do might constitute too much intervention to the ultra-purists. But wine is not some perfect gift from nature—it requires some guidance!"

"But what about the idea that too much intervention leads to all wine tasting the same?" I asked.

"That's baloney," he said. "First of all, it's true that more wines have similar taste than ever before, and that's because the cleanliness in winemaking has improved. Some people think flaws automatically equate to character. I think a flaw is a flaw. We're doing a better job than ever before of keeping flaws out, and we shouldn't apologize for that. But that doesn't mean there is no regional character in our wine. Quite the opposite, in fact. When you keep those ugly flaws out, you can allow wine to give a very honest representation of its place."

He laughed. "How did we get to a point where there is a true, consistent Finger Lakes profile? If clean wines had no character, you wouldn't be able to pick Finger Lakes wines out of a lineup! But, of course, you certainly can now."

During a rare break—Peter tends not to eat lunch—he invited me up to his lab and office. Half a dozen glasses sat on the counter; each contained a short pour of an unlabeled white wine. He asked me to sample each and seek out the differences. I found any variation to be very subtle—the wines were crisp and expressive. He explained that he was comparing Riesling samples from different parts of the Fox Run Vineyard properties.

"Just when you think you have it all figured out, you'll get a totally different result one year," he said. "That's why I try not to speak in absolutes too often."

He was brutal when assessing his own wines, especially his Chardonnay. He is a notorious critic of thick, hot-climate Chardonnays—so much so that he once famously dumped out a bottle of Chardonnay in the bushes to "avoid contaminating the sink."

"So if you don't eat lunch, do you eat dinner?" I asked. "I want to hear about your adventures."

"Oh, sure, we eat dinner," he said, offering to bring wine for the occasion. Then he added, "But don't expect me to bring some West Coast Chardonnay or something."

* * *

Of all the winemakers who had come from around the world to the Finger Lakes, Peter Bell was probably the most unlikely. On the eve of summer he and Joanna sat on the end of our dock outside our Keuka Lake cottage and recounted the near-death experiences and chance encounters that had set their course for a winemaking region they once knew nothing about.

"This is why we came here," he gushed, nodding at the oil-painting sun that was setting over the lake bluff. We had just finished a meal of local spring vegetables, which is about all that Peter and Joanna eat.

"That's not actually why we came here, but it's a lovely bonus on nights like this," Joanna said as we leaned back in Adirondack chairs. She added with a laugh, "By rights, we probably should be sitting in the bottom of the Strait of Malacca!"

Peter explained that amid several years of savvy travel habits, there was one very poor decision. "We wanted to get from India to Singapore so we booked passage on a rickety old tramp steamer."

"I don't think 'rickety' quite does it justice," Joanna interjected.

"This was not our brightest moment," Peter confessed. "It would have been a stupid way to die. During the last night at sea we awoke to find this wall of opaque smoke pouring out of the air vent in our cabin. We spent the rest of the night huddled on the deck in life jackets. That thing was listing badly and it couldn't have been very long from sinking. The crew somehow saved it, but we found out that it sank several years later. Fifty people died."

"We eventually made it to Australia," Joanna said. "That's when it became certain that Peter was going to make wine. We made such wonderful friends there and they helped us when we needed it."

Indeed, that assistance paved the way for Peter to study at Charles Sturt University in Wagga Wagga, Australia. The School of Agricultural and Wine Sciences had produced a number of world-class winemakers and it had become a hub of industry research.

After graduating, Peter took a job in New Zealand, but the fit just wasn't right. People he met explained that it took about five years to be accepted into New Zealand's somewhat insular culture, a strong contrast to the friendly and inclusive way of life they had enjoyed in Australia. Reluctantly, Peter and Joanna looked to head back to the Northern Hemisphere. But how, and where?

Peter was working with a neighboring winery when he bumped into an American. "I don't believe in predestination," Peter said, pouring a glass of his new rosé wine. "People chalk everything up to destiny and it's like, give me a break. Our lives are the result of an unknowable number of chance encounters. None of us can know where we would be if certain moments had happened differently. But for me, there was a chance moment that steered our lives in a very fortunate direction."

He sipped his wine before stressing, "This wasn't destiny, just extremely good luck. This guy senses my restlessness and happens to mention that the Finger Lakes of New York are making great Riesling and there might be jobs open. I thought about the advantage of propinquity—it's reasonably close to where I grew up in Canada. So I started making phone calls to Finger Lakes wineries."

I was beginning to understand why Peter had gained a reputation as one of the most helpful winemakers in the region. Over the past twenty years he had become a kind of answer man, consulting on dozens of projects and solving problems for colleagues. It seemed to me that Peter's collaborative spirit was born the moment he got that phone call from Australia, reviving his nascent winemaking career. Without some unexpected help, he would have been making beer.

In other regions, winemakers sign confidentiality agreements. In the Finger Lakes, they believe regional success helps everyone. But Peter's first job in the Finger Lakes nearly squashed that attitude.

In 1990 he was hired as winemaker at Dr. Konstantin Frank's Vinifera Wine Cellars, a historic winery that first made wine in the 1960s. Owner Willy Frank made it clear to Peter that, while he could take the wine in new directions, friendships with other winemakers wouldn't be tolerated.

"There were five years that I wasn't allowed to talk to my colleagues," Peter said as the last sliver of reddish sun slipped below the horizon. "If Willy would catch me talking to another winemaker he would go ballistic. It was paranoia, sort of this old-world mindset that information is proprietary and everyone else is your enemy."

He laughed. "So I did the only thing I could do. I made friends on the sly!"

Joanna nodded. "It's true," she said. "Other winemakers couldn't even visit to taste Peter's wines. But we knew this wasn't normal. It was obvious early on that we had come to a region with an outgoing spirit."

As Peter swirled his rosé, I poured another glass of 2006 Fox Run Reserve Riesling, one of the truly special Rieslings to come out of the Finger Lakes. Peter has been the head winemaker at Fox Run since 1995, the year when everything changed for him.

"It was like we had thrown off the shackles and everything was finally right," he said. "I started doing consulting jobs almost immediately after leaving Dr. Frank for Fox Run. I worked with a number of Finger Lakes wineries and even a few on Long Island. Our owner encouraged me to reach out. It felt entirely natural to work with other wineries."

He leaned back in his chair. "I loved it. I still do."

It's impossible to know exactly how deep the impact of Peter Bell's consulting has been, but no one doubts that his fingerprints can be found in wine cellars across the region. He brought with him the kind of technical training, study, and experience that few local winemakers had. And it was clear to me that he was one of the smartest people I'd ever met, wielding raw intellect as a weapon in debate or a soft needle in jest. Cornell University enlisted Peter to be a guest lecturer on a variety of wine courses and it's no surprise that one of his favorites was a class on a rather arcane subject: cognitive relativism.

Remembering his students' reaction, Peter cocked his head and said, "Cognitive *what*?"

And yet the mark of a special teacher is to take a complicated or foreign idea and transform it into something that is easily demonstrated and understood. Professor Bell sent a bottle of wine around the classroom that day, then asked each student to describe its aroma using a single word.

"Just about every single person had written down a different word," Peter recalled. "This wine smells like raspberries! No, blueberries! No, it smells like herbs! And that was exactly the point."

"They were all correct, weren't they?" I said with a smile.

"They were all correct," he nodded. "And they were laughing with each new description. That's cognitive relativism. Some things are true and we know them to be true." He picked up the half-empty wine bottle. "This is made of glass, not straw. But the way we perceive the wine is going to be different for all of us, for myriad reasons. And are you going to tell me that I'm wrong to think this wine smells like vanilla, just because you're thinking strawberries?"

I thought of the retired German winemaker Hermann Wiemer, a towering figure who had come to the Finger Lakes but was reluctant to share his knowledge. Peter Bell was one of the first to choose a different path.

"I've opened my veins," he said, "and maybe that's encouraged other people to open their veins, and we're all bleeding into the same stream now." The comparison flopped like a dying fish and Joanna nearly spit her wine out, laughing. "You know," Peter added, "that could be the worst analogy I've ever made."

We drained another couple of bottles on a night that had become perfectly still—the kind of night that makes all of those long frigid winter days worth the resulting seasonal affective disorder. It was obvious how much fun Peter and Joanna were still having in the Finger Lakes nearly two decades after arriving. She had gone to work at the local library as well as for a handful of social causes. Their two boys were recently out of college and already building successful careers of their own. Joanna worried that Peter's wine-consulting travels were too demanding, but she knew he still thrived on travel. He had expanded his consulting to other states—Ohio and Rhode Island—as well as to China and Europe. His projects took him to Hungary, France, and Spain, but it was his visit to Serbia that had concerned Joanna the most. She wondered if he could retain the energy necessary to help so many people.

"So you didn't get the winemaking training until you were almost thirty," I said, futilely searching the dock for any remaining wine. "What was your original degree in?"

"Anthropology. So I went to work in the best tradition of anthropology graduates."

"Doing what?" I asked.

"Making cabinets."

With the wine gone and the midnight hour approaching, Morgan and I reluctantly set about cleaning up the dishes and empty glasses. As Peter stood up he said, "I think you should check out Red Tail Ridge." He was referring to a three-year-old winery just a mile down Seneca Lake from Fox Run; Peter had helped make the wine while the owners built a stunning new facility. "They're doing some excellent things."

"Those are your wines," I said.

He shook his head. "Nope. They're doing the work and it's really impressive. Go see it."

* * *

I had begun to wonder: Which Finger Lakes success story owes the most to Peter Bell? The list is long. Hunt Country Vineyards, a family operation on Keuka Lake, brought Peter in to help the owners' son ascend to the role of head winemaker—and the early results were outstanding. On Seneca Lake, Miles Wine Cellars is locally famous for the playful ghost stories surrounding their property; much lesser known is the influence Peter has in making the wines. But considering the rapid development at Red Tail Ridge, it has to be considered Peter's most successful local project.

The story behind Red Tail Ridge always surprises customers: a couple moved from the California wine industry to start fresh in the Finger Lakes. It's easy to assume that a couple from the Finger Lakes might seek to move to the West Coast in search of warmer weather and a more prestigious wine region. In this case, it was exactly the opposite.

Nancy Irelan was the director of research for the massive Gallo Wine Company and had spent twelve years working her way up in the company and the industry. She had carved out a career that many of her colleagues envied, so they have been confused when she gave it all up. She and her husband, Mike, wanted to launch their own wine company, but the cost of West Coast land was prohibitive. Nancy had grown to appreciate Finger Lakes wines during her consulting visits to Cornell University over the years, and the cost of land made the region that much more appealing.

Nancy and Mike had no idea that they were buying property just one mile from the man who would help their wines gain the attention of critics almost instantly. When they needed a facility—and winemaking guidance—they would turn to Fox Run and Peter Bell.

As I turned up the hill leading to the new Red Tail Ridge facility, I marveled at the vineyards. Nancy and Mike wanted the steep entrance road to snake through the vineyards so visitors would see just how meticulous the grape growing was. Mike was in charge of the vines, and he had arrived in the Finger Lakes with two essential attributes: a desire to make the vineyard as visually attractive as those back in California, and an open mind about learning how to grow grapes in a cool climate.

But the best vineyards still need a skilled hand to make the wines, and Nancy came to the Finger Lakes seeking help. She had done many jobs in California, but she had never been a full-time winemaker.

This was my first visit to Red Tail Ridge's sparkling new building, which was on its way to becoming certified in the Leadership in Energy and Environmental Design program. This meant it was seriously expensive to build—and potentially a bargain in the long run, thanks to some very cool and difficult-to-explain energy efficiencies. It looked to me like a building plucked from the *Star Wars* universe, with massive glass windows and complicated gadgets all over the place.

Nancy and Mike greeted me downstairs before leading me up to a lab that looked suspiciously like the one up the road at Fox Run. Nancy wears short salt-and-pepper hair and projects all business, while Mike, with short dark hair and broad, athletic shoulders, is quicker with a joke.

"So nobody thumbed their nose at the Californians?" I asked with a smile as Nancy handed me a glass from a series of Riesling samples.

"This is such a great neighborhood," Nancy said. "I call it the 'hood. People are awesome."

"It's been open arms since we got here," Mike said. "If you try the same thing in California, everyone would probably slam the door in your face. You know, they'd say something like, 'Go figure it out on your own.'"

"I don't know if it's quite like that," Nancy said. "But out there it makes a big difference if you have a connection. If you went to school with someone in the industry you might get some help or guidance."

"Well, you can put it that way," Mike said, "but there's no doubt that in California it's much more individually competitive. Here, the region is trying to make wines that compete on a world scale, but that doesn't necessarily mean knocking your local competitors down."

The wines we tasted were the first that Nancy had made essentially on her own, and they were excellent. It was impossible to miss Peter Bell's influence, but some of the samples showed a slightly richer style.

"It could have been a disaster if I came here not looking to learn," she said. "I didn't have to ask, either. I had people offering anything we needed. And none more than Peter."

Red Tail Ridge was earning slightly higher magazine scores than Fox Run wines, and I wondered if that made things awkward between her and Peter. She brushed it off. "Peter has to make a huge lineup of wines. We're a much smaller production. He can do it all, and he does. I don't think it makes sense to look at every score without that context."

It was a diplomatic and sincere answer. Red Tail had become an extremely hot property with critics, who appreciated not only the quality of the wines but the professional approach that Nancy and Mike had brought. The Finger Lakes will never try to be California, but the high standards are something to emulate. Red Tail Ridge is going to be a leader. And even if customers don't notice, Peter Bell's fingerprints will remain on these wines. Most important, Nancy was able to take what she learned from Peter to build her own philosophy of winemaking.

"I get a little lonely over here!" Nancy said as I packed up to leave. "When I was over at Fox Run, before our facility was built, there was always laughter. But I'm sure I'll have plenty of reasons to go back. And you know, Peter's not the only genius up there. Tricia has been so wonderful with us."

She was talking about Peter's assistant winemaker Tricia Renshaw, and I realized that Nancy had just answered the question that had been rattling around my brain.

* * *

I wanted to tell Peter that I had figured it out. When I stopped back in at Fox Run, Peter and the crew were performing one of the countless enjoyable tasks that comes with making wine: they were tasting through the library of older vintages. "We could really use your help on this," Peter told me. "We're trying to track how these wines are aging. You think you can handle this?"

After around an hour of inspecting ten-year-old Rieslings, Lembergers, and more, Peter instructed me to join him in the lab. "We have a glass of something that is a very effective learning tool," he explained.

There were several glasses of red wine on the counter and Peter picked them up one by one, swirling and sniffing, until he arrived at a glass that arched his eyebrows. "Here it is," he said. "Give it a try."

I swirled the dark liquid and dropped my nose into the glass—then immediately jerked my nose back out. The smell was wickedly reminiscent of nail-polish remover. "Wow," I said. "What the hell did you do to this?"

He laughed and said, "It wasn't me. That was our best barrel of Pinot Noir—until it was overcome with ethyl acetate. I wanted you to know exactly what it smells like. That barrel is dead now."

I never felt like Peter was lecturing, and yet I always left Fox Run with more knowledge—and it didn't always pertain to wine. Through my conversations with the Canadian I have become well versed in hematology, chaos theory, and ichthyology (the study of fish, not an aversion to religion). But this time I wanted to enlighten Peter about something.

"I've finally figured out your greatest contribution to the local wine scene," I told him. "You know, your most significant local project."

He rolled his eyes. Peter prefers to talk about the success of others. His consulting wasn't free; he made some good money on the side in addition to a steady stream of altruistic pro bono work. But his desire to collaborate was one of the most significant reasons for the growing success of Finger Lakes wine.

"Your biggest impact is not a winery," I said. "It's a person."

"Oh, it is?" he said.

I grinned. "Tricia Renshaw."

He closed his eyes and shook his head slowly but firmly. "I can't take credit for her. I have nothing to do with her skills."

"She told me she owes you everything," I said.

"She's too modest. Do you know how she became a winemaker? Her trajectory is like *nothing* I've ever seen, and you can't credit me."

"I do know," I said, "and I think everyone should know."

SEVEN

The Prodigy Next Door: Tricia Renshaw

August 1, 2005
Canandaigua, New York

"There is nothing ridiculous about this," Tricia Renshaw said out loud to no one in particular. She was pacing her bedroom, holding the phone. "Nothing ridiculous at all."

And of course she knew that what she was about to do was completely, utterly, inherently ridiculous.

Wanting to change careers is common. Some sociologists have recommended everyone switch vocations every five years to avoid the kind of burnout that drains the worker and the workplace. Tricia had been groomed for a career in banking, then switched to teaching, and now something was giving her the courage to try something entirely different.

Or at least she thought she was being courageous—but her fingers couldn't stop shaking long enough to dial the numbers. Her torment was driven by her conflicting feelings that this was the right thing to do—and also completely absurd.

At age thirty-five, Tricia Renshaw had decided she wanted to make wine for a living.

This would not seem so ridiculous if she had studied enology, the science of wine. Chemistry, perhaps—or any kind of science at all. But Tricia had graduated from Nazareth College in Rochester with a degree in

French—the language, not the wine. She wanted to make wine but she was more qualified to do almost anything else.

She considered going down to the kitchen to pour herself a shot. But as she slowed her breathing to a manageable pace, she finally dialed the work number given to her for Peter Bell.

"Fox Run. Peter."

He had answered so quickly that Tricia briefly lost her composure. After a pause she began to string words together at a high rate of speed, hoping they would form a complete sentence: "I was talking to someone in your tasting room who said that occasionally you take volunteers, and maybe you'll need some this year, and I'm calling to find out if I could possibly come and hold a pail and scrub floors or something."

For a moment there was silence on the other end of the line, and Tricia feared that Peter had already hung up. She would have been relieved to see that he was simply smiling at Tricia's enthusiasm and raw nerves.

"Okay," he said. "Can you come by tomorrow?"

What? *Tomorrow?*

"Tomorrow! Of course!" Tricia was checking her schedule in her head, and then she grimaced. She had two girls, nine and six years old, and they were the only thing in the world more important to her than this phone conversation. It was the first day of August and they were going to be home all day on summer vacation.

"Wait, I'm sorry to ask," she said, feeling like a balloon on the verge of popping. "I have two little girls, and—"

"Bring the girls! I'd love to meet them."

Tricia felt a rush of lightheadedness and her feet turned into Jell-O underneath her. She landed softly on her bed, the phone held tight to her ear, an astonished, open-mouthed grin on her face. As awkward as it had started out, she could not have scripted this conversation any better.

Peter was accustomed to being approached by winemaker wannabes, from naïve romantics to whip-smart graduates from halfway around the world. His policy was always to offer encouragement, as long as he could disabuse them of any conviction that winemaking was easy and glamorous.

He got right to the point with Tricia. "We're bottling all day tomorrow," he said. "It's dull and repetitive, and you'll have a sore back. We don't take many breaks."

Without a moment's hesitation, Tricia answered, "I'll be there at eight sharp."

"Dress grubby," Peter said, and hung up the phone.

She dropped the receiver and stared at the ceiling. *What if I make a fool of myself? What if they don't invite me back?* It was only one day of bottling, after all. She could hate it. They could decide she was wasting their time. At the very least, she was finally following through on a promise to herself. While monitoring high-school detention months earlier, she had lectured a student to stop making excuses and work hard to achieve his potential. That day on the drive home she had promised herself she would follow her own advice. Now she was making the effort.

No matter what happens tomorrow, she thought, *this feels really good. And I haven't felt this good in a long time.*

* * *

A winery's bottling line is about as stimulating as decaf coffee. Most normal human beings find it tedious. Tricia loved it immediately.

Of course, the rest of the bottling line tingled with excitement as well. Several men worked the line; their typical day consisted of unloading boxes of empty bottles, loading them onto the conveyor, filling the bottles, monitoring the corking and labeling, and then repackaging them. That morning they added another task: staring at the gorgeous new girl.

She wasn't trying to drop jaws to the floor, of course. Tricia would have preferred to quietly blend into the line, but she was the kind of woman who looks better in jeans and a T-shirt than a dress. She was cursed with preternaturally good looks. Her light brown hair fell down past her shoulders, and she carried the figure of a childless twenty-five-year-old young professional, not a thirty-five-year-old mother of two. Her wide smile was positively infectious to the guys on the bottling line, who, despite their obvious attraction to the new girl, treated Tricia with courtesy and respect. They decided that she was like the classic girl next door, attractive and fun. But they knew she was there to work.

Tricia had decided that morning to drop the girls off with her parents for the day so she could focus on her work at Fox Run. Walking into the winery was a surreal thrill. She had chosen Fox Run based on a strange experience earlier that year when she had visited the tasting room on a Finger Lakes wine tour with friends. Fox Run offers regular tours of the grounds and winery, and during the walk through the vineyard Tricia had felt something oddly compelling come over her. She would later say it was a tranquil, clear message telling her that she should be working in the wine industry. She waited months to call Peter Bell because she had no experience and no real reason to want the job, other than her strong conviction that she was supposed to make wine. Given that she is not particularly religious, Tricia had a hard time explaining the idea. She had a hard time even understanding it herself.

Now that she was finally working in the winery, Tricia tried to control her emotions. What was banal for everyone else was new and exciting for Tricia, and it would have been plenty to occupy her first day at Fox Run, if only the line hadn't broken down.

At 10:30 that morning, with the bottling line in need of repair, the rest of the crew moved on to other tasks around the winery. Tricia was not trained to do anything else, so Peter came down from the lab with an idea.

"Want to taste some wines for me?" he asked. "And jot down your impressions of them, if you don't mind."

"Uh, sure!" she said, and then smiled in embarrassment. She had never seen a tasting note before—she had never written anything about wine—but she didn't want to tell Peter.

"The wine is tawny port," Peter said. "It's a fortified red dessert wine. There are eight samples."

"That sounds great," Tricia said, and started to go up the metal stairs to the lab. She'd made it three quarters of the way up when Peter called out to her.

"You do know how to write tasting notes, right?"

Tricia stopped cold. She turned around slowly.

"Not exactly!"

Peter was surprised to learn that Tricia had never seen a tasting note—not in a wine magazine, not even in a restaurant. "It's nothing complicated," he said. "Just grab the notepad and write down what you smell and then what you taste."

"I can do that," Tricia said.

"Take your time," Peter said. "Enjoy it."

Inside the lab, Tricia found the fortified wine samples, but not in wineglasses. They had been poured into small bottles with lines on the side and orange caps on the top. She figured the bottles were marked for measurements of some sort but she had never seen anything like it. At that moment she tried to suppress a sense of feeling overwhelmed. *I'm not a winemaker*, she thought. *I don't know the first thing about any of this stuff.*

Fighting off the feeling, Tricia grabbed a blank notepad on the counter and set about her task. Opening the first small bottle, she gently brought her nose to the top and inhaled. The aromas were so explosive that she flinched. She backed away for a moment, and then smelled the wine again. The wine smelled like rich butterscotch and toffee, which were just about the last things Tricia expected to smell in wine. After putting down on paper what she thought she was smelling, she tasted the first sample.

Taking a small sip, Tricia let the sweet wine coat her mouth. She felt a drip roll down her chin, and she was grateful to be alone in the lab. Then the flavors hit her and her eyes went wide as she tried to identify each distinctive taste. Cinnamon, definitely. Nutmeg. And then there was the butterscotch that she had smelled. Instead of spitting the wine into an empty glass or the sink, Tricia swallowed and felt it warm her throat. She closed her eyes and exhaled deeply. Never had a beverage been so satisfying, so inspiring.

Scribbling quickly, she moved on to the next bottle. This wine was vastly different and yet no less explosive. She smelled dried apple and clove, and then—mincemeat pie? Yes, it was undoubtedly mincemeat pie, and she said aloud, "What kind of wine smells like mincemeat pie?" Taking a long swig, she found flavors of apple, caramel, and fig. Then the mincemeat pie showed up, and she began writing furiously once more. For the next thirty minutes Tricia sniffed and tasted and scribbled to her heart's content. She had no idea how to fully express her thoughts about the wine, but by the end she didn't care. She was so moved by the experience that nothing could dampen her enthusiasm.

When she returned to the repaired bottling line downstairs, she was smiling so broadly that the guys thought she had just been hired full-time.

* * *

Peter Bell wanted to make sure he wasn't being conned. Most novices write only the most basic ideas about wine in their first tasting notes. They'll write that the wine smells "sweet," or tastes "bitter," or occasionally they'll say it tastes like some general fruit, like cherries.

Tricia's tasting notes could have been written by a world-class winemaker.

He marveled at the depth of thought in the notes. The fourth wine, Tricia wrote, was "slightly out of balance . . . a little hot . . . maybe too much alcohol." Of the sixth sample she wrote, "pure silk . . . smells like raisins and figs and the taste matches the smell gorgeously." She had identified the most nuanced smells and flavors, and Peter raised his palm to his forehead in disbelief as he read that Tricia had detected scents of mincemeat pie in one of the samples. He had been making trial blends all week in hopes of highlighting just such a quality.

Then he laughed as he discovered the one section of Tricia's notes that was more than a little unorthodox. She had struggled to describe how the flavors in the wine evolved in her mouth so she had drawn arrows, indicating the change from one flavor to another and then another. Peter thought it was brilliant.

After lunch he asked to speak with her privately, giving nothing away about how impressed he was with her notes. "I want to know," he said sternly, "if you've ever done this before."

"No, I haven't," she said, and for a brief moment Tricia worried that she had flopped. "I just tried to do what you asked me to do."

Peter shook his head and began to smile. "That's what I thought. So you want to be a winemaker?"

Again searching for the right response, she mumbled awkwardly, "I . . . guess?"

"Well, you are not just going to be a winemaker," Peter said. "You are going to be a judge, and you are going to be one of the best."

Tricia felt a lump in her throat and she knew she was about to cry.

"I want you to know," he said, "that you were born with the kind of skills that a trained professional could spend thirty years trying to attain. And they would never have what you have."

If you're going to spend time with Tricia Renshaw, you're going to spend time with her two girls. For Morgan and me, this was no problem. Morgan's job as a photographer entails hundreds of hours spent with young children each year, and I spent my high-school and college summers directing programs at a camp on Lake Chautauqua. But if others who come into Tricia's life are not accustomed to kids, they're going to have to get used to it. Tricia and her daughters are an inseparable package.

It has always been this way, and Tricia's devotion to her kids was only bolstered by the dissolution of her marriage. She doesn't talk about it—not even with the girls, and she talks about almost everything with them. Her ex lives in another state and sees the girls on occasion, but Tricia does the parenting. She is their rock and they, no doubt, are hers.

Tricia had abandoned her pursuit of teaching French shortly after she started at Fox Run. It had been an enormous risk. While she found working in a public school district to be banal, it had at least offered a steady paycheck and the promise of long-term stability. Making wine offered daily invigoration—and a much smaller paycheck, along with the instability of an industry increasingly saturated with new wineries.

On top of that, Tricia had to answer one important question: Could she learn the science of making wine? Her instincts would carry her only so far, and she knew she could never be a head winemaker without scientific training. Not long after Peter Bell had asked Tricia to be his assistant winemaker, she began the daunting task of book learning, classes, and online coursework. It would take several years, and some nights she wondered if she could even complete the work, let alone flourish in a scientific world that was entirely new to her.

Peter Bell might not have realized it, but Tricia tried to absorb every little detail when he talked about the science of wine. She found him even more helpful than her classes.

We met Tricia and her girls on a muggy July night for dinner almost three years after she first called Fox Run. This trip took us to downtown Canandaigua, the town on the northern edge of the lake with the same name. Canandaigua lies to the west of Keuka, Seneca, and Cayuga and, at fifteen miles in length, is about half the size of Seneca and Cayuga. It is not a celebrated wine-producing lake—it's best known for rivaling Lake Tahoe in property values.

The town of Canandaigua is charming, and especially so on summer evenings. The vivacious main street hums with the sound of farmers' markets and open-air orchestral performances. The lake, glistening down below the sweep of the hill, hosts sailboat races and leisurely cruises. Fortunately for people like Tricia, the properties set back from the lake were nowhere near as expensive.

Tricia lived in an old house directly across the street from the historic Sonnenberg Gardens, and she had invited Morgan and me to join her and the girls for dinner downtown, followed by a drink on her back porch. We arranged to have dinner at a restaurant on Main Street called Simply Crepes, a new place owned by a Rochester couple who had adopted their French-Canadian family's recipes.

Morgan and I arrived completely unaware of the Tricia Renshaw Rule: however much time she estimates you'll spend with her, double it.

Tricia and the girls wore almost-matching flower-print dresses and greeted us cheerfully just a few minutes past six. Elizabeth, twelve, was tall for her age with long brown hair and a confidence not usually evident in preteens. Nine-year-old Meghan was much shorter, with light-brown hair and cute, high cheeks that puffed up when she smiled, which was often. My first clue to Meghan's maturity came when the waitress brought our menus and said, "I can bring a children's menu." Meghan politely replied, "No, thanks. Do you happen to have French onion soup tonight?"

Tricia had decided to bring the girls into her career, and they were loving the adventure. She occasionally allowed them a furtive taste of wine, and she brought them to work on some of the days they didn't have school. Meghan was already an outstanding gymnast, and she enjoyed practicing parts of her routines on the oak barrels in the Fox Run winery. "It's a good place to work on my balance," she said, while Tricia shook her head slowly, evidently concerned that Morgan and I might not approve of oak barrel gymnastics. We simply laughed.

"Meghan hangs out on the barrels, and sometimes we play with the tanks," Elizabeth said, which prompted another wide-eyed look from Tricia.

"I'm not sure we want to share that story, honey," she said.

"But it's funny!" Elizabeth protested, and after I shot her an approving nod, she continued. "You know those huge steel tanks? When they're empty, they clean them out, but you're not supposed to go inside them. So we don't. But sometimes we'll throw balls and toys in there and bounce them around. I'm pretty sure they knew that, because one time Meghan left one of those squishy toys in the tank."

"It was a squishy orange caterpillar," Meghan said. "And they filled the tank with wine when it was still in there."

"And they looked down into the tank and they saw this thing floating in the wine," Elizabeth added eagerly. "So when they found out what it was they called it the V.H.C. wine, which stands for Very Hungry Caterpillar. No one knew why except Meghan and me!" The girls busted up, as did their mother.

"Okay, that's enough of the stories that can make me look bad," Tricia said.

We enjoyed our servings of various crepes—and Meghan got her bowl of French onion soup. Tricia explained that long before she began making wine, work was a grind, focused solely on providing for her kids.

"When they were younger, whenever I worked it was just to fill a very specific need," she said. "I took a job tending bar when we were short on school expenses. It was a terrible job, late at night, and I wouldn't get home until one in the morning."

She paused and seemed on the verge of getting emotional. "The hard part was that none of my early jobs taught my girls anything about work other than the fact that you have to do it. Now my girls see that if you don't give up on what you really want, work doesn't have to just be drudgery. You really can find something you love, and all of a sudden your life isn't just about finding a way to get to the weekend. You can love the work week just as much."

Elizabeth and Meghan brightened as their mother talked about having a job that she finally enjoyed. "It helps that she's really awesome at making wine," Elizabeth told us.

"Which wine is your favorite?" I asked.

Elizabeth didn't hesitate: "Gewürztraminer," she said, pronouncing it flawlessly.

"Mom fixes things now," Meghan said. "She fixed the washing machine one time."

"It's true!" Tricia said. "When I started working at the winery I started to learn how to do some things for the first time. I started using tools. I repaired equipment. I fixed lights. And it began to help me do things at home—I was able to fix the washing machine when it broke down. I feel like I can take on more challenges now, and my kids like that. They say I'm a can-do kind of woman!"

"Can do!" Meghan echoed.

As we finished our meal, we arranged to follow Tricia on the short drive back to her house. "I have a few barrel samples to share with you guys," she said excitedly. "I promise not to keep you long."

* * *

A gorgeous summer evening is different in the Finger Lakes than it is in California, or Arizona, or Texas, or Tuscany. Beyond the infinite canvas of the stars and the soft, warm air, there is a gratitude that is present and acknowledged if not spoken. The vicissitudes of winter never quite leave the mind of a western New Yorker, and a winemaker in particular. Having endured patiently, a winemaker in the Finger Lakes values the majesty of summer more deeply than his or her counterparts in many other parts of the world.

We relaxed on Tricia's back deck on what had become an ideal night, with only a few drops of the day's rain remaining on the wooden railings.

Elizabeth and Meghan stayed in the living room, playing with their pair of new kittens. Morgan and I snacked on cheese and baguette while Tricia stole away to her cellar. When she emerged she was carrying half a case of wine and nearly tripped on her way out to the back deck.

"I couldn't decide what I wanted to pour for you guys, so I kind of just grabbed everything," she said sheepishly. "I hope that's okay."

It was more than okay. We could see instantly that Tricia loves to share her wines, and I was guessing that she didn't have the opportunity to do so very often. When she's not at the winery, Tricia is heavily involved in her girls' schoolwork and extracurricular activities. She doesn't often host company.

We started with a glass of the aggressively aromatic Fox Run Gewürztraminer. Tasting wine with Tricia is a whirlwind experience. She buries her nose in the glass and takes several long, slow inhalations before swishing the wine in her mouth and studying it carefully. Then she comes out with a barrage of descriptors so precise and accurate that it is as though she is reading each ingredient on the back label. "Pine nuts," she said thoughtfully, staring at the glass of straw-colored liquid. "Of course that classic lychee. And then a whole bouquet of gorgeous fresh-cut flowers. Almond paste and curry."

Morgan smiled and said, "Me, too. That's what I get."

We laughed as Tricia began to explain how she first felt connected to wine. Given the story that she told, I was surprised that she didn't pursue a career in wine much earlier in life.

In 1988 she lived in Belgium for a semester as a nineteen-year-old exchange student. The meals were a challenge to an American weaned on processed convenience food. "I was staying with this family, and the mother was a fabulous cook, but a lot of what she made I couldn't fathom putting in my mouth," she said. "Calf's head stew, where they boil the whole head of a calf—things like that. Cheeks, eyes, brain. Finally one night they said we were having spaghetti bolognese, and I thought, 'Oh, good. At least I know what this meal is.'

"But then I saw what looked like a bowl of vegetable soup on a bed of noodles. And the smells were so strong, and I was almost on the verge of tears with another meal I didn't want to eat. There was wine on the table that night, but it wasn't something I was thinking much about. I just thought it was cool to write home to my friends and tell them I'd been drinking wine. I remember taking one spoonful from the soup and it was really hot. It had loads of black pepper and it was tremendously spicy. And after that one bite I quickly grabbed a glass of wine and tossed back a mouthful, and everything changed."

Tricia paused from her story, swirled the wine in her glass, and closed her eyes. "In that one instant I became so much more open-minded about food and wine. I finally understood what the point was. I saw that wine can make food taste better, and food can make wine taste better. As soon as the wine hit my mouth, I wanted more food, and as soon as the food hit my mouth, I wanted more wine. It was beautiful. It was a life-changing mouthful."

"So why didn't you go straight into winemaking?" I asked.

"My friends were not wine drinkers and we didn't have money," she said. "It wasn't even legal to buy a bottle of wine—I was only nineteen. So while that experience stayed with me, it kind of faded. When I got married, wine was something we drank when we had it, but we didn't have the budget to buy a lot of it. It was a luxury, not a regular part of life."

"But when you walked through the vineyards at Fox Run three years ago, and you felt that magic, did you think of that night in Belgium?"

"You know, I didn't," she said. "I probably should have connected it. Looking back on my life, I can see how all of these moments seemed to work together to lead me to Fox Run and making wine."

* * *

At midnight, three and a half hours after we had arrived at Tricia's house, Elizabeth and Meghan joined us on the back deck and announced that they were not nearly tired enough to go to bed. Making no attempt to defend the veracity of this claim, Meghan lay down on a bench and was almost instantly asleep. Elizabeth sat on the wooden rail next to her mother, leaning her head on Tricia's shoulder. It was a display of affection much more common between a mother and a six-year-old, and yet at twelve years old Elizabeth was comfortable enough to hold her mother's hand while talking about the various careers she might pursue in college.

We were swirling a second barrel sample of fortified red dessert wine, the very same wine that had smitten Tricia on her first day at Fox Run. The samples were rich and delicious, conjuring images of orange peel, Werther's candy—and a long list of other scents and flavors uncovered by Tricia. Peter Bell had turned a large part of the fortified winemaking over to Tricia. That, however, was the extent of any full-time winemaking duties she was willing to consider. In fact, Peter had gladly agreed to the kind of schedule Tricia had proposed: she needed to be there to get her girls on the school bus in the morning, and she needed to be there when they got off the bus in the afternoon. With her instinct and palate, Tricia could easily have gotten on the fast track to her own lead winemaking job, but she was years away from even thinking of such a move.

"Not until the girls are out of high school," she said, stroking Elizabeth's hair. "Right now I'm just waiting for someone to walk into the winery and say, 'Okay, it's over. Thanks for coming. Back to the gas station or the bar.' I mean, it's been like a dream for three years, but I had zero training when I came to Fox Run. I had no reason to believe I would be good at making wine. So what right do I have to push for anything more?"

"But what about in ten years?" Morgan asked. "Meghan will be done with high school, and Peter might want to retire." With the age difference—Peter is nearly a decade and a half older—a succession plan seemed logical.

"Peter thinks it's smart to groom a successor," she said. "As he would slowly work fewer and fewer hours, I could pick up more and more hours. That would work out nicely for both of us. But I have to say that I can't imagine Peter Bell not making wine. As long as he can get out of bed, I can't see him not making wine." She swirled the last sip of wine in her glass. "If Fox Run grows, I'd like to think it would make sense to have two full-time winemakers, and we could increase our focus on Riesling and fortified wines. I'm so invested in Fox Run that I can't imagine going someplace else."

Tricia finished her wine and announced that she had forgotten something inside. Returning just a minute later, she was carrying another unlabeled bottle of red wine—yet another new barrel sample from Fox Run. "Do you have time to taste one more?" she asked almost apologetically. "I know it's a little late, but I thought it would be fun to compare another."

Morgan and I laughed. "We always have time for another barrel sample," I said.

"Good!" She grabbed our empty glasses. "I should have warned you that I'll keep pouring until you leave. You'll have to see yourself out at some point, 'cause I won't stop."

As we set about uncovering the mysteries of this new sample, Elizabeth asked if she could try a sip of one of the wines. Tricia poured her a sip of Gewürztraminer. Morgan and I smiled as we watched Elizabeth dutifully dive her nose into the glass to smell the wine, then hold it thoughtfully in her mouth before swallowing. "I like it," she said. "It doesn't separate in my mouth. It stays together."

Tricia explained that Elizabeth tends to see wine in two groups: those that "stay together" in the mouth and those that "separate."

"She may not realize it, but she's talking about balance," Tricia said. "Some wines are out of balance because they have too much alcohol.

Some are off balance because the winemaker didn't do a good job of playing the acidity off the sugar. She can sense it."

Oh, the wonders of genetics.

Then Tricia explained that the reason we taste different flavors in wine is because the wine contains a component called "esters," and the tiny esters have many characteristics. This was starting to sound rather, well, scientific.

"When people say a wine tastes like peaches or lime, it's probably because the esters found in actual peaches and limes are present in that wine. What we eat and drink tastes good because of all those odor-active compounds, and they're what make wines so diverse."

"Sounds like you're making progress in getting that winemaking certificate," I observed, but she didn't seem optimistic.

"I hope so, but there are long nights. It can be frustrating, and I just want to feel like I fit in with Peter and other winemakers." She explained that she was about a year away from completing the program.

Sometime after two in the morning I extinguished the final drops in my glass (it was the same glass Tricia had poured a couple of hours earlier, as I tend to drink fortified wines slowly). Morgan and I stood up, stretched contentedly, and thanked Tricia for a glorious evening.

"You can stay here if you want," she offered. "We could open one more bottle . . ." We smiled and declined. As we made our way to the door I thought that Tricia had it backward: it was her employer that was the fortunate one in their relationship. Fox Run had lucked into an assistant winemaker with an almost impossibly rare gift, a bottomless enthusiasm for wine—and no desire to break away and take a head winemaking job. Her children ensured that Tricia would stay at Fox Run for many years, learning the science of wine from Peter Bell and using her natural talent to make high-quality products.

And as I turned back to see Tricia gently waking Meghan, I wondered if she would ever be as good at making wine as she seems to be at being a mom.

* * *

I had never heard the word *tawnification* before, and I considered my wine vocabulary to be pretty strong. But when Tricia said, "Let's go check out the Tawnification Room," I could only respond, "Sure. The what?"

It was a dreary harvest evening with a chilly mist falling. During this first week of October I had volunteered for a variety of Finger Lakes winemakers in my effort to learn about winemaking by doing every individual task performed by harvest crews. I'd spent nearly ten hours pouring rice hulls into freshly crushed Riesling, filling oak barrels with new Chardonnay, and cleaning up the detritus that inevitably litters the ground after a press cycle. Most of the work was done outdoors, and I was cold. So my interest perked up when Tricia explained, "The Tawny Room is also called the Warm Room."

During harvest, Tricia's parents watch the girls after they get home from school so Tricia can work long hours. Winemakers and their crews rarely get home before nine or ten o'clock during harvest.

We had just finished having dinner on the picnic tables outside the winery with the setting sun barely noticeable behind the clouds. Peter and Tricia had pulled a couple of bottles for their crew to enjoy with a collection of grilled sandwiches they had grabbed from the tasting room. The 2005 Riesling was a gem, just coming into its luscious peak. It was also one of the first wines that Tricia had helped make, and she was clearly proud of it.

Morgan had joined us for the meal and, as I was packing up my pile of dirty clothes from the day, Tricia asked us to stay a little while longer. "If you've never seen the Tawny Room, you've got to check it out. Most people don't know it's there. It's where we keep the barrels of fortified wine. Peter built it last year to house our tawny port–style wine." The look in her eye was reminiscent of that long July night, and I knew there was no turning her down.

While the rest of the crew headed back to the forklifts and pumps and press, Tricia, Morgan, and I quietly slipped into the back of the winery. Oak barrels were stacked toward the high ceiling on all sides of the room. Tricia approached the side wall, moved an empty pallet aside, and revealed a wooden door. She tugged it open and we saw a small room containing more oak barrels and some fiberglass insulation—and we felt a blast of heat. Tricia whipped her head around and smiled. "Here it is!"

She handed us each a glass and pulled the small plug from the top of one of the barrels. As she drew the first sample, I inhaled and took in the now-familiar scents of fortified red wine. Tricia had converted me; I had never enjoyed port until tasting the red dessert wines made at Fox Run. There were about a dozen barrels in the Tawny Room, all warm to the touch. These barrels each contained a different batch of fortified wine. Each bottling was a carefully wrought blend of portions of each. These were the barrels that Tricia had tasted and written her impressive notes on when she first started at Fox Run.

"You really have to know all of the barrels intimately," Tricia said as we began tasting. "One will have beautiful dried fruits, and another will show more fresh fruits and spices. They're changing all the time, and you have to track what's happening to them. You want to allow them to develop, but you also want to catch them before they begin to lose their freshness. I find it thrilling when we taste them and something's finally moved that extra couple of inches. There's something about making this style that allows you to add something of yourself to the wine."

"Why keep them warm?" I asked.

"Keeping them warm speeds up oxidation reactions," Tricia said, and then launched into a scientific explanation of the process. "Tawny port is the result of a fortified red being subjected to a long, controlled period of exposure to air. It's what Peter calls 'tawnification,' though you're not going to find that word in any dictionary."

Throughout the workday at Fox Run I had noticed Tricia speaking in more technical terms about the winemaking process. Tasting one sample earlier in the day she had described it as smelling like a "licked envelope." As I laughed at the unique accuracy of her description she said, "In other words, there's a lot of Epernay, which is a strain of yeast used in winemaking." Red Newt Cellars' assistant winemaker Brandon Seager later told me that Tricia "has Epernay-dar. Just like real radar. She can pick out Epernay yeast better than anyone I know."

"Don't look now, but you're starting to sound like a scientist," I told her.

This time she smiled more confidently. "I've been spending more time talking to the guys from the Cornell experiment station when they stop by the winery. And I should have my certificate soon. I'm working on a big paper where I have to play the role of a consultant." The budding scientist smiled again, then said, "And all of this is thanks to Peter. He believed in me and he's been so patient in helping me learn."

"Does the science aspect ever feel overwhelming?" I asked.

"Oh, absolutely. Every time I learn how to do something it becomes obvious that I know just enough to make it work, and I still have miles and miles to go. But it's getting better. I used to stay quiet when Peter would talk to scientists about wine. The guys from Cornell would come to the winery and I'd hear words I could never imagine even trying to spell. Now I like to jump in and contribute. It feels great."

"Like picking out the smell of Epernay?" I said, smiling.

"Yeah, or if you've ever smelled a wine that reminded you of a bad perm, that's hydrogen sulfide." She truly has the most impressive nose of anyone I've met in the wine business. Peter Bell says he told Fox Run's owner, Scott Osborn, that Tricia's nose was too valuable to lose when Scott was working on paring down the budget back in the spring of 2006. "If you think we can't afford to pay her, the truth is that we can't afford not to," Peter had said.

We spent the next fifteen minutes moving from barrel to barrel, tasting the warm red wine and discussing its varied characteristics.

Occasionally I'd poke my head around the sliding door, concerned that Peter Bell was going to wise up to Tricia having ditched out on work. She was gleefully unconcerned. "We've all worked hard today," she said. "Peter would be thrilled to know that we're tasting the fortified wine. We're technically working, you know."

"That's true," I said, though it would have taken some real temerity to claim that this was a difficult task. "Hard to believe this is work for you. I've had so much fun volunteering."

Tricia nodded. "I always say it feels like *I* should be paying *them*."

When Morgan and I finally decided to leave, we arranged to get together with Tricia and the girls for another meal—and another long evening of tasting wine. Tricia told us she would have more samples to share soon. We left Fox Run with a bounce in our step, already looking forward to spending more time with the Renshaw girls. Tricia left soon after we did. She wanted to make it home in time to help the girls with their homework.

EIGHT

The Unlikely Heir: Fred Merwarth

September 8, 1999
Freiburg, Germany

The professor's intense lisp seemed only fitting to twenty-one-year-old Fred Merwarth. It was already nearly impossible to understand him—why not a lisp to go with his absurd insistence on speaking Schwäbisch? Fred had figured that his excellent grasp of the German language would make studying abroad enjoyable. He had not counted on a professor who spoke the obscure High German dialect of Schwäbisch, and he had certainly not counted on having to take the brutally banal course called "History of the Catholic Church in Germany, 1865–82."

Sitting toward the back of the packed classroom, five minutes into the first day of class, Fred felt the urge to surrender. When he raised his head from his palms he realized that the entire front row was composed of nuns.

Jesus, he thought. *This might not be the most appropriate response, given the course, but . . . Jesus.*

When he finally walked out of class, the three hours of lecture having felt like three days, he wondered if he would be able to complete the course. He would have to find a way, but the thought of giving a final oral presentation was daunting. It was enough to cause Fred to ask himself why he had decided to study abroad in the first place. Most of the other American students had come to Germany with a career goal in mind, and the abroad program offered a supplement to their learning.

Fred had come to Germany without much career direction—his plan had recently evaporated. Having grown up on a dairy farm outside Philadelphia, Fred wanted to see the world. His parents had urged him to consider careers outside of farming. And, like his father, Fred had gone through high school with an open mind, but his heart kept pulling him back to the farm. When he decided to get a degree in agriculture from Cornell University, he knew he would take over the farm from his parents.

They knew it was poor timing when they sold it. Fred was in the middle of his studies when his parents decided the business model wasn't working anymore. They told him that selling the farm was the best option for the entire family, but that forced Fred to make some decisions of his own. He was on track to get his agricultural degree and now he had no idea what he would do with it.

He was about to find out, and the answer would come in the last place he would have expected to find it.

* * *

The town of Freiburg sits in the southwest of Germany in the Black Forest, just a few miles from Germany's borders with France and Switzerland. It was the ancestral home of Fred Merwarth's family, and he had decided to study in Germany to clear his mind and learn more about his heritage. This was the town from which his family had emigrated 150 years before. The coursework would supplement his German minor, but Fred did not expect this trip to chart out the rest of his life.

Apart from the classes, he was beginning to feel comfortable. Fred had been inspired to learn German after he heard the story of his great-grandfather, who taught American soldiers to speak conversational German before they went behind enemy lines in World War II.

Now, finally getting a chance to explore his family's roots, Fred felt connected to the historic old town. He found his German to be strong enough to carry on regular conversations with the locals. The land was breathtaking, and as a long-distance runner he reveled in seeing it from every angle. During his first week in Freiburg, Fred took three occasions to lace up his running shoes and jog until he felt like stopping. As a six-foot-two track star, Fred could literally run for hours. And he did. On one occasion he decided to turn off the main road and jog through the old vineyards that seemed to be everywhere. The vines dipped and dived down the steep slopes of the mountains around Freiburg. Fred was taken with the beauty of the vineyards and he was fascinated by how the growers seemed to find ways to plant vines in the roughest, most recalcitrant terrain.

This was not the type of agricultural planting that he was accustomed to back home.

Fred spoke no French, but when a group of students decided to take a tour just over the border into neighboring Alsace, he joined them. The group visited the ancient Alsatian town of Eguisheim, and Fred was drawn to it instantly. It felt to him like a town lost in time, with the history of the last few centuries still vividly alive. The narrow streets featured the smells of fresh-baked breads and the pleasures of casual conversation. A stork's nest dotted the top of the steeple of the church on the town square. Most of the forty students seemed less than enthralled, but Fred found himself wanting to see more of this anachronistic jewel. When the guide offered to take the students on a tour of a local wine cellar, only five students showed any interest. Fred eagerly accepted the offer.

The winemaker was a shy but affable young man, certainly not more than a few years older than Fred, and he spoke German. His family's winery was hardly a glitzy affair, with the cellar located underneath their old house. The tour guide swung open a creaky wooden door and the group descended a set of enormous stone steps into the dank cellar, ducking their heads as they reached the bottom.

Fred glanced around the small room. He had never seen anything like it. Around the edges of the cellar stood a series of thousand-liter casks for storing wine known as *stücks*—pronounced "shtooks"—and Fred wondered how anyone ever constructed such large barrels in such a small, dark space. As he continued to study the room the winemaker pulled out some glasses and began to speak.

"My family has been making wine in this house since the Romans left," he said. Fred did some quick math in his head. The winemaker smiled. "I'm a thirteenth-generation winemaker. We've been at it since about 1380."

The Alsatian poured the first wine and handed the glasses around the room. Unlike many other winemakers, this man did not give a long explanation of the wine. He did not instruct the students about what they should smell or taste. He simply poured the wine and waited quietly. Fred buried his nose in the glass and, unprepared for the power of the wine's aromatics, nearly sneezed.

The Merwarths were not a wine-drinking family, but Fred had begun to appreciate wine after joining a group of students who were enthusiastic about it. He had experienced a variety of aromatic white wines, but this was something entirely different. This Riesling seemed to reach up out of the glass to deliver a right hook of honeysuckle, slate, and petrol. He was in love, and when he swished the wine in his mouth it only confirmed what his nose had predicted.

Someone asked the winemaker about the huge casks that Fred found so impressive. "This barrel is the youngest," the man said, pointing to a rather rough-looking cask. "It's 150 years old." He pointed to another on the other side of the cellar. "This is the oldest. It's 310 years old."

Fred could not tell if the other students were moved, but he felt immersed in the winery's history. The winemaker poured another Riesling, then a Pinot Gris, and then the matriarch of the family entered the cellar carrying a loaf of bread fresh from the oven. "For our guests!" the old woman said cheerfully.

When it came time to leave, Fred asked if he could purchase several bottles of Riesling. Then he asked for a Pinot Gris, then a Gewürztraminer. Then, panicked that he would go through the wine too quickly, he asked for more Riesling and Pinot Gris. He ended up with a case of wine, barely able to afford the bill and drunk with excitement.

"Thank you," the winemaker said.

"I should be thanking *you*," Fred replied. He took one last look around the cellar and said to himself, *This is what I'm going to do. This is why I came to study abroad. I have no idea how I'm going to get there, but I'm going to make wine.*

On the day Fred Merwarth bought what was perhaps the most highly regarded winery in the eastern United States, almost no one seemed to notice. There was no press conference, no glossy news release, no gala dinner. He simply showed up for work and prepared for harvest as if nothing had changed.

He hadn't really bought the winery, of course. He and his family had simply taken on a debt equivalent to their life savings—several times over. The banks were convinced that the numbers were ripe for a successful transition; as long as Fred continued to make world-class wines he could be reasonably confident that the sales wouldn't dry up. If he faltered he knew he would spend the rest of his life digging out of a financial hole so deep he might never see daylight again.

Fear of failure is an intense motivator, and especially so when failure would mean the collapse of not just your own reputation, but that of the man who preceded you.

Fred had first gone to work for Hermann Wiemer in March 2001, less than a year after graduating from Cornell. He had taken several wine-related courses but he didn't have a degree in enology and he had told Wiemer that he was not interested in going back to school to get it. "I want to learn to make wine by doing it," he boldly declared during his first meeting with the German winemaker. His goal had been to find an internship in Germany, and he hoped that by speaking German he could impress Wiemer enough to help him find a place to study the trade in Europe. But Wiemer feigned ignorance on the matter, claiming that he had been away from Germany for too long to help Fred. "Why don't you work for me for six months and during that time we'll make sure we find you something in Germany," Hermann had offered.

"What B.S.!" Fred would say years later with a healthy laugh. "I found out he could have set me up anywhere."

By the time those initial six months had passed, Fred had already started down a path that would lead him to become Hermann's assistant winemaker. With each passing vintage Fred took on more responsibility, eventually taking a leading role in making some of the most prestigious wines in the Finger Lakes. But Hermann was looking to sell the winery and retire, and Fred knew his position at Wiemer could be in jeopardy. That is, unless *he* were the buyer. Which is exactly what the twenty-seven-year-old proposed in the summer of 2005.

To Hermann, it made perfect sense. Fred had grown into an elite winemaker in just a few years in the cellar. He had learned everything from Hermann, so there would be no temptation for Fred to revert to the more sterile techniques many students learn in school. Hermann could be sure that Fred would respect the traditions he had established. And Fred had no desire to change the wines—Wiemer was the first winery that inspired Fred in the same way that the old winery in Alsace did. He was still nursing a case of 1997 Wiemer Riesling that he had purchased before ever meeting Hermann.

And yet it made almost no sense at all. Like most people his age, Fred was hardly flush with cash. True, his parents had done well in selling their farm and branching into real estate, but Fred would have to assume a huge amount of debt in any transaction. And then there was the potential of a consumer revolt. After all, Hermann Wiemer's clients had grown so loyal because they knew the wines—and they knew the man who had so skillfully crafted them. At sixty-five years old, Wiemer had become a lion in the trade, and many consumers associated the wines with the man. Hermann could tout Fred's skills but there was no doubt that some customers would question the sale of the winery to a young man with a degree in agriculture, not enology.

Arranging the sale took more than two years. The banks had to be assuaged and Hermann had to determine what kind of role he wanted to play when he no longer owned the place. Ultimately, Hermann decided that he would consult on grape growing and winemaking decisions but he would only visit several times a year. Fred could call any time, but Hermann was going to travel the world. Fred would be largely on his own.

Of course, Fred would have company on the business side of the operation. His best friend, a charismatic Swede named Oskar Bynke whom he had met on the last day of class at Cornell, would run the marketing and distribution. Fred viewed Oskar as a vital part of the new team and he insisted that Oskar have a stake in the company. This would allow Fred to concentrate on the wines while the talented and energetic Swede could travel and represent the winery. Without Oskar, Fred doubted that he would have much of a chance in that crucial first year on their own. And Fred's wife, Maressa, a metalsmith and jewelry maker who worked in nearby Ithaca, would offer support as well—she even offered to perform some of the heavy labor during harvest.

But when Fred needed to make decisions regarding the wines, his would be the sole voice in the room.

And so, at the end of July 2007, Fred Merwarth signed the papers that made him and Maressa the proprietors of the Hermann J. Wiemer company. Hermann spoke privately with some of the winery's longest running clients to explain the decision. The labels didn't change, nor did the sign in front of the tasting room. Many customers didn't realize that Hermann was gone. In fact, if it weren't for one news article on the sale, the whole deal might have gone completely unnoticed. But the article was exactly what Fred had feared.

The writer called Fred for an interview, and Fred was nervous. He didn't want to embarrass Hermann. Making matters worse, the writer was aggressive and terse on the phone. "Why would Hermann do this?" Fred recalled the reporter asking—not exactly a constructive way to phrase a question. Then the writer asked Fred about taking on a monumental task "as a novice."

It was that word—*novice*—that cut Fred deeply.

Fred was furious—not with the writer, but with himself. "I never try to overstep my bounds," he told Maressa and Oskar. "I don't think of my age as an issue, and I try not to come off as cocky. But I probably sounded unsure on the phone. I probably sounded like a novice. That's the last thing we need. I have to change my tone a bit. I can't act nervous about taking over the winery."

With the sting of doubt still fresh, Fred decided to contact the members on the winery's mailing list with a calm but strong message. He explained to his small staff, "They need to know that it's me steering the ship now and it's not anybody else. We'll tell them that Hermann's efforts will be preserved and celebrated. If they're not happy with who Hermann chose to succeed him, I can't control that." While Oskar planned an aggressive new marketing and distribution strategy that would focus on large markets like New York City, Fred devoted his energy to the upcoming harvest, which would be the most important in the history of the winery. A weak vintage could destroy the market's confidence in Fred as an owner and winemaker. Inferior wines would signal that Fred was simply an ersatz winemaker, hardly capable of building upon Hermann's legacy. He had only one chance to pacify the doubters.

When the 2007 harvest arrived, Fred could not help but feel an intense amount of pressure. He confided to Maressa that he didn't think another excellent vintage would be good enough. "We have to find a way to make it better than it's ever been," he told her. "It can't just be the same. We need to show that Hermann made the right decision." Maressa responded by providing the hard-driving physical labor usually reserved for several men. Barely more than a hundred pounds, she led the crew in plantings and trimmings—even moving large rocks from the field. She was a partner in every sense.

Already accustomed to long hours, Fred was getting up earlier and working later. When the first lots of grapes came in he felt some trepidation—the extraordinarily hot and dry summer had produced deeply concentrated grapes, but that's not exactly an ideal scenario for Riesling. Fred had doggedly monitored the acid levels in the grapes to make sure they didn't come in flat, but he knew it would be a challenge to make the same electric wines that customers had come to expect from the Hermann J. Wiemer wine company.

One morning in the spring of 2008, with the juices finishing their fermentations, Fred felt alone for the first time. He had been working so hard to achieve a successful first vintage as owner that he had hardly noticed the solitude that can come with the job. Oskar and Maressa were constantly involved but the winery itself was a different place without the German patriarch. Now, tasting through the wines, Fred heard the sound of his own voice echoing off the steel tanks. For the past seven years he and Hermann would debate and discuss the wines.

Looking around the empty building, he could almost feel the silence.

* * *

Fred and Maressa Merwarth danced like an aristocratic couple. Their moves evoked sophistication and class. Amid a crowd that was simply content to dance in rhythm to the beat of the Chilean band, Fred and Maressa displayed their nicely honed cha-cha-cha.

It was not an ostentatious performance. They seemed much more interested in enjoying themselves than showing off. Maressa, a petite, graceful brunette with shoulder-length hair, moved easily in a midlength dress and scarf. She was laughing often. Fred, nearly a foot taller and built like a fishing rod, was dressed in a simple button-down shirt and slacks, his short hair cut plainly. As my wife and I admired their steps we occasionally noticed Fred miss a turn or step on his wife's feet. He wasn't gangly but did gangle occasionally—especially in comparison to Maressa, who danced like she had learned the moves in grade school. It was impressive.

The wedding of Anthony Road winemaker Johannes Reinhardt and Imelda Ryona had brought a large swath of the Finger Lakes wine community together on a mild but windy December afternoon in the last week of 2008. In the Anthony Road tasting room, Johannes and Imelda urged their friends to join them on what had become the dance floor, the shelves of wine pushed aside for the occasion.

For one day at least, no one asked Johannes about his immigration status. He had married Imelda in a quiet, humble service in a local church and now it was time to celebrate. The federal government was in the excruciating process of deciding on his appeal, and until the ruling, why talk about it? Johannes wanted to let loose, and for a tall German in a tuxedo, he was doing an admirable job. Imelda could have graced the cover of any fashion magazine in the world with her lithe figure fitting into an elegant white dress, her dark hair pulled up. They smiled as if the tumult in their lives had finally ceased.

Taking a break, Johannes stopped over to chat with Morgan and me. He wanted to know if we had met the new owner and winemaker of the Hermann J. Wiemer company. "You should say hello," Johannes said. "He's quite an impressive guy."

We waited for the band to break and then approached Fred and Maressa. They smiled warmly and we found ourselves listening to the story of how they had come to the Finger Lakes. High-school sweethearts, they were very close to their families and were excited that Fred's parents were planning a move to the Finger Lakes the following spring.

Fred invited us to come taste through the line of 2007 Rieslings, and when we asked about the 2008 vintage we were surprised when he said, "They won't be finished fermenting for a while yet, but I'd love for you to come taste those as well." I exchanged a curious glance with Morgan. Fermentations were finished everywhere else. Winemakers can speed them up using temperature control, and no one was doing long fermentations anymore because they were deemed to be too risky.

When the music finally kicked back up we could sense Maressa mentally tugging her husband back to the dance floor. We watched the Merwarths glide back to the floor to happily show us what an expert Latin dance should look like.

* * *

Driving down to the winery in January, I had just learned about a controversy that was going to make Fred's first solo vintage even more difficult to sell. I had known that, for many years, Hermann Wiemer had a poor relationship with much of the critical wine media including heavyweight publications such as *Wine Spectator.* When Fred took over the business he had hoped to foster a rapprochement with these publications, and the *Spectator* was the most important target. *Wine Spectator* enjoys the largest circulation of any wine publication, and its critic in charge of covering the Finger Lakes, James Molesworth, is a thoughtful, thorough writer who was beginning to take more trips to the region. Molesworth had written a fair and straightforward article detailing the sale of the Hermann Wiemer winery, but it was only published online. In the fall of 2008 the critic planned to tour the region for a series of pieces and reviews, and those who found out about the trip were angling for some individual attention.

But Molesworth kept the trip quiet, and only a select number of winemakers even knew he was in the region. Fred was not one of them. Only after Molesworth went back to New York City did Fred learn of the trip. Molesworth had not called Fred to ask for a tour or tasting and, even more egregious in Fred's mind, Molesworth's trip included a stop at Shaw Vineyards, a winery that is almost literally across the road from Hermann Wiemer. Fred thought the critic could have walked over to say hello.

I called Fred from the road to make sure our visit would not interrupt his day. He said he was ready for us, and he was also ready to talk about the *Spectator* snub. I cautiously mentioned that I was surprised not to see Hermann Wiemer covered in Molesworth's trip reports, and Fred began to explain what happened.

"I'm irate about it," he said, laughing softly and sounding nothing close to irate. "Okay, I guess I get irate in my own way. But I was fired up. I was expecting that Molesworth would have seen the chance to start new with our winery. I know that Hermann had upset a lot of people from the *Spectator*, but I really thought there'd be some effort by them to engage with me. They know Hermann is no longer at the winery. I mean, I figured at least he might call and say, 'I'm in the area.'"

"Why don't we talk more when Morgan and I get there," I offered. Fred did not strike me as a gossip and I sensed that he felt genuinely wounded by the affair. I wanted to give him time to collect his thoughts—I didn't want Fred to regret sharing a personal story, though I certainly was eager to hear more.

"Sounds good," he said, "but it gets worse." Then he laughed. "But we'll focus on the wines. See you soon."

Morgan and I always look forward to seeing the Wiemer winery, which is a veritable temple of wine in the Finger Lakes. Hermann had always appreciated architecture, and in the 1980s he hired a firm to convert a tall, aging dairy barn into a magnificent building suitable for making wine and welcoming visitors. The results were stunning. Hermann's guests enjoyed private tastings just a few feet from soaring tanks and rows of oak barrels. A small, lofted dining room, reachable by ladder, was built for dinner parties. The high ceilings gave the winery the aura of a cathedral, rays of light streaming in through high windows, and no doubt many visitors felt converted by the time they left. Even architects from other firms and other cities had studied the design, which evoked the famous German Architecture Museum in Frankfurt.

When we stepped inside we did what many guests tend to do: we drew a long, slow breath to take in the smells of fermenting grape juice. We arched our necks and glanced around the winery. What a sight.

Fred came bounding in gregariously, extending his gloved hand. He was wearing a dark winter hat and long rubber boots that covered much of his old jeans. "You ready?" he asked with a broad smile. "Let's see the Riesling!"

We had our wine geek hats on. It was time to see if Fred was living up to Hermann's winemaking legend.

Heading past rows of large steel tanks, we exited the main barn into a kind of wide, covered walkway. Five steel tanks lined this new room, and because it was walled off but not insulated, it was ideal for slow fermentations. This area fed into another building that looked much more like a standard winery, complete with more tanks and barrels. Fred handed two glasses to Morgan and me and he began drawing off a sample of Riesling from one of the tanks.

"I'm doing something a little differently," he said.

"You're allowed to change things?" I asked with a smile.

"This isn't a major change," Fred said, "but we think it's an improvement. Instead of blending all of our vineyard lots together, we're going to bottle a small amount of Riesling from each vineyard separately. We have three vineyards, and the Riesling from each site tastes very different. So your glass contains Riesling from the warmest vineyard, and it's still fermenting, so it's sweeter than it will be when it's finished."

Lowering my nose into the glass, I could sense immediately that it was a powerhouse. The amber-colored liquid gushed with scents of honey and grapefruit. In the mouth it was simply luscious. I noticed Morgan's eyes blink open wide.

The Riesling from the next tank might as well have come from a different planet. It was buzzing and tense. As I sipped it, the wine seemed to cut my tongue with its bracing acidity. This was a first kiss of a wine, a bit awkward and overeager, but undoubtedly filled with promise.

"See?" Fred said. "Now you can understand why I thought it would be so meaningful to bottle the Rieslings separately. They're just so remarkably individual. Hermann has been studying the wines from each vineyard ever since they were planted, and I've been keeping track since I started here. So we have years of experience to know what we're getting from each site. Hermann never bottled them separately, so I just decided that it's time."

"Starting in 2008?" I asked.

"Nope, 2007. We'll have two single-vineyard Rieslings from 2007, very small production, very special wines. Most of our production will still be the standard Rieslings, blended."

It was a risky move for Fred to make—not because his customers wouldn't want to taste Rieslings from wildly different sites, but because Hermann never did it this way. He knew that many Wiemer loyalists were looking for proof that Fred was simply going to carry on the tradition and not change it. I found it to be a clear change for the better, but it was a change nonetheless.

As we tasted through several more tanks I became convinced that this winery was making Riesling in a way that truly allowed the grape to shine. Fred had everything working in his favor to make world-class Riesling: diverse and premium vineyard sites, healthy but low crop yields, and the advantage of focusing heavily on one grape instead of trying to make wine from two dozen varieties. While Fred continued to make a handful of other wines, he devoted nearly two-thirds of the production at Hermann J. Wiemer to Riesling.

And yet, I was most impressed with Fred's demeanor. Ebullient but calm, he radiated knowledge. I kept having to remind myself that *this man has very little technical training.*

It would have been easy, and understandable, for Fred to take a modern route in his winemaking. Instead, he was pushing the most dangerous and anachronistic techniques.

Unclean conditions can turn a batch of wine into a funky mess. Wild yeast strains can cause similar spoilage. Fermentation can stop before the juice has fully completed its journey to wine. Winemakers like Peter Bell at Fox Run Vineyards have spent years perfecting the techniques to ensure that grape juice enjoys a clean, successful transition to wine. Consumers around the world have benefited from these efforts.

Fred was simply not interested in such winemaking interventions.

I asked Fred how he could afford to make white wines using only the most miminal amout of commercial yeast, the kind sold in a bag to make sure the wine comes out fresh and clean. This was no small matter. Fred was the only Finger Lakes winemaker I knew who relied primarily on natural or wild yeast.

"Here's how I see it," he responded, drawing another sample from a new tank. "Wines that are fermented naturally are absolutely the best representation of the land on which they're grown. No doubt about it, and that's what we're going for. If we want to convey a real sense of place in a wine, natural fermentation is the best way to do that. Now, you can use a commercial yeast to invoke whatever you're looking for, but then the wine isn't telling a clear story of its place. I'd rather let the grapes do their thing. Hermann never bought much commercial yeast when he made Riesling, and so it's second nature for me to go without it."

"But Fred," I interjected, "I've heard horror stories of what can happen to wine when the winemaker only uses natural yeast and not commercial yeast. I mean, I'm envisioning science labs blowing up and wine tanks bubbling over."

"Oh, I know," Fred said, laughing. "I've heard the stories too. But I've never had even one spoiled tank of wine and I've never seen wine get ruined by natural fermentation. I know it scares some people, but when it becomes the standard, you don't even think about it. The wines are so pure and you stop worrying about it."

Morgan swished another sip in her mouth, swallowed, and said, "Works for me!"

"But it's not just the yeast that sets you apart," I said, admiring the aromatic power of yet another unique tank sample. "Most winemakers would say you're nuts to let the juice ferment slowly. Almost everyone uses heat, and that speeds it up, right? Fermentations last a few weeks, tops."

"That's right," Fred said, nodding. "But we keep the tanks colder to allow the juice to ferment at its own pace. Did you notice the cooling jackets?" Morgan and I surveyed the giant tanks and realized they were sheathed with what appeared to be thick tinfoil armor. "It's our way to prevent it from getting too warm."

Fred led us to one more tank and once again he began to laugh. "I'll talk to other winemakers in January, or March, or April, and I'll mention that we still have wines fermenting," he said. "They look at me like I'm crazy. They say, 'How do you sleep at night?' And I just say that fermentation is going to happen when it happens. The wine does not need us to force it along. If it's three months, it's three months. If it's eight months, that's fine too. But when you rush the fermentation you risk blowing off some of the aromatics. When you let it happen at its own pace, you're encouraging those delicate, nuanced aromatics that make wine special."

This old-school approach even extended to Fred's red wines.

"There are so many winemaking fads that come and go," he said. "Oak chips are another example, or acid addition. We always take free samples from manufacturers who are trying to sell this stuff, and we'll experiment with small batches of wine just to see what happens. You should have seen us—it was hilarious. Hermann would add one of these products to a wine, and we'd mix it up and try to follow the directions but we'd never think it was very good. And sometimes Hermann would say, 'Add some more. Maybe we did it wrong.' And we'd screw around a little, but we always found that whatever supposed benefits these products were providing, we could find a better, more natural way to achieve the same outcome."

It was a compelling argument. As we headed for the tasting room to try the line of 2007 wines—the wines that Fred had obsessed over—I asked Morgan what she thought.

"Nobody is doing Riesling like this," she whispered. "Those individual tanks have such a wide range. Why haven't we spent more time here?"

"Fred," I said, "I'd love to see the individual sites where these grapes are grown."

"Absolutely," he said. "I think you'll find it fascinating."

We had reached the austere tasting room that connects to the original winery. Fred set three glasses on the wine barrel that serves as a table in the middle of the room. He smiled.

"Now, earlier you were asking about what is going on with *Wine Spectator* . . ."

* * *

For the few who knew it was happening, it was a thrill to have a high-powered critic touring the wine cellars of the Finger Lakes. James Molesworth has proven to be an amiable and accessible writer while covering some of the megawatt wine regions around the world for *Wine Spectator*. He's responsible for reviewing France's Rhône and Loire valleys, as well as South Africa, Chile, and the increasingly popular wineries of Argentina.

Unlike some other major-media wine critics, Molesworth does not travel with an open palm and an expectation of a free vacation. He pays most of his own way and he makes it clear to winemakers that his mission is to work hard, not relax on a wine-themed junket. As a result, he packs his schedule tightly and his visits to cellars often feel sterile and impersonal. After Molesworth has left, winemakers tend to remark on how "quiet and unreadable" he is when tasting through tanks and barrels.

In other words, Molesworth was earning his respect by resisting the urge to turn his work into a hobby, and it was difficult to doubt the integrity of his reviews.

On the *Spectator* website, Molesworth informed readers that his coverage of the Finger Lakes was going to "introduce you to arguably the best Riesling region in the U.S." Why, then, had he chosen not to visit Hermann J. Wiemer, with its reputation as a world-class Riesling producer?

Fred Merwarth did not share his mentor's disdain for the big wine media. Scores were not terribly appealing to Fred; his idea of wine was born in that small, family cellar in Alsace, and the notion of the 100-point scale seemed entirely out of place in the cold tasting room under the winemaker's house. But Fred also knew the impact that scores have on sales and reputation. Furthermore, he was impressed with what he read from Molesworth, and he appreciated a critic who didn't immediately dismiss the Finger Lakes as inferior. When Fred took over the Wiemer operation he figured he'd have a chance to set a new course for the winery's relationships with writers like Molesworth.

When Molesworth chose not to call or stop by, Fred felt like both sides had missed a big opportunity.

"So I emailed him," Fred told us. "I wrote, 'To a certain extent I know that our companies have not gotten along well. But please understand that my policy is that we don't submit samples unless the reviewer has visited the winery. You're welcome here anytime, and we'd like for you to come visit.' That was it."

"That sounds fair," I said. "Did James respond?"

"He did. He sent me back an email that said, 'It's good to hear from you. Our company policy is that we don't visit a place unless we have a history of reviewing their wines.'" Fred paused and began to pour the 2007 Magdalena Vineyard Riesling alongside the 2007 HJW Vineyard Riesling. Standing around the barrel in the Wiemer tasting room, this would be my first chance to see how Fred's inaugural solo effort had turned out.

"This sounds like a dilemma," I said, returning to the *Spectator* story.

"Yep. We're pretty much at an impasse, right? I have to submit wines for review before he'll come visit, but I won't submit wines for review unless he comes to visit first!"

I swirled the first wine and admired its deep amber color. "Do you worry," I said, "that it will hurt you by not being included in his coverage of his major tour of Finger Lakes producers?"

"Well, it's not what I would prefer," he said, smiling. "Here, tell me what you think of these single-vineyard Rieslings. I don't want to say anything to affect how the wine smells and tastes to you. The winemaker in Alsace never prodded us to smell or taste specific things, and I've never forgotten that. So I'll just be quiet."

Morgan had already closed her eyes and begun the forensic work of discerning scents and flavors. I started with the Magdalena, a vineyard known for its ideal location in a warm, protective site.

This wine was an aromatic assault, so full of scents that one could enjoy it for an hour without ever taking a sip. I didn't have the willpower, of course, to continue smelling without sipping, and I was not disappointed. This was the most lush, mouth-filling Finger Lakes Riesling I'd ever tasted. From common fruit flavors such as peach and apple to something more tropical, the wine seemed to wrap around the tongue and just stay there.

"Awesome," I heard Morgan say, breaking my focus. "I wish I had a better word for it."

We moved on to the HJW Vineyard Riesling, planted by Hermann more than three decades earlier. A touch lighter in color, this was a buzzsaw. The wine was sparked by such wonderful acidity that my mouth watered after swallowing. It was leaner, with more of that classic river-rock flavor that seems to emerge in Finger Lakes wines.

"This must be the same vineyard as the wine from the second tank," Morgan deduced. "The one we tasted earlier."

"That's right," Fred said, satisfied. "This is the first time our customers will have a chance to experience the difference you just saw."

"This is going to work," I said. "This is a brilliant idea." Then I thought about the unfortunate standoff with *Spectator*. "Isn't there a part of you that would love for this wine to be reviewed? Just to see?"

"There is," he said. "So I've decided to take the wines to James Molesworth."

"Does he know this?"

"Yep, but I'm not asking him to review the wines. That's up to him. I didn't respond to his email three months ago, because to me, there was nothing we could do to solve this. But last week I decided to try again. I said, 'I'm coming down to the city. I think it's important for you to see what we've done. I'm not asking you to review the wines but I want to show you what we're doing.' He thanked me for being willing to come see him."

"So when are you going?" I asked.

"Next week," he said. "At least we can start to repair the relationship. Who knows what he'll think of the wines?"

* * *

The huge aging barn looked like it could collapse at any moment. The massive walls still stood on the barn's edges, painted red but browning from the years, and the shingled roof had begun to sag precipitously in the center. What was once a beautiful structure could fall apart without careful attention.

"It reminds me that I have a lot of work to do," Fred told me on a cool, sunny morning when the grass was finally growing healthily.

To my eye, the barn appeared to be about the same size as the one that Hermann Wiemer had converted into his winery decades ago. We were standing at the intersection of Wiemer's two other vineyards—known as Magdalena and Josef—and we were ten miles to the north of the winery. This barn was beautiful but needed improvements. "Everything needs a little help over time," the winemaker said.

Nearly half a century ago a researcher from Cornell toured the Finger Lakes with a simple mission: he wanted to determine if there were truly "mesoclimates," which are small pockets of land that feature different average temperatures and weather patterns. The researcher determined that there was one spot in all of the region that seemed to be warmer than any other—by five degrees or more on average. It was the site on which we were standing.

This was the site where, all those years ago, Hermann Wiemer had discovered that vinifera vines could survive even a Christmas Massacre in the Finger Lakes.

"Think about what the warmer weather does to the vines here," Fred said as we walked down one of the long rows. "The grapes always get a little riper here, so the wines are a little richer and show that fruit. Compare that to Hermann's original vineyard back at the winery, where it's always a little cooler."

"Very different place to grow grapes," I said.

"Right, but it's just a few miles down the road! Most people can't believe you can take the same vines and do things basically the same just a few miles away and end up with two totally different wines. But it happens. The wines from Hermann's vineyard are always a little more steely, a little more crisp. We think that's pretty cool."

The vines on this site appeared to be very carefully cropped. Fred pointed to the shoots, where there would be a lot less fruit than most vines. "I don't mean to overstate it," he said, "but if you grow too much fruit you don't have a chance. And the truth is, there is still way too much fruit growing on most vines in the Finger Lakes." He made the diagnosis in the way a doctor would gently tell a patient he has cancer—not with a sense of pleasure, but obligation.

We made our way down a narrow trench and then back up to a steeper vineyard. This was the Josef site, nearly connected to the Magdalena site but bringing a personality all its own. It was an outstretched index finger of a vineyard, narrow and reaching high up the hill. This was where the grapes were prone to that potentially good kind of rot: botrytis, the kind that could concentrate the sugars of the grape and yield delicious sweeter wines.

Fred galloped like a child to a spot about a third of the way up the hill. I struggled to keep up.

"This is it!" he said, turning back to face me as he stood at the edge of one of the rows. "This is where everything changes in this vineyard."

"Changes how?" I asked.

"Well, you have to know your vineyard," he said. "I don't mean you have to know it in general terms. You have to know every part of it, because different sections behave differently. In this vineyard, botrytis starts at the bottom and works its way up the hill. So the bottom I always pick early and very carefully. The botrytis should stay at the bottom of the field. And then up on the hill, it's like a totally different site for grapes. Let's go!" He was bounding off again with the speed and endurance of the long-distance runner he is. I caught up to him about a dozen rows higher.

"I think the top section of the Josef vineyard, right here on up, is probably the best site discovered so far to grow grapes in the Finger Lakes," Fred said. He looked around, nodding slowly. "It has everything: slope, soils, sun exposure, air flow. Those grapes can just hang forever up there. They'll never get botrytis. We always pick this top section of Josef last. And you've got to remember that this way of working the vineyard has been years in the making. We've studied the grapes and what happens to them. We didn't snap our fingers and come to this magical understanding. It's taken a lot of meticulous observation, and now we know what to expect. So if you want to bottle single-vineyard wines, I think you need to truly know that vineyard the way we've come to know ours."

It was brilliant. Looking back down the hill and across the neighboring Magdalena vineyard, I was thrilled to see that this site had been planted to the grapes best suited to grow in the Finger Lakes. There was a small portion for Cabernet Franc, and Fred's version was honest and beautiful. But more than anything, there was a lot of Riesling. So much thought had gone into every little detail.

"Fix up that old barn," I told Fred as we finally made our way back. "It doesn't need a complete overhaul. Just a few improvements and it could be even better than before. I think you're just the man for the job."

* * *

When the scores from *Wine Spectator* finally came, Fred was buried in his work and he had no idea the numbers had been released. Oskar was spending another week courting potential clients in New York City, and Maressa was preparing for a jewelry show in Ithaca. They almost missed the moment.

Under a headline that began, "Outstanding Rieslings," Molesworth did his part to confirm Hermann Wiemer's wisdom in choosing Fred to succeed him. Molesworth wrote: "Historically among the best producers in the region, the winery is now under the guidance of Fred Merwarth, who took over from the eponymous founder in 2007. The vintage marks the debut releases of this winery's single-vineyard bottlings, which prove the important role that site selection and low yields play for Finger Lakes vintners who strive to produce world-class wines."

Alongside the review for the HJW Riesling came its score: 91 points, the highest *Wine Spectator* score in the history of the Finger Lakes for a nondessert wine. The Magdalena Riesling checked in right behind with a total of 90 points. Just a few months after Red Newt Cellars had broken through to 90 points, Fred's first vintage alone at Hermann J. Wiemer had gone one better.

I wanted to congratulate Fred, but I wanted to choose my words carefully. I had the sense that Fred was interested in the scores because they could be seen as a signal to the wine industry and to consumers that the winery was succeeding without Hermann. I also knew that Fred was a confident winemaker who hardly needed a critic's score to validate his work. But given the pressure he had been under, I figured this was cause to open a bottle of sparkling wine.

"I can't help but pump a fist and raise a glass on the *Spectator* scores—just don't tell Hermann!" I finally wrote.

That evening Fred called to thank me for the heads up. "I called Maressa and said, 'I just got an email from Evan and it sounds like the scores are good.' When I saw them . . . It was nice. It was really, really nice. Just like you, I did a little fist pump."

It was as much emotion as the cheerfully even-keel winemaker tends to show, and I could feel his relief. He had wanted to make his first vintage better than his historic winery had ever done and he had pulled it off. It wasn't simply the *Spectator* scores that said so; his single-vineyard wines had become a hot topic in the wine community. Scientists at Cornell had asked Fred to give a presentation explaining how two vineyards just miles apart could produce such wildly different Rieslings. Blogs lit up. Fred was asked to do a variety of interviews to talk about his first vintage as owner.

New clients were lining up to buy Wiemer wines, and Oskar's Swedish connection was bearing fruit in Europe. Sweden's most widely read wine magazine published a cover story on Hermann J. Wiemer wines under the headline, "Welcome New York to Sweden!" The writer heaped praise on these "fine Obamaland wines that show so much character."

"That's pretty cool, isn't it?" Fred said with a laugh. "There's only one thing left for me to do that I'm not exactly looking forward to."

"What's that?" I asked.

"I have to call Hermann. I'm going to have to tell him about the *Wine Spectator* scores."

"Won't he be thrilled?"

Fred paused. "Well, he doesn't even know I submitted the wines."

* * *

The music started the moment Hermann's leather boots stepped onto the winery floor. Perfectly timed, a trio of opera singers dressed classically in tuxedos launched into a rollicking performance.

It was the night of the Hermann J. Wiemer thirtieth-anniversary celebration. Fred and Maressa invited about three dozen people to the party: Hermann and a small group of his friends; Fred's and Maressa's parents; Oskar's Swedish friends from New York City; and a few others. Morgan and I arrived to find the winery crowded with long, elegantly set tables covered in white cloth. Maressa's classy touches were everywhere—in the jewelry around her family's shoulders and wrists, in the fresh flowers that made up the centerpieces, in the handwritten name cards for each seat. We were going to dine among the vast stainless-steel tanks, which only added to the atmosphere. Servers wove in and out with mouthwatering appetizers.

"Hey," Morgan whispered as she took a toasted baguette covered in plums, microgreens, and goat cheese, "how did we get invited?"

I didn't notice at the time, but the private dining area in the top of the winery had become a stage. Hermann wanted that spot to be special, tucked away and reachable by ladder. Tonight it served as the perfect stage that looked out over the tables and tanks. We noticed Hermann, looking sharp in a sport coat, nice pants and those long boots, strolling in with a wide smile.

I had no idea I would love opera.

Turns out that Maressa's uncle is an opera singer. Not just any opera singer, though. He's a lifelong, touring, performed-at-Carnegie-and-recorded-with-the-greats kind of opera singer. He sings with his wife and another tenor, and together they had us captivated, nearly forty people with necks arched, looking up at the stage with the attention of a crowd saluting a flag. The songs were upbeat, occasionally funny, and I noticed that even Hermann was clapping and stomping along at certain points. In between songs, when we weren't cheering wildly, we poured glasses of the newly released Hermann J. Wiemer Sparkling Cuvée.

After about half an hour the performers announced a break so we could all sit down for dinner. Morgan and I sat directly across from Maressa, stunning in a blue dress, and Fred, in dress pants, white shirt, and pink tie. When the revelry of the opera settled down, I was curious to see how Fred and Hermann would interact—or if anyone would give a speech. Hermann was seated at a different table across the winery and seemed to be enjoying himself, but he was surrounded by his oldest friends and the winery's longest-running clients. I worried the event might feel segregated by generation.

About halfway through the meal a man sitting next to Hermann stood up to announce a toast. He was dressed in a chic striped blue and white suit and appeared to be roughly Hermann's age. In fact, with his stylish suit and jewelry he appeared to be dripping in money. "That's Johannes Neckermann," Fred whispered. "Hermann's best friend here. Two Germans making their way in America."

Neckermann was regarded by everyone at the winery as Hermann's toughest critic—and biggest supporter. He spent several minutes talking exclusively about Hermann and the success he had achieved. It had the feel of a retirement speech, not a celebration of a new beginning. But then Neckermann turned to face Fred and Maressa.

"We all know that Hermann made the best choice, the right choice, in Fred," he said. "And so now we raise our glasses to you and the new family of the winery. We are so happy for the future of Hermann Wiemer." Fred's father, a sweet and humble man, appropriately bellowed, "Cheers!" Everyone applauded. It was a seal of approval from the winery's most important customer.

Settling back into dinner I asked Fred if Hermann would speak. "Probably not," he said slowly. "Johannes knows Hermann so well that he can speak for him. So I'll probably give a little toast at the end of the meal before we bring back the opera."

Hermann had told friends jokingly that he had "forgiven Fred for the *Spectator* thing." When Fred called to give Hermann the news about the scores, Hermann brushed it off without much reaction. And while Hermann famously loathes wine critics, I found myself hoping that he would say something to the gathering that night to acknowledge Fred's achievements.

As we savored the main course of duck breast and sweet local sausage, Fred said, "No magazine score could ever be more important than what Hermann has to say about the wines. Getting his approval is still the ultimate."

Morgan and I sat back to digest the meal and sample the new late-harvest Rieslings when Fred headed for the stage. Following some remarks from Oskar, Fred spoke without a script about his desire to maintain the direction of the winery. "I know that so many of you appreciate what Hermann has done, and we want to respect his legacy and extend it. We know that Hermann . . ."

Fred noticed that Hermann had stood up, and the tall German began to speak.

"We changed the taste of New York," he said, looking up at Fred before turning to the rest of us. Everyone had stopped eating; the room was silent. "It's true. We changed the taste of New York, Fred, and you're going to continue doing that. I know you will."

Hermann smiled and sat down, and before Fred could sheepishly respond, the room burst into applause. This time the applause was extended and raucous. I looked at Fred—he was humbly grinning and nodding as the sound echoed across this beautiful building. It was a perfect, and total, confirmation. I noticed that Hermann had joined the applause and was smiling broadly now. These two men, so vastly different, yet so singularly committed to the purpose of Finger Lakes wine. What a contrast and yet—what a match. Hermann had earned his adulation, even if his time as a winemaker had been a bit rocky on occasion. But he was mostly a supportive friend now. Fred had the stage, and we couldn't wait to see what he was going to do next.

NINE

The Black Russian: John McGregor

August, 1992
Dundee, New York

He wasn't embarrassed about it, but Bob McGregor wasn't planning to advertise this little winemaking experiment he had been conducting. He had spent more than a decade trying to figure out how to grow red wine grapes on the shores of Keuka Lake, but nothing seemed to work. A phone call in 1980 from a highly regarded grower in Maryland had gone like this:

"Bob, I have a handful of new grape plantings that you can try if you want."

"What are they?"

"Russian, I think."

"Russian grapes?"

"I think so. Weird names. Saperavi, Mtzvani, Rkatsiteli, Sereksiya, and Sereksiya Charni."

Silence. "What the hell are those?"

"I don't really know. Some are white. Some are red. Do you want to give them a shot?"

More silence as Bob considered the possible ridicule he might endure for messing around with such oddball varieties. *These should be the names of hockey players, not wines*, he thought.

Then he thought about how he lost all of the Cabernet Sauvignon in his first year. "Those Russian grapes can probably handle the cold a little better, right?" Bob asked. "Eastern Europe can get some nasty winters."

"I would assume that's right."

"Okay, bring them over," he said, then added, "but let's keep this between us for now."

McGregor's first stab at these varieties had been a disaster. Mtzvani was more a weed than a wine grape. The two red varieties, Saperavi and Sereksiya Charni, produced intensely dark wines with a kind of fake, canned grape juice quality along with heavy tannins and ripping acidity. And while the whites were showing some potential, this was always about finding a suitable red wine grape.

But Bob McGregor couldn't afford to give up. While the wines were a mess, these grapes were indeed surviving the long winters, just as he had hoped they would. His winery, McGregor Vineyard, needed a red wine to compete in the marketplace. And given his intrepid researching skills, he was going to have to keep experimenting.

Some days Bob wondered why he ever left his job at Kodak in Rochester. He was chasing a dream that might be unattainable, and when he stumbled in pronouncing the names of these strange grape varieties, he wondered if he would have been better off staying in the film business.

It had been a half-sober, late-evening encounter with an eccentric winemaker that convinced Bob McGregor to set money aside and leave Kodak. During the late hours of one of winery owner Walter Taylor's infamous parties on Keuka Lake, Taylor wandered over to Bob. His eyes darting around the room, he told Bob that the future contained a string of wineries all along the banks of this Y-shaped lake. Bob, drunk on excitement—and perhaps more than a little drunk on sugary blush wine—decided on the spot that he would eventually leave the business of photo chemistry in favor of grape chemistry.

Now here he was, trying to make sense of two red wine grapes that almost no one had ever heard of. Even worse, Bob's research had failed to uncover a single bottle of Saperavi or Sereksiya produced anywhere else in the world that had earned critical acclaim. Why, he wondered, should he expect to make the first?

But he was going to have to find a way. The wine industry was slowly expanding. Wineries needed to succeed in one of two ways to ensure long-term survival: they had to have critical success or a large, devoted following. Bob figured that gaining a following would be much easier with critical success. Finger Lakes wines had never scored well with writers.

On that summer day, Bob McGregor couldn't even fathom submitting this bizarre red wine for professional review.

As Bob wandered back to the winery building he looked out at the bluff that separates the branches of the lake's Y. It was seventy miles from his old work station at Kodak, which featured views of coughing chemical stacks. The landscape was inspiring, but Bob was concerned. Now in his fifties, he didn't feel that he had much time left to figure out this whole red wine business. His whites were showing very nicely, sure, but he had to be able to make something else besides Pinot Noir.

Then, as he entered his winery, he saw the oak barrels and laughed. Even the barrels had been a disaster. "Man, we're screwed," he chuckled to himself.

* * *

American oak barrels were rarely used for wine in those days, but Bob had found that French oak made his strange red wines even worse. He had decided that instead of making the wines separately, McGregor Vineyard would blend them—and they'd stop using French oak. But finding American oak hadn't been easy.

Eventually Bob found a whiskey barrel maker who was willing to make a deal. He was charging $50 a barrel, but when he found out that Bob wanted to use the whiskey barrels to store wine, the price doubled. Bob felt he had no choice but to pay it.

So here he was, on a glorious summer day, laughing at his own stubbornness. He could have simply focused on white wines and tried to make a decent living. But the dream of a big, rich red wine still tempted the man.

His young winemaker drew a sample of the blended red wine, and Bob swirled it in his glass. This time something was different. The grapey character was gone. In its place were the scents of exotic fruits and even tart fruits like cranberry. There was also something that evoked smoked bacon.

Bob loved smoked bacon.

He practically spilled the wine as he eagerly sipped it, hoping to discover that the taste, too, had changed. It had. The monstrous tannins were still heavy, but less so, and the cringe-inducing acidity had begun to mellow out. This was by no means a great wine, but for the first time, Bob was thinking that it could be. It had evolved from something utterly unremarkable into a rather distinctive, quality wine.

"What the hell happened?" he barked excitedly.

"Might be the combination of American whiskey oak barrels and more time to age," his winemaker offered.

"Well, whatever it is, we've got to keep doing this. We can sell this. This can work."

Maybe, Bob wondered, these grapes simply needed time to mature in the vineyard. And maybe the wine needed more time in the bottle to develop.

As they continued to evaluate this new creation, his winemaker asked, "What do you plan to call it?"

"I don't know," Bob said, his mind racing. "I'm sick of trying to say Saperavi and Sereksiya. No one will have any clue how to pronounce it." He thought about calling his son, John, a brilliant college student who always seemed to have useful ideas.

They pondered it for a moment more until Bob said, "Simple. This black, Russian wine names itself. It's Black Russian Red."

He just hoped that his customers would be open-minded enough to try it.

Making love in a vineyard must have seemed like a romantic idea, but I couldn't believe it offered much pleasure in practice. I wasn't about to ask the amorous couple how it was working out.

All I saw at first were arms. My good Samaritan instinct stopped me cold because for a moment I thought I was witnessing a fight. The hands, visible over several rows of Riesling vines, were gesticulating wildly—I could make out four in total and thought it looked roughly like a pair of inebriated boxers throwing aimless punches. Then I saw a shirt. Then another. This was no winery-side boxing ring. This was a happy couple removing each other's clothes as if they were on fire.

The man next to me had whispered that he thought there was a brawl starting, but now he gasped. "I don't think they're fighting," he said. "I think they're—"

"Yes they are," I replied, and began to walk as surreptitiously as I could in the other direction.

"I can't imagine that's a comfortable place for that," the man said, his feet following mine but his gaze steadfast on the action.

"Yep, they're probably plastered," I said, desperate to turn the focus to something—anything—else. "But hey, it's perfect weather. Could be the best day of the summer, huh?"

As we strode quickly away I wasn't surprised by what we had witnessed, given the nature of the McGregor Clan Club picnic. The locals like to call it the Woodstock of Finger Lakes wine.

The McGregor Clan Club had grown to be one of the largest wine clubs in the Finger Lakes despite the relatively small volume of wine McGregor was producing. But it wasn't simply the size of the club that provoked the envy and admiration of other winery owners. McGregor Clan Club members supported the winery with a steadfast ferocity that was difficult to explain. Hundreds of people had become members, and nearly four hundred of them had gathered to party on the slopes above Keuka Lake for the annual picnic. Even other successful local wine clubs struggle to draw more than a couple dozen people for major events.

The revelers had even brought food. It had apparently become a Clan Club tradition to bring a dish to pass. This gyrating and laughing mass of people had assembled from myriad places, including Long Island, New York City, Michigan, and Washington, D.C. And that was just from the license plates we noticed on the walk in. I tried to imagine a Clan Club couple preparing to depart from several states away:

"Is the car packed, honey? Remember, this is an eight-hour drive."

"We've got everything but the casserole—don't forget!"

There were hippies at this Clan Club picnic. There were also bankers, and construction workers, and guys in meticulously pressed dress shirts. And yet, in the heat of summer, the many outdoor tables were not segregated based on aroma or social class. Morgan and I grabbed an open spot at a table where a long-haired man in a NASCAR tank top, mesh hat, and cutoff jean shorts was chatting gregariously with an older couple dressed in what I could only assume was their Sunday best. Across the table a middle-aged couple occasionally chimed in; they looked more like a couple ready for a round of golf at a country club than a round of drinks with this wine club's menagerie.

I noticed their discussion had alighted upon the very subject that had sparked my interest in McGregor wines. "It's the acid," the man in cutoff jean shorts was saying. "Black Russian has a lot of acid, and it needs a long time to settle down. Critics don't know what to make of it because they always taste it when it's young."

I marveled at wine's ability, shown time and again, to demolish social barriers.

We settled into our seats just in time to take in the McGregor Clan Club auction. A man dressed like Jimmy Buffett pulled out a guitar and led the crowd in a rendition of the Neil Diamond classic "Forever in Blue Jeans," only he changed the words to "Spark-a-ling Riesling." I found it schlocky. Then I decided it was brilliant when someone bid $300 for a half case of old McGregor Sparkling Riesling, a wine that very possibly was already dead.

I was most interested in the old Black Russian wines that would be auctioned. Clan Club members professed an abiding affection for the rare Black Russian, even if they all had unique reasons for enjoying the wine. No matter. It had united them on this glorious August afternoon, and some had come with checkbooks in hand, prepared to bid on aged bottles.

In fact, when Clan Club members talk about what first convinced them to join, they often credit this unusual wine. Bob McGregor had shown the wisdom to consult competent winemakers while trying to handle the mysterious Russian varieties. It had evolved from a freakish curiosity—a pariah in its early days—to an object of passion for club members.

Of course, wine lovers who weren't members in this club could never seem to figure out the Black Russian's allure.

To appreciate just how impressive this auction was, one must first understand that even people who have heard of Finger Lakes wines don't often believe the region to be capable of producing profound reds. This opinion is now wrong, but it is only recently wrong, and if habits are hard to break, then reputations are only more so. The average Finger Lakes winery's best red wine doesn't sell for more than $20. The Black Russian is released every year for right around $60.

Now, return to what our long-haired, cutoff shorts–wearing friend was saying: the Black Russian is a wine that needs years in the bottle before it can reach full maturity. Whether it was true made no difference at this auction, because everyone *believed* it was true. The club members traded stories about elaborate meals shaped around a bottle of ten- or fifteen-year-old Black Russian Red. You could uncork one early but you'd simply be committing infanticide, they asserted.

Most of the auction featured wines that were not the Black Russian, and after a while my attention began to flicker. I somehow missed the big announcement: the McGregor family had unearthed a stash of the oldest known Black Russian, and they were prepared to sell it.

Amid raucous applause, I noticed a beaming older gentleman

making his way toward the front of the crowd. "What did I miss?" I asked the man next to me.

"You missed quite a bid!" he said. "That man just paid nearly a thousand dollars for the Black Russian!"

* * *

John McGregor looks like the kind of guy that Hollywood casts to play the hot scientist in the movies. He could probably never grow a full beard but his baby face only belies his age, as most would guess him to be considerably younger than his thirty-eight years. His black hair is always pulled back into a ponytail that stretches to the middle of his back. I've attended a number of high-end dinners with John in attendance, but I've never seen him wear a suit.

This is not what the stereotypical archeologist looks like.

John was on his way to being a globe-traveling fossil hunter before the lure of his family's business brought him home to the Finger Lakes. His father was ready to get away from the wine business, and by the time John had spent just a few months working at the McGregor winery, Bob McGregor had transitioned from selling Pinot Noir to picking up a bottle every afternoon at four o'clock for that night's meal. This was John's operation now.

Morgan and I had gotten to know John and his wife, Stacey, at various McGregor Clan Club events; we had been given a membership as a gift. While I rarely swooned over the wines, I was routinely left slack-jawed at club events like the annual picnic. Club members showed such obstinate devotion to the wines and traveled such distances that you'd think the McGregors were sneaking bottles of first-growth Bordeaux into club packs.

John had promised to offer some answers to the mystery of the Black Russian when we joined him for dinner on a perfect summer night. Better yet, John told us he'd uncork an older bottle to show off its charms. We arranged to meet at the only restaurant that carries old Black Russian: the Village Tavern in Hammondsport, where Morgan and I had first experienced the beauty of aged Finger Lakes Riesling.

When we arrived we found John and Stacey at the bar, and John greeted us with a devilish smile. He revealed a bottle of 1998 McGregor Black Russian Red. "I told you we'd have some fun!"

John decanted the wine as we sat down and immediately launched into his views on a very sensitive subject in the Finger Lakes: bias.

"It's so nice to open a bottle like this with people who are open-minded," John said.

"We're thrilled to get the opportunity," Morgan replied. "My mother found a bottle of 1994 Black Russian, but it had been sitting out in the sun in her house for ten years."

John winced. "Well, there are no such storage issues with this one! You know, the wine world is so accustomed to its ways that it's hard to convince people to try something new. Give someone a glass of Black Russian Red blind, and they probably won't know what it is, but they'll really like it. Then tell them what it is and where it's from, and they'll find a way to decide that they don't like it after all."

He grabbed the glass decanter, which now held the wine. It was opaque, an inky purple that hadn't begun to show the brown edges of aging wine. He swirled the wine in the decanter and shoved his nose into the opening, inhaling deeply. "Wow, we picked the right bottle," he said.

The Village Tavern's general manager recognized John and Stacey and stopped by to chat. He inquired about John's father. Later during the meal I asked John how important it was to keep the winery in the family.

"It's everything," he said. "We're well aware that most local wineries can't do it. My dad was just a home winemaker with no real idea of what he was doing when he got this thing started."

"I'll bet he had never heard of Saperavi and Black Sereksiya," I said with a laugh, referring to the grapes that are blended to make Black Russian Red.

"He deserves a hell of a lot of credit for being willing to give these grapes a try," John said. "It was the definition of the road less traveled, and you know what? For all the people who like to say this is nothing more than a strange wine, I say they're wrong and my dad was right."

He reached for the decanter and said, "I think it's ready, don't you?"

Bob McGregor's two-pronged plan for success hadn't come together, but that hadn't prevented the winery from thriving. The devoted following had developed organically without glowing reviews from top wine critics. I knew that John was trying to change that.

As John poured the wine into our glasses, Stacey pointed to her husband's ponytail and said, "What I love about wine is that it's open to anyone, no matter how they're dressed or what they look like. Wine is the great equalizer."

John was nodding. "I've hung out in the tasting room with ripped-up jeans, tie-dyed shirt, and a headband on, with my long hair, and I could talk to anyone about wine. All they knew when they saw me was that this was not a pretentious place. But if they judged me before talking to me, they were surprised to know that I could talk about wine. Our picnic is the same way. It sucks when people look at some guy in a tank top, drinking wine, and think, *That guy probably knows nothing about it.* If you've got a hang-up about someone's clothes and appearance, that's your loss. You'll be missing out on a lot of great conversations about wine."

With a pause in the conversation we had our first chance to taste the wine. The first thing I noticed was that it was extremely aromatic and still very fresh for being in its second decade of life. The second thing I noticed was that this wine was nothing like the classic dark Cabernets that so many consumers drink. Instead of the common characteristics like plum, currant, and blackberry, this Black Russian was bringing cranberry, pomegranate, and a variety of other fascinating scents that I couldn't instantly identify.

No one spoke as we finally tasted it. I wasn't surprised to find that the flavors matched the aromatics, but I was surprised to find so much acidity. Many deep, dark wines feature lower levels of acid, but this wine was extremely racy and mouthwatering. John must have noticed my eyebrows arch as I took that first sip.

"Got some kick, doesn't it?" he said, laughing.

"It's so alive," I remarked. "But it's not what you expect it to be."

"And that is what we love about it," John said, satisfied.

I recalled the conversation I had overheard at the Clan Club picnic, when the discussion focused on the raging acidity that shows up in young Black Russian wines. Even after more than a decade, that electricity was still there—but it had evolved from what must have been an awkward thunderbolt to an interesting crackle. I wasn't sure I loved the wine, but I loved the idea of something so unique.

Critics were far less kind. After taking over the winery, John began submitting more wines to major wine publications like *Wine Spectator*. The stellar 2005 harvest convinced John that the time had come to send the Black Russian in for review. The *Spectator* critique delivered this devastating conclusion: "Smoky finish leads to a slightly medicinal hint. Not for everyone. Drink now."

Then came the score: 80 points. There shouldn't be anything wrong with an 80-point wine, but consumers tend to view 80 points as the threshold for a barely drinkable product.

John had been deeply wounded by the review, and I found it admirable that he didn't try to hide it.

"It really gets to you, huh?" I asked.

"It's tough, sure," he said, slowly twirling his glass.

"But you seem like such a nonconformist that a critic's review wouldn't bother you," I said.

"Well," he said, then paused. "I'm human." We laughed uncomfortably. "Absolutely I care. You'd like to think that, even though you don't lend a lot of credence to those things, if you send the wine in to be judged then you're going to like the results. This one hurt."

His tone changed to one of resentment. "And really, how could anyone urge people to drink this wine now? C'mon, it can't age at all? That's just ridiculous. This wine *needs* time to settle down. You can't tell people to drink it now."

He leaned back and his tone softened again. Stacey gently rubbed his hand. "As you can see, I get a little bent out of shape about this. I'm tempted to send in our 2007 Black Russian because it's probably the best we've ever made, but I don't know if I can deal with another round of bullshit."

"But everyone talks about 2007 like it can finally change people's minds," I said.

"I know. I'll decide soon. I'd love to get that recognition, because I think if anyone deserves it, my dad does."

Shifting the conversation, Morgan said, "We're already looking forward to your next Clan Club picnic."

"This next year will be a test to see how strong our club is," John said. "The economy is so bad, but people still make the trip. A guy flew in from Hawaii just to come to the Clan Club picnic. How freaking cool is that? It blows me away. Every picnic I like to find a spot away from the action and just take a moment to check it all out. I try to soak it in. We are involved with creating something that brings total strangers together. They talk about it and plan it for a whole year. They come because they've made friends from other states who also come every year. And it's humbling to know that it started with our wines."

We patiently drained the bottle of 1998 Black Russian, and I began to wonder what old wines John would dig up for the next big auction.

As I thought about the possibilities, Morgan asked, "Is anyone else planting the grapes that you use to make Black Russian?"

It was an important question, and it's one that I had asked when I spoke to one of the first McGregor winemakers earlier that summer. Dave Whiting, the owner and winemaker at Red Newt Cellars, had worked three harvests at McGregor back when the winery was putting the first blends together for Black Russian Red. "Why," I had wondered, "isn't anyone else trying to make this wine?"

"Those grapes are so unique to McGregor that you would have a hard time duplicating what they do anywhere else," Dave had told me. "It's not that other winemakers don't like the wine, but our customers would have no idea what it is. The McGregors have invested years in their customers, and now they have people who know what Black Russian is." Then his eyes lit up as he concluded, "That's pretty special."

Before we departed, John wanted to know if we had met a man who had become a fixture at the annual picnic and auction. He urged me to track down this collector who lived out of state. "Trust me," John said. "He's worth the time."

* * *

Many people will never comprehend the idea of paying hundreds of dollars for a single bottle of wine. When 750 milliliters of wine can cover the cost of a mortgage payment, even many avid wine drinkers will argue that things have gone too far. Why not spend the cash on a case or two instead of a bottle or two? Indeed, the escalating cost of high-end wine has created a gulf dividing only the most lavishly well-heeled consumers and everybody else. The misunderstanding of wine as an elitist product almost always starts with the trophy collections of arrogant poseurs who care little for the wine's origins or the winemaker's vision.

In light of this, the simple conclusion is that there is no collector, no wine lover, quite like Paul DeStio.

A sixty-eight-year-old retired inventor and plastics researcher, Paul has spent enough of his income on wine to cover the cost of the world's most treasured bottles many times over. He could entertain guests with vertical tastings of the first-growths of France if he pleased. When the heralded Château Latour earned a perfect score for the 2000 vintage, Paul never considered paying the release price of $475, even though he easily could have. His collection could feature California's growing list of cult Cabernet Sauvignons. Even the priciest Pinot Noirs of Burgundy have been well within his considerable wine budget. But when Paul scratched out the biggest check he's ever written for wine, the $850 did not pay for any of these viticultural prizes.

It paid for the 1991 McGregor Black Russian Red.

"It probably made my wife a little nervous," Paul told me sheepishly as he surveyed the cellar he built to house his wine library.

I found Paul to be exactly my kind of high-end wine lover: unburdened by the pressure to show off famous bottles to friends, in love with the story of wine. He exuded energy as we talked about how a man from Middlesex, New Jersey, came to treasure Finger Lakes wine.

"We took a vacation to the Finger Lakes years ago," he said, kneeling to check the vintages on older bottles. "We felt like we had discovered a secret with Finger Lakes Riesling, and just when we thought the red wines were lagging behind the whites, we tasted the Black Russian. I remember turning to my wife and saying, 'Wow, this is terrific. What *is* this?' We joined the McGregor Clan Club, and we've been coming back every year."

His wine cellar is a clever temperature-controlled room that he created in the basement of his modest house. Wooden racks cover three walls, wines from around the world nearly touching the eight-foot ceiling. He uses a computer database to track his cellar, which is nearly at its capacity of 624 bottles.

"How many bottles are Black Russian Red?" I asked.

Paul laughed and said, "Only 136. We've had to drink some of it!"

He could tell I was surprised. "Some vintages haven't held up," he said with a shrug. "But that's okay. Most have just continued to get better. Our friends who love wine used to be skeptical, but we'd tell them, 'Come over to the house. Just come over and try some mature Finger Lakes wines before you judge how they'll age.' Well, don't you know that they think it's astounding, just as we once did."

"I thought you were excited to have that little secret to yourself!" I said.

"We're not very good at keeping secrets, I guess! Older Rieslings can really be special too. We have some of those down here. But the Black Russian is our New Year's Eve wine and it makes an appearance on plenty of special occasions."

I shook my head and smiled. Collectors like Paul are more rare than 100-point wines. The world's highest-scoring wines are undeniably delicious and many enthusiasts spend their fortunes and their lives chasing the big labels. No one would blame Paul if he were among that crowd. But aside from a few recognizable bottles from Napa and Italy, Paul's cellar seemed to feature the ugly ducklings of the critical press. I wondered if he was aware of that.

"Oh, sure," he said with a knowing chuckle. "The wines I love don't fit in a wine critic's box. The Black Russian especially. It's just too different. They don't know anything about it. They think it's freakish. I don't blame them, either. They review a consistent set of varieties, and these Georgian grapes aren't among them. But I can't get enough of the exotic flavors and the acidity. Different can be interesting—and different can be good!"

I didn't dare ask Paul if he was willing to open the scarcest of his treasures—the last remaining bottle of the 1991 Black Russian. I could see that he was thoughtful about when to open mature bottles, and it's never easy to decide when to uncork the last of a special vintage. But I wondered if the McGregor family would be able to turn up a lost bottle or two of the 1991 for the upcoming picnic and auction. I asked Paul if he was planning on attending.

"We never miss it," he said. "It's always fun to see what the McGregors find to put up for bid."

Then, with that knowing laugh: "And if you hear them announce that they're auctioning off a bottle of mature Black Russian, look around. You'll find me debating whether I want to grab the checkbook again!"

* * *

No one was talking about scores at the Clan Club picnic the following year. The major publications had reviewed several rounds of Finger Lakes wines from the 2007 vintage, and John McGregor had finally made a decision about submitting the Black Russian for professional review.

He wasn't going to do it anymore.

I'm not sure his club members gave much thought to it, anyway. The rough reviews in the past had never affected their purchasing decisions, and while the Black Russian had been ignored by some critics, some of the other McGregor wines had landed better scores.

As we sipped a variety of wines on a scorchingly hot day, I again pondered why the critical reviews bothered John so much. If the critics didn't understand his wines, certainly the Clan Club did. Club members had been pouring in faithfully every year to attend this event, and nothing written in a wine magazine had stopped them yet. On this day, my second Clan Club picnic, I could see that no economic downturn or negative press was going to keep club members away. That should be enough for John, I thought. He ought to wear those ugly scores like a badge of honor.

Then I glanced across the rolling field and saw John staffing the food line. He was serving pig roast alongside his father. They were laughing with an older couple, no doubt longtime members of the club and part of the extended McGregor family. And I realized that John views each score as a direct critique of his father's efforts. Even after Bob McGregor had retired, John interpreted each review of McGregor wines in intensely personal terms. His successful winery was built by family and survived on the idea of family, extending far beyond John and Stacey and this twenty-five-mile lake. The McGregor clan looked out for one another, and John would always defend his family's—and especially his father's—efforts.

When the auction rolled around, John stood up in front of the crowd. After leading a few rousing cheers, someone shouted, "Where's that cult wine?" As clan members laughed, I wondered if it was fair to refer to the Black Russian as a cult wine. John answered my question.

"You know, it might be a cult wine," he said. "Think about it, everyone. How else would you describe it? It's just so unique."

"It's *our* cult wine!" the eager bidder called out.

"Well, you can't drink a glass of the Black Russian and say it's like the best Cabernet you've ever had," John replied. "It's not that way. I'll bet most of you had your first glass right up the hill in our winery, and I'll bet most of you had that first glass with Stacey or myself pouring." The auction tent burst into applause.

John had not been able to uncover any of the 1991 Black Russian for that auction, but he did offer up several bottles from the mid-'90s. I was surprised to see Paul DeStio sitting back, smiling as if to say, *I have to let someone else enjoy it too.* Each sold bottle brought new applause. It was one heck of a party.

They were pouring Black Russian by the glass that day, but I confess that I have no idea what I thought about the current vintage. It didn't matter. That could have been a 100-point wine in my glass because all I remember is enjoying the day and the people. And I remember seeing John McGregor, laughing with his blood family and his wine family, unburdened by the pressure of pleasing the wine press, perfectly at home. There is no score that can be placed on such satisfaction.

TEN

The Geologist and His Rock: Tom and Susan Higgins

May 10, 2005
Central Finger Lakes, New York

"Someone is going to shoot you. With a gun, Tom. A real one. And I can't say that I'll blame them when they do."

Susan Higgins was talking to her husband, who had awakened that morning to find that he had fallen asleep the previous night with his face in a book about soil composition. This had become a normal occurrence. Today he had planned to do some prospecting, but Susan was—understandably—concerned about it.

"I'd call it 'trespassing,'" she told him. "You're going to be tromping around people's private land. They've been known to shoot trespassers."

Tom, a sturdy-shouldered and handsome thirty-year-old, pulled his wavy hair out of his eyes. "I have a plan," he mumbled. "If anyone sees me I can just tell them that I'm an inspector with the state."

"And what if you like the property?" Susan responded. "You come back the next day and tell them that you just happen to want to buy it?"

"Well, it's not for sale, anyway," Tom said. "Nothing seems to be for sale right now." Then he smiled at his wife, who was staring back at him with piercing blue eyes. "But you're right. This is a bad idea. I just feel a little desperate lately."

Susan, a beautiful woman with medium-length brown hair, put her hands on Tom's shoulders. "I know you do. But you've already just about given my mother one heart attack. I don't want to have to call her to say that her son-in-law has been shot while gallivanting on private land."

Tom knew he would never live the heart attack down. He had decided in 2002 that he was leaving his career in information technology to pursue a life making wine. They were living in Yorktown, New York, but he had been born in Colorado and had lived in several states, and he was willing to go anywhere to learn how to do it. All of his schooling had come in the field of IT. He knew that he loved Pinot Noir, but he didn't know anything about how to make it. Susan, a tough and successful corporate management consultant, urged him to quit work; she too had tired of the 4 a.m. phone calls from Tom's company and she knew he was miserable at work.

But when Susan called her mother to inform her of Tom's plans, her mother put the phone down and nearly suffered a heart attack. Susan would downplay the episode when talking to friends, saying, "I'm not sure it was an actual heart attack, but she ended up in the hospital. She just needed a little nitroglycerine. But I guess Tom's career change nearly killed her."

Susan's business acumen would make the transition easier. She drew up a five-year plan for a new winery while Tom began his training. He went to France, learning from world-class winemakers, and then to California, where he worked under America's most storied producer of Pinot Noir, Josh Jensen of Calera Wine Company. He was away from home for most of two years.

Ultimately the Finger Lakes became their destination for three significant reasons. Tom had family in the Finger Lakes area and had spent part of his childhood there. The climate was nicely suited to Pinot Noir. Most important, it was affordable.

An acre of potential vineyard land in California was selling for an average of $100,000. In Washington State an acre cost $75,000. In Oregon, a rising star in the world of Pinot Noir, an acre cost $40,000. In the Finger Lakes the average acre cost $5,000.

Susan could keep an apartment in the New York City metro area, where she would base her management consulting work. She could come to the Finger Lakes on weekends to help run the tasting room. Eventually she could move to the Finger Lakes full-time, but for now she could live separately and use her income to fund the winery.

Everywhere Tom went he received the same advice: find limestone. From several dozen winemakers in French Burgundy to the folks at Calera, the message was simple. They told Tom that the world's best Pinot Noir is made from vines that grow in limestone-based soils. At first it sounded strange, but as Tom tasted more wines, he found a salient difference in the Pinots that came from limestone.

This little bit of information had turned the Higgins' kitchen table into a scene from an Indiana Jones film. There were maps sprawled everywhere. Tom had hunted down the geological survey maps of all counties that bordered the Finger Lakes. Scattered among the maps were handwritten lists. Some featured Tom's must-have characteristics for a piece of land (slope, proximity to one of the lakes, fair price), while others revealed the best-case scenarios (land with an existing building that could be converted into a winery, access to a main road).

But mostly Tom was fixated on the limestone.

He had begun working west to east, visiting plots of land that looked promising based on the maps. Often he was disappointed. He found that, after digging into the soil, most land didn't have much limestone at all. The few sites that did were so far from a lake that a vineyard would not likely survive.

As Susan looked at the maps, then her husband, she said sweetly, "You're still going to go trespassing today, aren't you, Tommy?"

"Yes, honey," he said. "Sorry."

"That's okay," she said, rubbing his shoulders. "Just keep in mind that if you get shot I'll have no idea where to find your body."

* * *

Tom Higgins finally found the limestone he was seeking in perhaps the most unlikely of places. Frustrated with the lack of viable options, he had intensified his research into local geology. And then he discovered a massive deposit of the coveted stone.

On Wall Street.

Turns out that the famous curbstone that lines Wall Street is made of limestone—and Tom discovered that it came from the Finger Lakes. The source was a large limestone quarry on the northeast side of Cayuga Lake, which was a part of the region he hadn't yet explored.

This discovery energized Tom, who had picked up work as an assistant winemaker at the highly regarded Atwater Estate on Seneca Lake. He had begun to wonder if he'd ever find a suitable piece of land, but now he couldn't wait to see this part of the Finger Lakes.

Susan was away at work so Tom made the drive alone. He headed to the top of Cayuga Lake and headed south down the east side, and he was surprised to find himself getting a little nervous. So many limestone-scouting missions had gone poorly, and he couldn't help but wonder if he'd be disappointed once again.

As he pulled into the town of Union Springs, just a few miles from the quarry, Tom couldn't believe what he was seeing. He slowed down to get a good look at a long, thick wall lining the edge of a large private property. The wall was made of limestone. He passed a group of old houses that clearly had limestone foundations. Then, in the middle of town, he saw a schoolhouse made entirely of limestone.

It was simply everywhere. And if he could see it in the buildings he figured it had to be hidden under the ground, too.

Now he just needed to find some properties that were for sale. Tom called a real-estate agent and provided a simple list of criteria. He hoped to find his perfect plot within days.

He was about to be disappointed once again.

* * *

The easiest way to get scammed is to tell someone you're planning to build a winery. It has the same effect as announcing you only carry hundred-dollar bills and you need six garages for your fleet of luxury cars.

Most new winery owners are floating on a deep pool of debt. Some wine regions feature big-money backers who provide a deep reserve of cash, but the Finger Lakes has never seen a flood of investors. Building or buying a winery in the Finger Lakes guarantees hard work, stressful harvests, and plenty of red ink.

While Tom and Susan weren't living an impecunious life, neither did they have gold coins spilling from their pockets. But they found that real-estate agents and property owners simply assumed that anyone seeking to build a winery must be rich. Time after time, a property owner would show a piece of land for $5,000 per acre—only to double the price after learning of the Higgins' wine dreams. They had set a tight and focused budget of $50,000 to acquire property, but when they found something in that range the final price would mysteriously reach six figures. In this part of the region the earth was riddled with limestone but it wouldn't matter if they couldn't find something for a reasonable price. And Tom blamed himself.

He approached each negotiation with a sense of trust that made him vulnerable. Instead of keeping his intentions private when asked, Tom would volunteer his intention to build a winery. He had seen property owners take advantage of this knowledge many times—sometimes as late as the final paperwork—but he couldn't overcome his instinct to assume the best in everyone. Susan worried that her husband was sweet but naïve, and Tom appreciated the balance she brought to their relationship. After eight months of failed searches, Tom resolved to make sure to bring Susan in for negotiations.

On a warm and still evening the first week of May, he was mentally fried. His real-estate agent showed him two pieces of property that were priced so offensively that Tom was prepared to shut the search down. For a while, at least. He feared that he and Susan might become so tired of the process that they might overpay for a bad piece of land just to get moving.

Too many people have predicted that we're going to fail, Tom thought, *and we're not going to do something stupid to make them right.*

The late-day sun sinking over Cayuga Lake was so idyllic that Tom almost wondered if he were being taunted. Everything he wanted was right here, but he couldn't make it work. Pulling over to the side of a county road, he dialed Susan on her cell phone in New York City.

"I can't do this anymore, Suze," he said quietly. "Not like this. Our agent won't listen to us. We've seen thirty properties in almost a year and most are terrible. The rest are money traps."

"Just clear your head and get away from it," she said. "You're going to go crazy if you keep thinking about it."

"You're right," he said. Hanging up, he headed down the hill toward the main lake road. He drove slowly with the windows down, trying to enjoy the sights and smells of a spring evening.

As he drove north on the main thoroughfare, toward the famous limestone quarry that built Wall Street, he noticed a sign on a hill in the distance. As he got closer it grabbed his attention: "For Sale By Owner," it read.

Stopping by the side of the road, Tom stepped out to take a look at the property. The smell of freshly cut grass hung in the air. Tom enjoyed the smell—the smell of work, he thought—and he immediately enjoyed the feeling of inspecting a property without the salesmanship that he endured from the agent.

The upper portion of property was densely covered with trees on a rather steep slope, feeding down to a flatter section of land. His imagination conjured a winery and tasting room on this lower portion, with vines taking the place of the trees. He walked several yards up the hill and turned his attention to the ground.

There it was, poking up from the earth, the entire length of the hillside. The chunks of limestone at his feet betokened the treasure below the surface.

"Can I help you?" Tom turned to see a short, thin man walking in his direction. The man spoke gently and amiably, extending a hand. Tom received it warmly and said, "I'm sorry to bother you—I was driving by and saw the sign."

"That's what it's there for!" the man replied.

They walked the land as Tom fired off a set of questions. The man was a retired college professor who had farmed this piece of land—as well as surrounding properties—organically for the last decade. Tom tried to hide his excitement, but this only made the property more attractive; some farmers who use heavy chemicals can pollute the land in such a way that makes it nearly impossible to grow healthy grapevines. That wouldn't be a problem here. The farmer intended to sell only 1.3 acres but he would consider selling all seven, which would be plenty for a new operation. After all, Tom would have to purchase grapes for a few years when he launched the winery while the new vines grew in.

The property even had public water, a serious bonus. Tom then asked the most important remaining question. "How much are you asking?"

"Six thousand an acre," the man replied calmly. It was a higher price than most properties, but given its attributes the price was more than fair.

That is, unless it was going to rise.

"So what are you looking to do with it?" the man asked.

Tom squeezed his eyes shut and exhaled slowly. He felt his instinct taking over once again. *Susan is going to kill me*, he thought.

"We want to start a winery," he said.

The man's eyebrows perked up. He nodded, then smiled. "That sounds awfully nice." Tom was waiting for him to revise the number. Finally the man said, "Well, I hope the price sounds fair."

Tom laughed softly as he felt relief washing over him. "Yeah, well, I think so," he stammered. "Listen, I've always been a handshake kind of guy, but I should call my wife. Maybe we can continue this discussion tomorrow night?"

"I can shake with you on that," the man said with a wink.

Tom made his way back down to the car, taking care not to trip on the limestone that occasionally got in his way. Then he stopped, sighed, and pulled out his cell phone. He wondered if Susan would believe that he had just found the home of their new winery.

There was no time to think. I could only react. I had just placed something in my mouth so foul that my body moved immediately to reject it.

It was a small cluster of grapes infected with sour rot. The taste was entirely new to me, though I would guess it perfectly matched the flavor of a runner's sock, freshly peeled from his foot after a ten-mile jog. I would have known not to put the rotting cluster in my mouth had I smelled it, but in this case I had mistaken the cluster for a healthy one and popped it into my mouth with a gentle toss.

My instincts taking over, I lurched to my right and spat the cluster with such ferocity that it must have created a breeze in the hair of the gentleman working next to me. I was relieved to see it miss his head by inches. We had just met half an hour before—I didn't even remember his name—so I thought this was a nice introduction.

As I gasped for breath I mouthed, "Sorry!"

"Sour rot!" he said with a knowing nod and smile. "That'll teach you to eat too much on the sorting line."

My only previous experience on a sorting line had been at Anthony Road Wine Company, where winemaker Johannes Reinhardt had feverishly selected his crop for a special dessert wine. But many wine producers in the Finger Lakes do not sort the grapes that are harvested; they rely on vineyard crews to pick out bad berries while the fruit is still on the vine. When the crop is in they crush it and it starts the journey to the bottle. Any flaws in the grapes go along with them.

Before their first harvest came in, Tom and Susan Higgins determined that every cluster of grapes would be hand-sorted. They were thrilled when friends and family asked to participate with the harvest, but that didn't mean they would always have a crew. If no one was available, they would do it themselves. They discovered exactly what kind of sacrifice that commitment entailed on the very first pass at sorting when they finally went to bed at 3:30 in the morning. They had started before noon.

What a difference it makes. I tried to imagine a small batch of grapes infected with sour rot making it into the crushing bin. The wine wouldn't be ruined, but the vibrant fruit taste would be blunted and made more acidic. And as I cautiously returned to the sorting line I noticed that Tom was still laughing.

"As a customer of yours, this is great," I said. "As a volunteer on your sorting line, it sucks."

"Well, most of our volunteers think it's enough to smell the infected berries," Tom said. "They don't find it necessary to eat them."

With the exception of the rare sour berries and the hardened dehydrated berries, the crop looked stunning. The Pinot clusters were small and tight and looked almost black. Tom had cleared the hillside of trees but his own vines wouldn't bear fruit for another several years, so he was purchasing fruit from some of the finest vineyards in the Finger Lakes. And, like winemaker Morten Hallgren of Ravines Wine Cellars, Tom was paying by the acre—making sure he was getting a small and stellar crop.

They had taken the most expensive approach possible to the winemaking, but it was all part of Susan's business plan. Tom didn't think his wines would gain a following if they were mediocre, so they budgeted to make sure he could have everything he needed to impress his first customers.

It seemed to be working. With a production of 90 percent Pinot Noir and 10 percent Riesling, the wines from tiny Heart & Hands Wine Company were slowly getting attention. The early sales were stronger than Tom and Susan expected—especially considering that

Tom crafted his 2007 Pinot Noir in a borrowed facility while the winery was under construction.

They chose "Heart & Hands" because it refers to the Irish Claddagh ring and they found it not only a fitting symbol for their efforts but a nod to Tom's Irish heritage. We were sorting grapes just outside the cozy tasting room and winery, which had been built into the side of the hill. That allowed the winery to benefit from the natural temperature of the earth—a handy way to avoid purchasing an exorbitantly expensive temperature-control system.

Susan had joined the volunteers to sort, and it occurred to me that she must rarely enjoy a day off. She was still living just outside New York City during the week, working as a corporate consultant. Her job sent her across the country to handle clients. And yet every weekend she made it home to work the tasting room and, during harvest, to sort grapes. She was clearly just as comfortable in jeans and a sweatshirt as she was in a power suit.

Even from the sorting table I could see the limestone emerging from the naked hillside. When I asked Tom about it he smiled. "If I was excited the first night I stopped here, you should have seen me when we cleared the trees. We couldn't have asked for more."

Eventually our small but enthusiastic crew filled the bin with worthy Pinot Noir grapes. "Want to jump in?" Tom asked me. "We crush by foot here. The old-fashioned way!"

It wasn't easy to get into the bin without falling. I climbed gingerly over the side and positioned my feet so I would slide into the tall rubber boots that had been left inside. Sitting on the edge, I felt my feet inside the boots and I jumped down. One foot started to slide, but I caught myself and earned some polite applause. For fifteen minutes I stomped happily, the crew returning to the sorting line and sending more grapes my way as I cleared space in the bin. I could see why Susan favored her weekends. This felt like old-world winemaking, raw and manic, with everyone personally invested in the outcome.

* * *

Just five miles south of Heart & Hands Wine Company is a small town called Aurora, and even though it sits on one of the region's major lakes, it might as well be on the moon for residents of the western Finger Lakes. My wife grew up two lakes to the west. She had never been to Aurora, nor had most of her friends.

Strolling into town, Morgan and I asked each other how this could be possible. The town was almost eerily serene, as if it had been plucked from a Bob Ross painting. The yards were perfectly cut, the decks swept, and the view of Cayuga Lake dazzling. High on a hill the famous MacKenzie-Childs pottery and furniture company provided a sophisticated air. There was a sense of charm that was absolutely atavistic, and we told Tom and Susan that this little village would be a magnet for wine tourists—if anyone knew it existed.

"We hope that's true," Tom said. "People think this side of the lake is so far away. I tell them that we're not lonely out here. We're pretty easy to find."

The four of us eventually headed for our dinner destination: the Aurora Inn, one of the first restaurants to carry Heart & Hands wine. It also happened to offer a nice look at the lake and an unstuffy, upscale atmosphere.

We toasted new beginnings over a bottle of vintage French Champagne as Susan explained her attempts to bring sanity to this endeavor.

"I'm less of a risk taker," she said. "So the fact that I can keep my consulting job going makes all of this a little less scary for me. Tom put in so much hard work in a lot of places—and these were not easy places to get into. And now, seeing how committed he is and how much happier he is . . . it's worth it, even if I'm a bit more frightened than he is." She smiled at her husband and put her hand over his.

"Is it tough when people doubt you?" Morgan asked.

"Well, it's one thing when people say it's risky," Susan said, "but there were people who told us we were flat-out crazy. Or even irresponsible. That stung. We've heard people predict that we'll fail. But I'm a pretty competitive person, so that was just a little more motivation to make this work."

"You can't blame anyone for doubting us," Tom added. "But my view is that you can go ahead and doubt, but you should support us too."

"And there are still people who think I'm doing something wrong by working," Susan said. "They can't believe that we choose to split the week up and live apart. I've been told that this isn't how you build a business—it's how you destroy a marriage."

She sipped her Champagne before continuing. "Rarely do people say something to our face. We hear about it secondhand." Then she laughed softly. "There are expectations that people from our generation shouldn't do it this way. I guess I'm supposed to be home supporting Tom and making dinner every night. And you know, that is exactly how we'd end up unhappy. That's just not us."

Tom grinned at her coyly before turning to me. "I wonder if deep down Susan thinks we *are* a little crazy for doing this."

She didn't hesitate. "No way. You are happier now than you ever were doing anything else. That makes me happy." But she admitted that there is a moment, every week, when she questions the decision. "Sunday nights. It's getting harder to leave on Sundays. The work is fun. I always thought it was a cliché that you have to love what you do, but I finally feel that way about the winery. We're both pretty independent people, but there are times that it's extremely tough to get in the car."

"It won't always be this way," Tom said, seeming to talk directly to Susan, as if Morgan and I weren't there. "Someday it will change. Soon."

We enjoyed the meal slowly as Tom picked a pair of bottles from the wine list. He didn't order his own wine, which didn't surprise me. Like the best winemakers in the region, Tom and Susan share adventurous taste.

"I hate to press this," I said, "but there is one part of your plan that might give fuel to the doubters. They already thought you were nuts to leave your IT job. Then you build the winery in the Finger Lakes instead of on the West Coast, and you concentrate on the most difficult red wine grape! That's compounding the degree of difficulty, isn't it?"

Tom laughed. "It's not like making wine in Siberia! I mean, we're daring, but we're not stupid. We're here because Pinot has real potential and we believe in it."

We capped the meal with an unnecessary slice of local fruit pie before Tom and Susan insisted we join them back at the winery. The three-story building was home to their private apartment upstairs, and as we entered the tasting room I noticed the massive door. "You guys spared no expense on the entrance!" I said, surveying the carved, reclaimed wood that gave the building an elegant touch.

"This was one of the small, big things," Susan said. "We've never been about trying to create a super-glamorous place to make and taste wine. There's plenty of that out there. We've been to the most beautiful wineries in the world and it's special—don't get me wrong. But we knew early on that we wanted our winery to be a comfortable place." Then, almost sheepishly, she added, "Of course, it turns out that we can't afford to go glamorous! But that's not our style. And I don't think it ever would be. So we aim for the subtle touches."

Tom ducked behind the tasting bar and emerged with a dust-covered half bottle. It was a 1961 Bordeaux. My wife, a devoted fan of aged wine, nearly passed out at the sight of it.

"We don't buy this idea that the Finger Lakes can't make special wines that last a long time," Tom said as he poured the Bordeaux into four glasses. "We're not expecting to make wine that will be sailing along in fifty years, but we can do better than five, I promise you."

The room went silent as we sank our noses into the wine's aromatics. It was so alive that it was nearly boastful. Finally Tom said, "Please don't think I have enough of an ego to assume I'm trying to reproduce something like this." We laughed as I said, "Don't worry. This isn't even Pinot."

"Everything has been tough," he said as we nursed the wine. "There's no doubt that this line of work is not set up for . . ." Then he stopped. He twirled the glass in his hand ponderously. "I realize we're drinking a 1961 Bordeaux, but I got it for a steal. What I'm saying is, people can start a winery with a great deal of wealth and do it very well. It's just reality that money helps. I've always tried to persevere through the fact that I've never been blessed with a lot of money. I try to do the best I can with what I have, and I try to make it work."

"You've convinced me," Morgan said.

There was something distinctly unselfish in the Higgins' approach. Here in this limestone-rich corner of the Finger Lakes, Tom never spoke about cornering the market on special property and keeping it all to himself. In fact, he and Susan had already begun telling anyone who would listen that northeast Cayuga was ripe to become "Pinot Row." That mentality fit in seamlessly with the open doors and open minds that had become so prevalent in the region.

He also was deeply curious about how other wineries were making Pinot in the Finger Lakes. To find out, Tom had devised a blind tasting. It was coming up, and it was the kind of event that can make winemakers proud—or awfully embarrassed.

* * *

Morgan and I had no idea what to expect when we arrived at the Stonecat Café on a rainy evening. Tom's event had grown to become the largest tasting of Finger Lakes Pinot Noir that the region had yet seen. Twenty wines were bagged up, their labels kept secret.

My only expectation was to feel foolish when the wines were revealed. Blind tasting can be more than a little humbling.

The Stonecat, located just a few miles from Red Newt Wine Cellars and Bistro on Seneca Lake, is unlike any restaurant in the region. It combines outdoor seating with a converted garage. There is a come-as-you-are vibe and every night, local wine professionals come as they are. In the past decade the Stonecat had become the nightly hotspot on Seneca Lake.

Tom had convinced the owners to clear part of the restaurant for his grand tasting. He had pulled several long tables together to allow enough room for the twenty bagged bottles. A large group of winemakers and winery owners gathered on the edges of the room, squeezing to stay out of the rain. Susan was out of town on business, so Tom would run the event on his own.

"We all know that 2007 was an excellent year in the Finger Lakes," Tom told the group. "I'm thrilled that so many of you contributed your wines so we could see what's been going on." He gestured at the rows of empty wineglasses and said, "Let's have some fun!"

And we were off. Everyone grabbed a glass and the tables were swarmed with curious winemakers, but the initial maelstrom subsided as each person found a chair to sit and contemplate. Morgan started at the front of the line while I worked backward, taking my time with each wine and scribbling detailed notes.

I was not exactly encouraged by the first three wines I tasted. They bore a transparent cranberry color and tasted thin and simple. By the time I had moved onto the next, I had forgotten much about the previous. Only my notes saved me.

After the ominous beginning I was thrilled to find that several wines in the middle of the table stood far above the rest. In fact, I wrote that these standouts would show favorably at any blind tasting—not simply among the lesser lights of the Finger Lakes.

As I tasted and scribbled my way to the front I found myself wondering what the professionals were thinking. I was conflicted.

These Pinots were largely disappointing—some even delivered a strange, acrid citrus note. But some were quite nice, and that group of three—well, the potential was indisputable.

When I had written my last note, Morgan marched over and whispered forcefully, "Fourteen!"

"What are you talking about?" I asked.

"Fourteen is Heart & Hands Pinot! I have no doubt in my mind."

This was new. Morgan loves wine but admits that the details tend to fade in her memory as time passes. Something about Tom's wine had embedded permanently. That is, if she was right.

"You'd better hope it is," I whispered with a mischievous smile. "Have you told Tom?"

"Absolutely not!" she replied, then turned to see him preparing the wines for the big reveal. "But I'm certain that's it."

My own notes on the fourteenth wine indicated that—for once!—Morgan and I agreed on a wine's superiority. It was intensely structured, so it made sense that this could be Tom's wine. After all, he was one of the few winemakers daring enough to crush the grapes on their stems, which can add a green note to the wine. But often the result is not a green note at all, but a spicy flavor and more mouth-puckering tannin.

As Tom pulled the wines out of their bags one by one, the individual winemakers talked about their approach to making Pinot in the Finger Lakes. Most seemed to treat it like any other red wine grape, and the results were uninspiring.

But there was a thrilling surprise coming up next: the first of my "big three" was an unfiltered Pinot Noir from Damiani, the excellent small producer from just up the road. The grape grower looks a lot like the almost-Iroquois Sam Argetsinger, and it turns out that Sam and Phil Davis are close friends. Both men are doing outstanding work with their vines.

The second standout came from Ravines Wine Cellars, no surprise at all. The grapes for the Ravines Pinot come from some of the same vineyards that contribute grapes for the Heart & Hands Pinot—for now, anyway. In just a couple of years the Heart & Hands vineyard will be bearing its first fruit and Tom will have the opportunity to make Pinot from multiple sites. This tasting was showing how much of an impact the top vineyard sites can have.

I kept my eyes on Morgan's when Tom finally arrived at the fourteenth mystery wine. She turned to me and nodded. He unbagged the bottle.

She had nailed it.

I knew this was a special moment for my wife. She has a wonderful palate but she often lacks the confidence to assert her ideas. We were going to remember this.

It was that much more special for Tom, who spent several minutes fielding the praise and questions from his colleagues. Whether or not these winemakers realized it, Tom had already become a leader in the local industry.

"And we're not even getting the benefit of the limestone yet!" Tom said, laughing. "We're still buying all of the fruit!"

Tom had not asked us to score the wines, so as the tasting wound down we ordered some food and retasted some of the Pinots.

"We've learned something very valuable tonight," Morten Hallgren told me as we compared notes. "We learned that good weather in a year like 2007 is not enough. You have to be committed to this grape, and if you're not, you're still going to make mediocre wine. And there is a lot of mediocre wine here." He shook his head. "I don't understand it. If you don't care enough to make great Pinot Noir, you're much better off making something else."

Dave Breeden, the head winemaker at highly regarded Sheldrake Point Vineyards on Cayuga Lake, was also unimpressed. Tom asked Dave for his assessment on Finger Lakes Pinot Noir. Dave laughed and said, "I think I'll just stick to making Riesling."

Later I pulled Dave aside to ask him to elaborate. He didn't hesitate. "I was talking about my own wines, first and foremost. They're not our strength. We do our best. But there is someone in this room who is absolutely doing the right thing, and that's Tom Higgins. I'm not easily moved by Pinot Noir, but he's already doing it."

Fox Run's assistant winemaker Tricia Renshaw put it this way: "Tom is changing the way people think about Pinot Noir from New York."

"Do you think more winemakers will try to make it around here?" I asked.

"I think probably fewer!" she said with a laugh. "He's setting a high standard in a really short amount of time. I don't know if many other wineries would be willing to go to the lengths they go to for their Pinot."

"You know," I said, "their first goal was to just find a special piece of property and survive."

"That's what I've heard," Tricia said. "I think they're going to do more than just survive."

Leaving Stonecat, the lesson was not at all complicated. Most wineries ought to rip out their Pinot vines if they can't invest the care and energy that the grape requires. There are too many wines that are simply a waste of time—the grower's, the winemaker's, the consumer's. But the best Pinots were already demonstrating the kind of potential this grape shows in ideal cool climates.

Several days later, a review came in from the "Prince of Pinot," a wine publication that focuses entirely on Pinot Noir. Of course, it's a publication that didn't look to the Finger Lakes for outstanding Pinot—until the Heart & Hands 2007 Pinot was released: "A very, very impressive wine like nothing I had ever previously tasted from the Finger Lakes region. Given the proper weather, viticulture management, and in the hands of a talented winemaker, the potential for premium Finger Lakes Pinot Noir is exemplified here."

Tom's reaction was immediate: "This is nice, but we're too new to spend much time on this kind of write-up. We have several long decades ahead of us."

And even if the critics like what they are doing, Tom and Susan know they need the approval of the average customer. They need devoted fans who will return to purchase their wine every year. It is the only way they will be able to build a thriving business.

So many red wine drinkers long ago decided not to bother with the Finger Lakes. Tom and Susan were going to have to change their minds.

* * *

After a long and slow Saturday, Tom and Susan were getting ready to close the tasting room when an older couple showed up at the door. Jim and Dotty Touschner had lived in the Finger Lakes for decades but they had all but given up on the wine. They were red wine drinkers and, as much as they appreciated the reputation that local Rieslings had gained, they tended to stick to red wine with dinner.

But after fifty-two years of marriage, they were open-minded enough to break up their routine and try something new. And, when they read about a small new producer called Heart & Hands, they figured it would be worth an afternoon's drive to go try it.

I had seen Tom and Susan handle customers who arrived right when the door was locking. They never turned anyone away. "Building a business means making yourself available," Susan told me. So they weren't going to send this cute couple home—dinner would have to wait.

The winemaker offered Jim and Dotty the full tasting, which meant a private tour of the barrel room and the chance to taste the wines directly from those barrels. Tom led them through another set of doors. Feeling a drop in temperatures, Dotty elbowed Jim and said, "I'm glad I kept my coat on!"

"Oh, sorry about that," Tom said. "It's 55 degrees in here, which is perfect for storing wine but maybe not perfect for tasting it."

"It's no problem at all," Jim said.

Removing the top from one of the pristine new barrels, Tom drew a sample of Pinot and filled two glasses. He handed one to Jim, then the other to Dotty, who could hardly believe what was happening. She considered herself to be a wine drinker, but perhaps not a true wine enthusiast; she enjoyed wine with dinner but she'd only tasted wine from a bottle.

"You take wine right out of the barrel and put it right in the glass?" She turned to her husband. "That's amazing!" He was already sipping the wine as she stood wide-eyed, whispering again, "That's amazing!"

"It's actually something we do all the time," Tom said. "Have you ever tasted from the barrel before?"

"I certainly haven't!" she said.

"Dotty, if you keep talking you'll miss your chance to taste his wine," Jim said.

As Tom poured sample after sample, comparing wines from new barrels to wine from aged barrels, Dotty never stopped smiling. "I know you say you treat everyone like this, but you're treating us like family," she said.

Dotty explained that she and her husband had been drinking wine almost exclusively from California and New Zealand because their daughter had married a man from New Zealand and moved to California. They felt a connection to those wines in a way they had never felt with Finger Lakes wines. "But this Heart & Hand wine is something special," she said.

"Heart & *Hands*," Jim said, stressing the plural.

"That's what I said, Dear."

For an hour they tasted and talked—the latter more than the former. Tom enjoyed the conversation. He knew it was in his best interests to build a relationship with every customer; he didn't have a budget for advertising and his tasting room was outside the main alley of wine tourist traffic. But this private tasting was more than just good business. Tom could talk about Pinot Noir for hours—in his mind, no other wine was nearly so fascinating.

Eventually Jim and Dotty decided to leave, but not before buying several bottles. "How long have you been married?" Dotty asked.

"About eight years," Tom said.

"Well, only about forty-five more to go!" she said, referencing her own marriage's longevity. "Just think of how much wine you can make in that time!"

Jim grabbed Tom's hand and shook it vigorously. "We'll be back."

"Will we ever!" Dotty gushed.

Most visitors say that, but not everyone means it. That's why Tom and Susan were surprised to see Jim and Dotty back just a few months later. Jim explained that they had recently celebrated their fifty-third wedding anniversary on a double-date with their daughter and her husband, who were celebrating their twelfth. Each year they choose a special bottle to mark the occasion, and each year the wine comes from either California or New Zealand. This year they had surprised their daughter with a bottle of 2007 Heart & Hands Pinot Noir. They wanted Tom and Susan to know that it made for one of the truly special occasions of their fifty-three years together. They had returned to replace the bottle.

ELEVEN

The Contradiction: John Ingle

October 2, 1971
British Columbia, Canada

This was not how it was supposed to feel. John and Jo Ingle had chosen a life of adventure. They had completed college in Denver and tried to transition into adulthood with normal jobs, but they wanted more.

And, John admitted, he was a little scared.

He had used his English degree to get a teaching job, but the experience was almost instantly overwhelming. John was intimidated by the prospect of not being able to make the impact he thought he would make. Quitting could mean serious financial hardship. Fortunately, he was born with good instincts for finance, and that meant always having a backup plan.

Unfortunately, the backup plan wasn't very lucrative.

The Ingles had been intrigued by a growing movement that stressed organic food and a more natural lifestyle. They could choose their own destination and adopt such a lifestyle. They loved to travel, so they got into a pickup truck and headed north. Eventually they expected to stumble upon an idyllic piece of land sporting a "For Sale" sign. They could use what money they had to buy the land, and after that, life wouldn't carry many costs.

In the beginning they simply desired to be on the road and as far away from home as possible. Home was the Finger Lakes, where John's family owned a small cabin on Canandaigua Lake. They had spent the past month driving through Wyoming, Oregon, and Washington. Neither of them had been to British Columbia, which seemed like an entirely new world at the time. That's where they went next, open to whatever they might discover.

So no, this was not how it was supposed to feel. It was supposed to feel impulsive, and euphoric, and recalcitrant. Instead it just felt empty.

"Now what?" John said, intending it to be rhetorical.

"We could regroup back home," Jo replied. "We could stay at your family's cabin. Who knows—maybe we could buy some property there."

"And do what with it?" John asked. "We're not farmers. We don't know dirt from soil. We've talked about growing some food, but we've never done it. We'd be going home with no plan."

"Right," Jo said. "And maybe *that's* more exciting than anything we've been searching for out here."

There is not much in the Finger Lakes that resembles Napa Valley, but the tasting room and winery at Heron Hill on Keuka Lake appears to have been pulled directly from the northern California wine trails. The property rises above several dozen acres of vineyards and is framed by a steep and dramatic forest. Built in a Greek revival style, it boasts an observation tower that allows visitors a breathtaking vantage point to take in the lake and surrounding hillsides. Cream-colored stone adorns the sprawling structure, which includes a restaurant and patio for wedding parties.

"So this is the upper crust of Finger Lakes wine country," a friend remarked on a day of casual summer tasting.

It occurred to me that I had never met John Ingle, the owner whose name is scrawled on several special bottlings from Heron Hill. "Yeah, I'd say this is the upper crust," I said. "But I have no idea what's funding it."

In Napa, the most glitzy facilities are often owned by investment bankers or doctors or lawyers. Heron Hill was a mystery.

I had seen several photographs of John Ingle and could only guess that he was about fifty years old—certainly not much older—and a private guy. Unlike some winery owners who had become ubiquitous in the tasting room and with wine writers, Ingle was rarely around.

I checked in with the public relations staff—Heron Hill has all the accoutrements of wine luxury, from the polished tasting-room bars to the überprofessional management team—and I was told that it would take some time to set up an appointment. They explained that John was busy trying to hire a new winemaker. He had recently dismissed Thomas Laszlo, a Hungarian-born winemaker who had led Heron Hill's team for seven years. Ingle told the *New York Cork Report*, "When we went through the first round of applicants it was like a world tour. We want someone who wasn't part of the Finger Lakes industry. We're looking for new blood, new energy and new ideas. Part of what brings progress is bringing in outside winemaking." It was a refreshingly solid approach in a region that tends to struggle with important business decisions. Ingle was busy interviewing candidates from France, Virginia, Michigan, and elsewhere.

My vision of John Ingle was a man accustomed to wearing a suit, staying late at the office, and running his winery with a corporate approach. When I finally had the chance to meet him in early fall, I discovered that my vision couldn't have been more wrong.

* * *

"Wear boots." That was the only directive given to me before my scheduled meeting with John Ingle at his home on Canandaigua Lake. It was a crisp and clear autumn afternoon, and I decided that if I needed boots, I'd need some beat-around clothing as well. But I couldn't quite figure out why.

Ingle's house was about a half-hour's drive northwest of his winery, built on a hill overlooking Canandaigua Lake. Canandaigua is one of the smaller lakes in the region, known more for the high prices of its waterfront property than for grape growing. I knew that Ingle owned a vineyard on his property, which was the source for several of Heron Hill's single-vineyard wines. I expected that we would take a walk through the vines, part of the usual show that wineries give to writers.

Following the directions, I turned off a main road up a winding path and found Ingle's mailbox. There wasn't much to see past the mailbox; a quick rise in the earth obscured what lay beyond. It offered some nice privacy for a high-powered winery owner, I thought.

As I pulled over the rise, a wide expanse opened before me. I drove left past a sloped vineyard, which fed into another parcel of vines, this one lined by fruit trees. I slowed down to get a better look and found myself dizzy as I surveyed the land. Hills seemed to rise and fall in all directions, some covered with high grass, others by various forms of agriculture. None of this was visible from the main road just a short drive below.

Eventually the path wound its way to a house, where John Ingle was waiting for me outside. He was smiling broadly as I got out of the car. He handed me an unlabeled bottle of dark juice and what appeared to be an acorn squash. "These are for you!" he said. "We're making a new juice of seedless concord grapes grown on this property. Kind of an experiment. And this is a carnival squash that should be just about perfect. It came from right over there." He pointed past the house.

I thanked him as I noted that he was wearing jeans, a fleece, and a pair of work boots. We were not going to be sitting down inside.

"It's a beautiful piece of land," I said.

"Oh, you haven't seen anything yet," he said. "We do okay up here. Not bad for a guy in his sixties."

Having only seen him in photographs, I would have guessed that John Ingle was younger. In person I could have been convinced that he was forty-five. His soft brown hair didn't show any hint of silver and his face bore fewer lines of age than those of many of his contemporaries. I had expected to meet a corporate titan; instead I was left feeling the way I did when I met the Iroquois-speaking grower Sam Argetsinger.

"I'm sure you've heard this," I said, "but it's hard to believe you're a day over fifty."

"Well, maybe living off the land preserves you," he said with a smile. I wondered if he were offering a carefully rehearsed marketing idea.

We took a short stroll over to the vineyard closest to his house. As John spoke about the grapes I realized that he was not simply the owner of one of the most highly regarded wine companies in the Finger Lakes. He was the grower for at least some of the grapes that became his wine. Most winery owners can offer a basic show-and-tell, mixed with corporate buzzwords, when talking about grape growing. John didn't have to fake it. He was talking about the various reasons that mowing between the rows can have a deleterious effect on the vine's life. They can't teach you that in a PR seminar.

"Did you plant these vines yourself?" I asked.

"Oh, yes," he said. "And believe me, there were plenty of mistakes early on. I was a kid with a cool idea, but grape growing is agriculture and I had no training. I was not a farmer."

He laughed. "I was a hippie, and if you've met many hippies you know that they want to save the planet but they're not very good at business."

For a guy with no agricultural background, the property looked like an experiment station that had gone mostly right. The row of fruit trees that lined the vineyard near the house offered apples, peaches, and quinces. John grabbed an apple and flipped it to me. We crossed over to a line of maple trees, where John had set up a makeshift stand for producing maple syrup.

"Looks like it's straight out of the '70s, doesn't it?" he said. "Well, it is! I can get about fifteen gallons a year the hard way."

I kept reminding myself that this was the CEO, not one of his employees. Past the maple stand John showed me a door built into a gentle hillside, where he had constructed a root cellar. We ducked our heads as he flipped on a light in the small space. It was filled with baskets, each one overflowing with dirt-covered root vegetables.

"The rain this year was rough on the grapes, but it made for amazing potatoes," he explained. "They never stopped."

Back outside we turned toward the lake, which came into breathtaking view. His neighbors couldn't see much of this impressive property, but the boaters could. Opening a gate, John was eager to show off his gardens. The tightly spaced rows grew eggplant, onions, celery root, squash, and more that I didn't have time to note.

"How come no one has seen this before?" I asked. "People see your name on the bottle at Heron Hill and they think you're just the money behind the wine."

"There is no money!" he said, laughing. "Really, we're doing okay. My wife and I came up here because we thought we could make a life. I was just going to grow grapes and sell them, which we did for a while after we finally figured out how to grow them. But when we couldn't sell them we decided we should just make the wine ourselves. That's when I stumbled onto the property over on Keuka Lake. But I was never stupid enough to think I could make the wine myself. It was hard enough to grow the grapes."

"So you never planned to start a winery?"

"Absolutely not. Our first goal was to be self-sufficient. We almost are. When we left college and our first jobs didn't work out, we fell back on Plan B. I always tell my kids that you can do anything you want, but you have to have a Plan B. Well, this was ours."

"And what does it mean to be self-sufficient?"

"About three-quarters of what we eat comes from right here," he said. "There was a massive ice storm in 1991 that knocked out power for two weeks. Shut everything down. And you know what? We loved it. We never wanted it to end. We had everything we needed and we just lit a fire and stayed in the basement."

"Why haven't I heard this story before?"

John paused and looked around his property. "I don't like attention for attention's sake. I think most people who are hungry for publicity, well, it's a lot of B.S. We do okay without turning this property into a museum. But I'm willing to talk about it occasionally because there is one message that I do want people to get. I want people to know that they don't have to rely on other people for their well-being. You can take care of yourself. You just have to choose to do it."

As I was nodding he said, "C'mon, there's a lot more to see."

Back toward the house John led me into a dusty shed. At first glance it was like a greenhouse, with artichoke plants sprouting enormous bulbs. Sifting through the plants John showed me a press for apple cider and two drawers, which opened to reveal some white grapes that John was converting into golden raisins. "I love my golden raisins," he said. "It takes me about forty-eight hours to make a batch. We eat them just about every morning this time of year."

Outside we passed a pen that was home to about two dozen chickens. John pushed one aside to show three green eggs. "They go great with ham," he deadpanned.

By now I had lost my bearings and could barely remember where everything was. We were walking near a creek bed when we came upon a green truck sitting outside a small cabin. "So the man in charge of Heron Hill drives an old beater?" I asked.

"Not for years. That truck made it back and forth from Denver nine times. About twenty years ago it was going to give out, and I told the truck, 'Just make it back home to the Finger Lakes one more time. One more time, and I'll never drive you again.' Somehow it did and I kept my promise. I parked it right here and it hasn't moved since that day."

We stepped inside the cabin, where it was cold and austere. There was a bed and some wooden furniture—the toilet was in the outhouse behind the cabin. "My wife and I lived in this cabin for two full years," he said, almost marveling at the thought of it. "It was the most simple living. Those might have been the best two years of my life."

"So how did it come to this?" I asked. "The Heron Hill facility is stunning. But getting to know you, it almost feels like a contradiction. Am I wrong to think that?"

John was amused. "It's like I said: most hippies aren't successful in business. When they are it can be surprising."

"But your tasting room and the building don't feel like your style."

"Maybe not at first. But our tower is meant to look like the old silos in the Finger Lakes. Take a look sometime. The stone came from local sources. It's a very sustainable operation, like our grape growing."

"You don't talk much about sustainability in your wines."

He squinted and shrugged. "We'll talk to customers about it if they ask. We put information on the website. But it's not a marketing gimmick like some wineries have. If you do something well you don't have to brag about it."

"But surely," I said, "that facility was not always that size. You had to decide to go big."

"We did, and it happened in 2000. There was a burst of tourism and we had to decide whether we wanted to keep going as we had always done it, or if we wanted to go whole hog and create something truly special. We decided to go for it. We hired Thomas Laszlo, and I commissioned an architect to do the building."

"Do you regret any of it?" I asked.

"I don't think so. I'm not always comfortable with everything, which is why I spend most of my time up here!"

The success of Heron Hill had allowed the Ingles to live as public or as private a life as they pleased, and John's wife was particularly private. He didn't mind acting as the winery's public face at times, but he didn't seek out high-wattage events. When he did meet with customers he would tell them that the wines from Ingle Vineyard had a family tradition. What he did not say was that he and Jo never thought they would stay—not for long, anyway, after coming home in 1971. They lived in an old family cabin and took the opportunity to purchase twenty acres when it became available. Plan B seemed to make them happy, and they never drew up a Plan C. They added gradually to the property, and the winery provided a steady enough income to survive, before the eventual dramatic expansion in 2000.

I followed John back up to his driveway, where he asked me to take a short ride in his pickup truck. When I opened the passenger door a wave of foul odor burst forward. I tried not to grimace, but John noticed and said, "Oh, sorry about that. This is B.B.'s house." In the backseat, sleeping on a blanket, was a rugged black lab.

"I'm going to show you the new piece of land that I just bought," he said. "We have 168 acres, and I just added 50 that I've had my eye on for a long time. It finally became available, and I know just what I want to do with it."

"And that is?"

"Absolutely nothing."

The truck darted off the driveway and up a hillside, past the Ingle Vineyard blocks. The grass-covered terrain stretched ever higher, and the truck fit snugly into a path John had carved into the fescue and weeds. "This is the toboggan run," John announced as the truck dove forward and then back up another slope. "You're not nervous, are you? Don't worry—this truck can handle it!"

Finally a small building came into view high on the hillside. As we approached it, John explained that he built the new cabin for his family and close friends only. We got out to see the simple deck that showcased one of the most expansive lake views I had seen in the region.

"This is going to be the only building on this entire fifty acres," he said. "I built this so my wife and I could bring friends up here to enjoy a glass of wine and get away from the world. Not many people know it exists, and we prefer it that way."

"Do your kids ever visit?"

"They certainly do!" he said, lighting up. "We have four adult children, two boys and two girls. And you know, sometimes I think I'd like to have even more freedom than I do now. I'm not motivated to run away from the wine business, but this won't be forever. So I'm working on my two daughters' husbands. One is interested in the business side, and one loves the vineyard side."

Then he grinned coyly. "But you can't push kids too hard, you know."

We gazed out at the lake in silence for a few minutes as John tossed a stick with B.B. The dog happily galloped into the high grass, pausing occasionally to inspect a strange sound or unusual smell. Finally John chuckled and said, "There is one thing I fear."

"What's that?"

"Commercial development. It's creeping ever closer." He looked across the hillside, which seemed ripe for some high-powered builder. "I don't mind neighbors, but I don't want to live in a subdivision."

"Well, with this fifty acres, maybe you won't have to," I said.

He smiled. "That's the idea."

* * *

My wife and I were sitting down for lunch at Heron Hill's revamped restaurant when I thought about how John Ingle fit into the Finger Lakes wine community. Perhaps more than anything else, the region's wines had improved thanks to collaboration. John Ingle was hardly Boo Radley, but he wasn't nearly as visible in the wine community as some of his colleagues.

And yet maybe this was another case of leading by example. The wines are excellent—particularly the bottlings from the Ingle Vineyard, which boast more of an earthy character. The expansion to the tasting room was built with local materials. The vineyards were farmed with admirably sustainable techniques, which John shared on occasion during growing seminars.

He was happy to help his peers when they would ask.

And the production had hardly grown out of control, anyway. Heron Hill had gone from about five thousand cases to about twenty thousand, which is manageable with a large staff. Ingle had seen opportunity to grow without losing his grip on quality wines. Instead of growing the wine production to unrealistic levels, he grew the overall business; we noticed the staff setting up to host a wedding reception on the other side of the facility.

Back in the winery, the new head winemaker was working through his first Finger Lakes vintage. John had decided to hire a Frenchman, Bernard Cannac, who had recently worked on Long Island. It had been a rigorous search process that impressed John's competitors.

We were about to dig into our salad when I noticed a familiar pickup truck making its way up the road. "That looks like John Ingle," I remarked to our waitress.

"Yep, that's John," she said. "Right on schedule. He has a fresh load of vegetables that he grew. He insists we use whatever he can bring to us on our menu."

"How come that's not detailed on the menu?"

The waitress shrugged. "I guess that's not his style. He'd rather not talk about some of that stuff."

Someday someone will, years from now when John Ingle is no longer running Heron Hill. Whether the winery is eventually turned over to his children or whether he hands it over to someone with a similar ethos, someone will boast about the efforts that John has made. Someone will explain to customers that a hippie taught himself how to be a farmer and then a winery owner and then a successful businessman. But not yet. As John might say, there's little time for talk when there's plenty more work to be done.

TWELVE

The Ukrainian and His Descendants: The Family of Dr. Konstantin Frank

Fall, 1952
New York City

Few people noticed the taciturn Ukrainian man sitting in the back of the bus. Dr. Konstantin Frank was a polyglot, but English was not one of his better languages. On this particular afternoon the fifty-four-year old, who had been washing dishes in New York City, was thinking about the journey ahead.

He had saved enough money to pay for the bus fare to move his family. Unlike many Europeans who arrive in the United States, Konstantin had little interest in the big city. He had come to the states in search of a more comfortable life, but he preferred a quieter place to raise his three children.

With a Ph.D. in viticulture from the University of Odessa, Konstantin was on a mission to take his grape-growing expertise to a place where it could impact an entire industry. His thesis had focused on growing high-quality grapes in cold climates. When he first learned about the Finger Lakes he had joked that the upstate New York region was positively mild compared to the climates in which he had worked in Europe. Today he was headed for Geneva, New York—the heart of the Finger Lakes.

Dr. Frank could hardly have known the adversity that lay before him, nor would he have dared to predict the great success that would lift up his winery. He certainly was confident that his ideas would bear fruit—wonderful, glorious fruit on the slopes of the lakes—but it's one thing to grow grapes, and quite another to grow a lucrative enterprise.

As he sat on that bus he had no idea that he would have the good fortune to meet a man named Charles Fournier. Charles ran a company called Gold Seal, which focused on a variety of wines but not the old-world European varieties that Dr. Frank believed would thrive in the Finger Lakes. Charles had already begun the work of growing those European grapes, but he could not figure out how to get them through the winter. Konstantin would famously tell Charles, not long after their first meeting, "If you give me a chance, I will prove to you that we can grow vinifera in the Finger Lakes." Within minutes of their first meeting Charles would hire Konstantin to be the Director of Vineyard Research at Gold Seal.

For a Ukrainian immigrant with no money and few possessions, the job at Gold Seal would provide the resources to allow Dr. Frank to prove his theories correct. For years, grape growers and farmers had been growing lower-quality grapes that would survive the cold winters. Dr. Frank argued that it wasn't the cold weather but disease that killed the grapes, which he blamed on poor growing practices. The locals would still resist the changes, even though Konstantin would prove that so much more was possible.

He would have loved to know that his trip from New York City to Geneva would find his permanent home. Yes, many of his grape-growing efforts would fail, but only because he would plant literally everything he could acquire. From the drought-loving Ruby Cabernet to the Bulgarian grape Kara Bumi, he would try it all. But it would become clear that a small set of varieties, led by Riesling, would be simply ideal for the region. The conditions for Riesling are similar in the Finger Lakes to what Dr. Frank had seen in places like the Rhine River regions in Germany or the slopes in Austria, but there were enough differences to allow Finger Lakes Riesling to establish its own identity.

Ultimately his legacy would be the winery that bears his name, producing its first wines in 1962 and its first commercial vintage in 1966. Konstantin would never tire of telling people, "I told you so." And who could blame him? He was never interested in diplomacy and he was not afraid to make enemies. His reputation would be built on the success of Finger Lakes grape growing. He would spend the rest of his life trying to convince his peers that the Finger Lakes didn't need to look to other places for high-quality wines.

His dreams ran wide and deep, but they could not possibly have included a thriving wine region with more than 100 wineries just fifty years later – much of it thanks to his efforts.

That day in 1952 it was a story that was all yet to be written. As the bus pulled into the dusty Geneva parking lot, Konstantin shifted his thoughts to the next day's work. He would later tell his family that despite his enological training, it would take some time to find the job he loved. Step one was paying whatever bills might come.

He stepped off the bus ready to work. His new bosses were instantly suspicious of his claims that the best European grape varieties would thrive under his tutelage. They joked that as committed as Konstantin was to those grapes, perhaps he should be committed to an institution.

His first paid job would include—as he would proudly explain years later—picking blueberries. It was a start. For Konstantin, and his family, and for an entire region.

Dr. Frank Vinifera Wine Cellars was on fire, and not in the metaphorical sense. A large tasting room and special events building was totally engulfed in flames. The first few people who pulled into the parking lot to see it knew immediately that there was no saving that building. The firefighters' mission would be to save the rest of the property and buildings that surrounded it.

I got a phone call as I was showing up to work at the ABC News affiliate in Rochester. It was 4 a.m, and the only thing we knew was that a large fire was burning and fire crews were fighting it. In that part of the Finger Lakes—southwest Keuka Lake—there aren't too many houses near the wineries, but the fire was large enough to attract people driving home from night-shift jobs.

"All of Dr. Frank's is burning down," one person said frantically, calling our newsroom and begging us to find out what was going on. "Get down here!"

I had never met Fred Frank, the grandson of Konstantin Frank and the current owner of the business, but I emailed him to try to find out what was happening. Over the course of the next two hours we heard from more passers-by who described the fire as "spectacular." I planned to head down to the winery with a photographer the moment I could get off the morning news anchor desk.

Finally, Fred called and wanted to speak to us live on the air. He was deeply concerned that potential customers might think the entire property was destroyed—the two main tasting rooms, the separate winery, along with the 2,000-square-foot special events building that had caught fire. "There are a lot of erroneous stories already circulating on the Internet," Fred said. "We did have a fire. It did damage our new tasting room, but none of our other buildings were damaged. We continue to operate with our two additional tasting rooms. The winery and the warehouse sustained no damage."

Before we ended the conversation Fred added, "We are open today for visitors. We are open for regular wine tastings. We hope that there are more people like yourself that call us for the real story instead of relying on erroneous stories like the ones saying that the whole winery burned down. We're continuing business. We will continue to win more gold medals. That's what we do best—make great wine."

As we ended the call I felt sorry for Fred. Businesses can suffer when misinformation spreads, and he wanted to blunt the flow of what he perceived to be inaccurate reporting. I also couldn't help but feel that he sounded strangely detached, almost like he was reading lines from a script. I wondered if he was downplaying the scope of the damage, but I figured we would find out when I arrived at the Dr. Frank facility.

The fire had almost certainly taken away a piece of history—and the Frank story had grown and changed. In the early days, Konstantin's peers viewed him with derision and disbelief. They mocked his attempts to grow old-world grapes. He clashed with researchers at Cornell, who viewed his ideas as too risky. But now his name was synonymous with quality wine. The reputation was forged in the 1970s, when more consumers noticed Dr. Frank's quality wines, but it truly blossomed in the 1980s and 1990s.

Production levels had also changed dramatically. The winery had become one of the largest volume producers in the Finger Lakes.

As we turned up the hill that led to the Dr. Frank facility, I turned my focus to the fire. I could see a scorched black shell standing against a brilliant and cloudless sky. We stopped by the side of the road to get a closer look. The next building over was untouched by flames and somehow undamaged by smoke, even though it couldn't have been more than twenty feet away. Firefighters had done an improbably effective job at controlling the fire.

But the huge special events building was reduced to ashes. Only that charred frame remained. Investigators would later determine that an electrical problem was to blame. I noticed Fred walking over to greet us; he wore a light spring coat and looked impressively composed for a man who had spent a stressful and sleepless night. His balding red hair was neatly combed and underneath his spectacles he showed none of the bags that typically betray weary eyes.

"Thank you for coming," he said, extending a hand.

"Sorry about all of this," I said. "Must have been a long night and morning for you."

"Well, we're open for business," he said without much facial expression. He spoke slowly and deliberately. "It's important that people understand that they can still come and taste wine. We're bottling wine today in our winery—I can show you if you'd like."

I asked whether the fire had destroyed any sentimental items.

"It's very sad," he said. "But the firefighters did an outstanding job. As you can see the fire was entirely contained. We have two separate tasting rooms that are still functional and open, even today."

"I understand that people need to know that the main buildings survived the fire," I said.

"Yes they did. There have been erroneous reports all day, but we're open and we will still be part of the weekend wine trail event."

"Right," I said, "but was there any significant loss that you can't replace?"

"Well, we will be meeting to talk about the insurance situation, but it will take a long time to rebuild. We had only recently opened this extra tasting room and special events building. I imagine we'll do it all again, even better and nicer."

"So there was nothing related to family history lost in this fire?" I asked.

He paused and considered the question. "A Governor's Cup Award trophy melted," he said, referring to the award given to the annual winner of the New York State Food and Wine Classic, a prestigious prize. "And there were some personal artifacts of Dr. Frank. Some old photographs and letters, I believe."

Fred took the opportunity to show me around the buildings. He continued to stress their availability for tastings as he showed me the bottling line, cranking away in the winery. We shot several on-camera interviews for that evening's newscasts, and before we left Fred thanked me once again for coming.

"It's very helpful for us," he said.

"No problem," I replied. "It's an important story and we're glad to tell it."

Driving away, I couldn't help but wonder about those personal artifacts, the history that had been lost to the flames.

* * *

I have often wondered if the art of letter writing died with the sending of the first email. In ragged old folders I maintain a collection of long, flowery handwritten notes and letters from family, friends, and ex-girlfriends. Morgan likes to poke fun at the implied gravity in each missive, but I hold on to them because they have become relics that will be very curious to our children. And I confess that I miss the thoughtfulness and care that was required in written communication before email.

With this in mind, and still thinking of what might have burned in the Dr. Frank fire, I was thrilled to learn that the Cornell University Archives maintains a collection of letters that help fill in the story of Dr. Konstantin Frank's mission.

The letters reveal the correspondence over three decades between Charles Fournier—the man who hired Konstantin, and a friend of Konstantin until his death—and Philip Wagner, a winemaker, winery owner, and grape grower in Maryland. Wagner was a newspaper columnist who became known for introducing French-American hybrid grapes to growers in the United States. Wagner believed in the quality and value of hybrid grapes, and he sold hybrids to grape growers across the east coast.

The stack of old letters was a treasure to me and I pored over each page like a child finishing the last of the Harry Potter novels. Much of the correspondence covered business transactions, but the personal relationship between the two men is prominent throughout. They wrote fondly of fine dinners, special bottles, and regular visits.

But it was Konstantin who caused some friction between Fournier and Wagner.

The first ripples of discontent appeared in a letter dated November 5, 1965. Wagner unloaded his frustration about Konstantin's public campaign to eradicate hybrid grapes. He wrote:

> Did you see the piece in the Buffalo paper, about Dr. Frank. In one sense it was good publicity—a fine photo certainly.

> But I note that he had the gall to push publicly for a legal prohibition of the hybrids, and it will surely be unwise to get your name connected with anything like that since his claims are not supportable scientifically.

This letter seemed to confirm one of the most bizarre rumors I had ever heard. Konstantin's disdain for hybrids was always clear, but over the years the stories about his opposition to hybrids have seemed to take on far-fetched proportions. One such legend holds that Konstantin sought to prove that hybrids were poisonous, and he used poultry to demonstrate, forcing chickens and pigeons to consume either the grapes or the wines made from them, depending on who was telling the story. The tale continues that the birds became sterile or bore offspring that suffered from birth defects.

It always seemed like quite a hyperbolic story to me—until I discovered the old letters.

Konstantin had never attempted his own experiments, but he pointed happily to a series of experiments conducted in France in 1951. French winemakers knew that hybrids could threaten their business, so they fed wine and dehydrated grape mash to chickens as a way to demonstrate potential dangers. The chickens died, as anyone might expect they would, considering that replacing water with grape juice and swamping an animal's liver is a sure way to kill it. Twenty years later, Cornell University conducted new trials and proved that hybrid grapes were not deadly, but Konstantin never stopped talking about those French chickens.

The warmth evident between the two men began to recede after Wagner first complained about Dr. Frank. The letters continued for years, but the discussion focused less and less on social occasions. Wagner occasionally complained about Konstantin's anti-hybrid positions, and when Wagner wrote publicly, he tried to paint the increasingly revered Dr. Frank as a grape grower whose talents were overhyped.

Fournier defended his friend in the letters, particularly when Wagner fired shots at Konstantin's grape-growing ability. In July of 1982 Wagner wrote that, during a visit to the Finger Lakes, he noticed that Konstantin's famous vineyards looked ragged. Fournier countered:

> As far as Dr. Frank is concerned, he has not been in good health now for several years, but he seems to be able to get around and do some work. His vineyard has often looked ragged because part of his experimental plants are near the road.

Later in the letter, Fournier returns to the poultry.

> As far as his chicken and pigeon stories, he has quieted down a bit, but of course, cannot help mentioning them from time to time.

Until his death in 1985, it seems that Dr. Konstantin Frank never gave up his quest of dissuading growers from planting and harvesting hybrid grapes. The dozens of letters between Fournier and Wagner also touch upon the immigrant's lack of business savvy. For all of his remarkable success growing old-world grape varieties, Konstantin never figured out how to turn that success into a thriving business.

He could never move past his love of experiments, because they always held the potential of proving another naysayer wrong. Instead of paring down the number of plantings, Konstantin continued to fool around with hot-climate grapes, and he seemed more interested in growing those grapes than in growing the company. His impact on Finger Lakes grape growing had long since been established by the 1980s, but he had failed to translate that success into cash.

Fournier noted this problem in one of his letters, writing:

> He has been making enough wine for his sales, and I think that his inventory is getting a bit too big. He has transferred his company to his family, Willy is president—he knows wine well, he's an excellent salesman but unfortunately, his father hasn't let him do anything.

When Konstantin passed away in 1985, everything changed.

* * *

If you are going to make claims that most people would find unbelievable, it helps if you convince yourself that the claims are true. For all his myriad talents, Willy Frank's biggest asset might have been his ability to believe the hype. Pretty soon, he had just about everyone else believing it, too.

Wine writer Jay McInerney discovered this on a visit to the Finger Lakes a decade ago. Willy wanted to talk about sparkling wine. The region was ideal for sparkling wine production, he told McInerney. That's why Chateau Frank was expanding their production of the wine. He was not going to apologize for Finger Lakes sparkling wine; Willy loathed the disclaimer "for a Finger Lakes wine . . ." And he felt confident enough to put the word "Champagne" right there on the bottle of Chateau Frank sparkling wine.

But Willy wasn't content to tell writers like McInerny that Finger Lakes sparkling wine was potentially as good as French Champagne. That claim would have been an undeniable stretch on its own. Willy declared that Finger Lakes sparkling wine was better.

I met Willy Frank one time before he died. His high-pitched, heavily accented voice carried such energy that it nearly demanded I love the Dr. Frank wines as much as he did. He seemed frustrated that the rest of the wine world did not yet view the Finger Lakes as the great cool climate wine region that he did.

Willy was the businessman that his father never learned how to be. He spent days on the road, introducing the wines to new markets and customers. He strove to make the Dr. Frank label synonymous with some of the great European chateaux. When Konstantin died, Willy decided it was time to rip out the dozens of oddball varieties that his father had planted. He narrowed the focus to well-known varieties, pushing Riesling to the front of the production line. From 1985 to 1995, production at Dr. Frank gradually increased.

Then Willy brought in his son Fred, who had been trained not only in the vineyard, but in the business world. Fred made an immediate impact by pushing production levels much higher.

Three generations of Franks had seen wine production rise from a mere 5,000 cases annually to more than 50,000 cases. The company bought additional vineyard acres, expanding the operation to multiple lakes and sites.

And yet with production racing forward, Willy and Fred made sure their family winery maintained the same lofty reputation that Konstantin had first established. Willy's tireless travels spurred some of his colleagues to think of him as a kind of east coast Robert Mondavi, a fearless champion for the brand and a prosthelytizer for the Finger Lakes. It has taken some time, but the wines from across the region—instead of one or two producers—have finally begun to approach Willy's grandiose descriptions. During the 1970s and 1980s, there was no louder (and certainly no prouder) voice than Willy Frank's. I often find myself wondering if people who doubted Willy in those years are now finally understanding what he was talking about. His energy made the entire region relevant, even if that only meant planting a seed that would take years to germinate.

The critics have never wavered in evaluating wines from the Frank family. The wines don't earn the very highest scores from the Finger Lakes, but a number of bottlings routinely bring home big numbers and are among the top handful. This is no simple accomplishment. Fred told me that it's easy to lose quality for the sake of production, and yet the critics continue to pin high scores on the Frank wines.

For the past decade, Dr. Frank has been the undisputed brand name leader in the Finger Lakes. Konstantin never seemed to care about such things, but there was a new direction at Dr. Frank.

* * *

The new special events building that had risen to replace the one destroyed by fire was already looking remarkable. As I approached the winery on a warm winter day I could see the outline of an impressive structure cutting against the steel gray sky. Crews had performed a rather rapid resurrection.

"It's going to be bigger and even better than before," Fred Frank said as he greeted me in one of the tasting rooms on the property. "We've lost business as a result of that fire. People would drive here from out of town and they would be disappointed that this facility was not here, but it's going to be open in just a few months. Spring of 2010."

Fred wanted to take me to Chateau Frank, which is Dr. Frank's sparkling wine facility. He explained that Chateau Frank was created by Willy, and adds roughly 4,000 cases to the annual production, bringing the yearly total of Dr. Frank brands to well over 50,000 cases. We made the short drive in Fred's truck and headed downstairs to the sparkling wine cellar.

The poorly lit room included a wall made entirely of unlabeled wine bottles, stacked high and wide. It created a stirring visual effect while also saving space. I rubbed my hands to warm them in the chilly air, and Fred pointed out, "We don't have to do a thing with temperature control down here. This is an ideal place for wine. The temperature never changes."

I tried to count the bottles but the columns seemed to extend endlessly. "We're slowly increasing production of sparkling wines," he explained, and then launched into his ideas about why it's essential for a producer like Dr. Frank to produce a high volume of wine.

"If people want Finger Lakes Riesling, they can't get it in the Midwest. Go to dinner in Iowa and you'll never find a Finger Lakes Riesling on the menu. How about California? You're not going to find Finger Lakes wine there. So it benefits everyone in the Finger Lakes if we can get more vinifera wines into more places. This region has to do more than simply sell wine to people who live here, and that's what we're trying to do. And then when more people pick up a bottle of Dr. Frank Riesling, for example, they'll want to learn more about all Finger Lakes wine. It's a slow process but we think it's important."

"But isn't that a distribution problem more than anything else?" I asked.

"That's an awareness problem, and that will only be corrected when there's enough Finger Lakes wine to get into these new markets."

Then Fred brought up a winery in Washington State, Chateau Saint Michelle, which had forged a partnership with a famous German winery. This German producer, Dr. Loosen, offered winemaking expertise and the prestige of their reputation in exchange for a stake in the profits generated from the joint wine. This was a partnership created to benefit both sides financially, not unlike the famous pairing of Napa's Robert Mondavi with Bordeaux's Lafite-Rothschild. Fred seemed to lament the fact that no Finger Lakes producer had ever entered into a partnership with a famous foreign partner.

"But those partnerships aren't really about great wine, are they?" I asked. "I mean, the wines might be good, but these are marriages of financial convenience, right?"

"They sell a lot of wine, and they're very effective," Fred responded.

"And we're not going to be able to attract that kind of valuable European partner without a larger scale of production."

"So is that your ultimate goal?"

"We're not pursuing anything like that," he said. "But we're trying to put ourselves and the region in a healthy position."

It is often said that every man becomes his father. Fred's comments indicated to me that he was well on his way in that regard; after all, there might not be Finger Lakes wines on a store shelf in Iowa, but there are indeed Dr. Frank's wines on store shelves in Michigan and Virginia and many other states. Willy created markets where none had previously existed. Fred was building on that theme.

On the short ride back over to the tasting room I asked Fred if there is any specific wine region or producer that he enjoys most. "A lot of people in the wine industry tend to drink beer at home," he said. "But of course I drink wines from around the world. It's important to do that when you're working to create world-class wines."

As we sat down in the empty tasting room Fred told stories of Konstantin's exploits. He insisted these were not embellished tales but the truth that captures the essence of a great man. From the time that Konstantin visited California to warn his counterparts that they needed to change rootstock or risk losing their vineyards ("Of course he was not taken seriously, and it led to a great financial loss for the American wine industry"), to his strong work ethic ("Dr. Frank worked a menial job, but it allowed him to buy that bus ticket"), Fred had a roster full of stories to share.

The history of Dr. Frank's includes the attraction of—and then the loss of—some of the Finger Lakes' best winemakers. Peter Bell made the wine at Dr. Frank for five years before leaving. Morten Hallgren left Dr. Frank to tend to his own operation at Ravines Wine Cellars. Johannes Reinhardt worked at Chateau Frank, but left before a year was up. Darren Bowker came home from Oregon to work at Dr. Frank, but left to take the head job at Villa Bellangelo on Seneca Lake.

Fred got defensive when I asked why so many talented winemakers had chosen not to stay at his family's operation. He insisted that Dr. Frank deserved credit for attracting such world-class talent, and who could argue?

Finally, after Fred talked about the pressure of increasing production in a region with potentially rough winters, I asked with a smile, "Could Dr. Frank be happy making 5,000 cases again?"

"No," he said. "We wouldn't be able to have all the family members work for the winery at that level of production. But it's not just our family that needs more production from the winery. The big challenge that we have is that Finger Lakes wines are not known outside of this state. For that to change, we have to have more volume of wine, first of all, and have the quality and the marketing to get noticed."

Fred's son Kyle is getting his degree in Wine Science from Cornell, and the family plan is to have Kyle eventually take over the head winemaking duties. As much as things had changed at the Dr. Frank winery over the years, it remains a family-led operation. Fred's sister Barbara still consults with the winery, despite turning down the head winemaking job in 1990. After Barbara's decision, and as each new winemaker eventually left, the family put together a plan for Kyle to move into the job. Fred speaks often about the value of multi-generation wineries, and Kyle will represent the fourth at Dr. Frank.

Perhaps this aggressive approach to expand production will yield the results Fred is seeking. No one would doubt the benefit of pushing Finger Lakes wines into new markets.

I shook Fred's hand and thanked him for his time. There was a part of me that wanted to ask to see the wine library underneath the property, but I knew it wasn't the right time. Rumor has it that the Frank family has kept a stash of some of the first bottles ever produced by Konstantin. Some day, I thought, it would be cool to see one.

Little did I know that one was about to fall into my lap.

* * *

I could barely believe the photograph, sent via email from a friend. The bottle in the picture said Dr. Konstantin Frank 1966 Johannisberg Riesling, but it did not make sense that a restaurant was selling such a bottle forty-three years later.

In Florida.

My mind raced. How did the restaurant get this wine? How did they know it was still worth drinking? How could it possibly be worth drinking at forty-three years old? If it was real, could I get one? And what would it smell and taste like?

A half case of Dr. Frank 1966 Riesling had been unearthed deep in the prodigious cellar of Bern's Steakhouse in Tampa, Florida. In the 1970s, Bern Laxer built a wine collection for his restaurant that was unrivaled in its diversity. Bottles came from the most storied regions, such as Bordeaux, as well as the less-heralded places like the Finger Lakes. Some unknown day in that fruitful decade, Bern acquired several bottles of the Dr. Frank wine during his travels. The bottles went to rest in ideal storage conditions, not to be touched for more than thirty years.

The current sommeliers at the restaurant knew it was a special group of bottles when they uncovered it during an inventory check, but they might not have known that it was the first commercial vintage at the historic Finger Lakes producer. The oldest bottles of Finger Lakes wine that appear on any restaurant wine list are typically found at the Village Tavern in Hammondsport on Keuka Lake. Those bottles date back to the late 1980s and early 1990s.

This was like discovering the Finger Lakes version of Lucy.

Outside the Dr. Frank facility, where a few odd bottles reside in the cellar, no known bottles exist of this wine—or any preceding the 1980s. I contacted the Bern's sommeliers to find out whether they might part with a bottle. They told me that they had sold a bottle to a dinner party in early December, where it was met with high praise, as impossible as that sounds.

The head sommelier explained that this was the last of the Dr. Frank collection and the restaurant would agree to sell me the bottle. He said that no one knew it existed because they don't publish their full wine list. "If we boast about rare bottles, there's a run on them," he said.

Friends occasionally ask why I cherish well-aged bottles, even when they tend to be past their prime. The answer would be found in that bottle of 1966 Dr. Frank Riesling—if it still had any vigor.

The bottle arrived safely and I decided to open it with two friends who had nearly as much curiosity as I did: Lenn Thompson, the founder and publisher of the *New York Cork Report*, and our Science Editor Tom Mansell. My wife joined us on a cold Western New York Saturday.

Lenn, a tall guy bursting with energy, walked in and immediately said, "Let's see this thing." I handed him the bottle, which included a gorgeous label depicting German grape harvesters wearing classic old clothes. It evoked *The Sound of Music*, and I liked it much more than any label currently in use in the Finger Lakes. Fred had told me that they abandoned the original label because it didn't display the Frank family name prominently enough.

"This is so cool," Lenn said, inspecting both sides of the label. He found that the back text was even more fascinating than the drawing on the front. I wondered if Konstantin himself had penned the text, which read as follows:

> "Natur Spaetlese"
>
> The delicious, fruity wine in this bottle represents a breakthrough in the wine industry in the eastern United States. The grapes for making this "Natur Spaetlese" wine have been harvested many days after the general picking of grapes was ended. Without amelioration or any

> other additions or ingredients. Only this over-ripeness is responsible that these wines developed their natural finest actual bouquet and the most noblest individuality. After years of painstaking research in our vineyards overlooking beautiful Keuka Lake, one of the picturesque Finger Lakes of New York State, we have finally achieved the impossible and proven that our "Natur Spaetlese" wines made continuous since 1957 exclusively from the European grape varieties of genuine wine grape can be the peers of some of the "GREAT GROWTHS" of Germany, France, and many another part of Europe.

Tom Mansell, a baby-faced scientist wise beyond his twenty-seven years, noticed that the top of the cork was covered with black mold. As we carefully removed the closure we saw that the mold stopped about halfway down and the rest of the cork was clean.

"It looks like a spent shell," Tom noted. "But it's in really impressive shape."

Most captivating of all was the wine's color. Over time, oxygen turns white wine orange or even brown. This 1966 wine was a glorious pale yellow. It had every appearance of a wine that had been bottled in the last twelve months

"This is going to be a lot better than vinegar," Lenn said with a smile, reminding me of my earlier prediction. I poured short glasses for the small group in the room and we buried our noses into the wine.

The aromatics were gorgeous and mature. My poor wife was stricken with a winter cold and couldn't smell a thing, but we could. Baked apple, creamy almond, and petrol. We were dazzled.

Of course, we were considerably less dazzled when we put the wine in our mouths. Its acidity was sharp and off balance, but the flavors neatly matched the nose and an ending note of that creamy almond helped mellow the sensation.

Our criticism of the wine quickly dissipated. We were simply thrilled by the experience. "There isn't anything like this, anywhere," Lenn said.

As Tom returned his nose to the glass he observed, "This is probably the oldest remaining Finger Lakes wine in existence. It's almost certainly the oldest wine still worth drinking."

It didn't prove that 1960s Finger Lakes Rieslings were world-class, but it demonstrated that Konstantin had the right idea when he endured the ridicule that came with planting Riesling on the slopes above the various lakes. This artifact before us told a simple, wonderful story: the winemaking in 1966 was less precise than we'd expect today, but it was happening in the right place. The wine was like a window into the past, a chance to experience the challenges and triumph of an awakening region. As for Riesling, this was the right grape in the right spot.

I thought of what had changed in the time since this wine was bottled. I thought of the Frank family, driven and competitive, pushing the scale of production. I thought of where Dr. Konstantin's family winery was headed, and I hoped for more world-class wines in the future.

But in that moment, none of that mattered. The only concern was the history in the glass, which will always be part of the Frank legacy.

THIRTEEN

The Tierce Brothers

THERE'S SOMETHING INTOXICATING ABOUT A SUMMER MORNING'S drive with fog rolling off the Finger Lakes. When the sun cuts the fog and the lake edge comes into view, the destination becomes irrelevant. The drive is its own reward.

On the third day of summer I was making just such a drive, but with the added excitement of what lay at the end of my travels. At Peter Bell's invitation I would join a small group of winemakers for the Tierce blending trials—they had come to refer to themselves as the "Tierce Brothers." We would meet in the bowels of Red Newt Wine Cellars and work all day.

This was like a film fanatic getting invited to join Steven Spielberg and George Lucas for the editing of *Star Wars*.

My excitement was tempered by the nausea-inducing news that Anthony Road Wine Company had just posted a job opening for the head winemaking position. They were posting Johannes Reinhardt's job, and it confused a lot of people in the industry.

Peter Bell explained that it was all part of a new strategy. The German's immigration status was in serious trouble. The American government had continually rejected his application for permanent worker status, each time deciding that while Johannes is an excellent winemaker, he's simply taking a job away from an American. The bureaucrats refused to consider the fact that Johannes's employer had set very strong training and experience requirements for the job, and no American with those credentials had applied for the position.

Johannes's recent appeal had been rejected once again, which would force him to return to Germany to reapply for temporary status as he made his last-ditch appeal to the U.S. Labor Department. Johannes's lawyer, working with the owner of the Anthony Road Wine Company, had devised this new strategy—a final effort to get the German his green card. They decided that the winery would post Johannes's job—and they would hire any American who could match or exceed Johannes's training, qualifications, and recognitions. It was a chance to prove to the American government that this talented German was not stealing a job from a winemaker born in the United States.

We all knew what was on the line, and we admired Johannes for keeping his cool throughout what must have been a devastatingly tumultuous process. He knew he might soon be forced to leave the United States, walking away from the friends who had grown into his family. It was going to be on everyone's minds, but we resolved not to bring it up during the Tierce blending trials.

As Peter explained, today was going to be about Tierce.

Since the birth of the Tierce project in 2005, it's been difficult to explain the concept to wine-industry professionals outside New York State. In the Finger Lakes, collaboration has become a powerful and necessary ethos. But in other winemaking regions it typically doesn't work that way. Quite the opposite, in fact.

In Italy, winemakers have very nearly sabotaged their own efforts by tarnishing the reputation of one of the country's greatest red wines. The small Tuscan hill town of Montalcino is home to Brunello, a wine made of the world's richest Sangiovese grapes. In the cutthroat race to impress critics, a handful of the biggest winemakers in Montalcino broke the rules. Brunello must, by law, be 100 percent Sangiovese. In March of 2008, prosecutors in the central Italian town of Siena obtained evidence that some winemakers were cutting a small percentage of their Sangiovese with Bordeaux grapes to enhance the color and texture. Those winemakers didn't trust their own efforts to create world-class wines. They didn't trust the capabilities of the Sangiovese grape—even in the place where it thrived. They wanted to increase production levels. They were desperate to get ahead of their neighbors. When their neighbors found out, they didn't confront the cheaters privately. Instead, they decided to leak the scandal to the prosecutors and the press. Within days the reputation of *every* winemaker—even the nearly two hundred Brunello producers who steadfastly followed the rules—was in jeopardy. Wine buyers started to question the integrity of what they were drinking. Sales stalled. When my wife and I spent a week in Tuscany that April, one of the smallest Brunello makers told me that his colleagues had cut off their own legs by trying to trip up the competition.

In this context it would be difficult to imagine the Tierce project happening almost anywhere else. It began in early 2005 when Johannes asked two of his colleagues to share their resources and ideas on a joint Riesling. Johannes, having broken free of the constraints of the old-world traditions back home, wanted to offer his expertise to his friendly competitors, and he hoped to learn from their contrasting styles. He didn't know what they would say, but he felt it was time to float the concept to two of the winemakers he admired most: Red Newt Wine Cellars' Dave Whiting and Fox Run's Peter Bell.

Both men said yes immediately.

"There's no downside to sharing knowledge," Peter told Johannes. "I've yet to find any reason not to share what we know. On top of that, the people making bad wines are dragging the entire region down. It's just a better idea to open your doors and share what we know, even if it helps a competitor."

Privately, Johannes felt that Peter's response went a long way in vindicating his decision to leave his parents' winery and come to the United States to make wine. He wondered what they would think about such a partnership, but he didn't really care.

The winemakers had first decided that each of the three wineries would offer an equal amount of its finest Riesling to create the blended wine. But it wasn't quite so simple. The winemakers brought multiple Riesling samples, taken from the massive stainless-steel tanks in their facilities, and the blending process involved hours—sometimes days—of trial and error.

In the early days of the program, some critics scoffed that the collaboration stripped away the diversity and individualism of the wines. How, they asked, could a blended wine sourced from a wide range of vineyards show a sense of place? They worried that the unique characteristics found in the wineries' individual Rieslings would melt together to create something bland.

But what they discovered was that Tierce had successfully taken the attributes of each winery's Riesling, combining to create a wine with a regional profile. It didn't carry the magic of a distinctive single-vineyard wine, but that was never the point.

Then the project got an unexpected boost when *Wine Review Online* published its editors' choices for the nine Wines of the Year. There, in a list that included French Champagne and Napa Cabernet Sauvignon, was the 2005 Tierce Riesling. The reviewer wrote: "The very best Finger Lakes Rieslings are bone dry. They offer riveting flavors and can proudly hold their own with top dry Rieslings from Alsace, Australia, Germany, or anywhere else in the world. Of all the exciting Finger Lakes wines I tasted, Tierce was the most enthralling."

Other publications seemed stunned the collaboration was permissible at all. "This type of collaboration simply isn't done," wrote the *Finger Lakes Wine Gazette*, adding this hyperbole: "It's forbidden." *The Detroit News* observed, "Winemakers have done a rare thing in the Finger Lakes."

Peter had informed me that today would be a different kind of blending session. For the first time, the winemakers had chosen not to make a blended Riesling, instead opting to take advantage of the hot 2007 vintage to make a blended red wine. There were more options for blending, and there would be more pressure to get it right. Given the track record of the Tierce Riesling, I wondered if this was a risk they should be taking. Finger Lakes red wine does not have even a shadow of the reputation of its Riesling.

I walked in and found Dave and his assistant winemaker Brandon sitting at the bar in Red Newt's bistro. Johannes, accompanied by his new assistant, arrived a few minutes later, followed by Peter and Fox Run's assistant winemaker, Tricia Renshaw. They were carrying jugs and bottles filled with the various wines they had chosen for the blending. Already I could see that I had made a mistake with my attire for the day. I was wearing a black golf shirt and charcoal pants with shiny black shoes.

"Nice duds," Peter quipped. "Don't worry—wine comes right out in the wash." He looked like someone who had dressed in the dark at a Hawaiian thrift store.

Dave led us to an unmarked door in the hallway past the bistro and we descended into the winery. A dozen stainless-steel vats gave the chilly air the pleasant, unmistakable aroma of young wine. Barrels and cardboard boxes were scattered among the vats, and on the edge of the room a long table was set for the blending. Short wineglasses crowded the table—I figured there were at least fifty—and spit jars filled out the rest of the space.

We had the kind of energy that calls to mind a group of twelve-year-olds sprinting out onto a baseball diamond, ready for the first inning. My goal was to stay out of the way. I planned to remain silent and simply absorb as much as I could. Even the most devoted wine lovers don't get to witness events like this, so I planned to respectfully enjoy it.

I grabbed a chair and sat next to one of the steel tanks, a safe distance away from the table. *I can't break anything if I can't touch it*, I thought.

Johannes was having none of it.

"Get over here!" he said. "We've set a place for you." When I hesitated, he said, "Your perspective is going to be valuable to us. C'mon, you big baby!" Most winemakers I've met would be uneasy with a writer in the room during such an important task. This group demanded I actually pitch in.

We started by pouring each of the wines brought by the winemakers. There were a dozen, composed of Cabernet Franc, Lemberger, Syrah, Merlot, and Cabernet Sauvignon.

Once everyone had the wines in their glasses the conversation halted and we began round one. I cautiously watched as the winemakers buried their noses deep into the first set of glasses. I did the same. Everyone seemed to have their own approach, so I dispensed with my nerves and set about my job. I sniffed, I swirled, I studied the color. After an initial taste, I spat and tasted again, hoping to encounter every layer of the wine. Then I scribbled my impressions down in my notebook and moved on to the next.

The wines were stunning in their individuality. A common complaint—and often a fair one—is that red wines from the Finger Lakes tend to offer little complexity, so even the good ones are rather thin and predictable. On this particular morning, it was clear that amid a sea of mediocre red wines were some gems that demonstrated the grapes' potential.

The hardest part was convincing myself to work, to move on to the next wine, and to spit. In my notes on Red Newt's Cabernet Franc, I wrote: "So damn good I'm not spitting as much as I should."

I knew that if I didn't start spitting more, I'd be the drunk guest at the nondrinking party.

The next several hours saw a mix of exhilarating moments and frustrating roadblocks. The second round fooled me into believing there would be a quick resolution, a master blend easily decided.

Each one of us had the task of putting together our own nine-part blend. Tasting blind through the nine-part trials, I was thrilled to see that the winemakers liked some of the characteristics of the wine I had put together. I had chosen to use multiple parts of Anthony Road's Lemberger, a variety that is relatively new to the Finger Lakes but shows tremendous promise.

As we worked through each blend, the descriptions of the wines flew around the room with such velocity that they were practically bouncing off the stainless-steel tanks.

"I love the blueberry pie flavors in blend four!"

"Ooh, that's good, but I'm looking for more of that tobacco that we see in the second."

"What else do you get in blend five?"

"Orange peel."

"Cracked black pepper."

"Just a whiff of nutmeg."

It was no surprise that Tricia Renshaw was leading the discussion on what each blend tasted like. I watched as they debated without getting overly heated. It was a monumental task made more challenging by the fact that these winemakers brought their own styles and preferences. Ego tends to prevail in such scenarios, but ego was essentially absent in the Red Newt cellar.

Finally Johannes made a suggestion that involved one small tweak to one of the blends, and everyone seemed to agree that it was the answer. There was a palpable sense of momentum in the room. After sorting through the many beakers and bottles, Johannes returned with a blend and a smile on his face to match. He sent it around the table.

I was terrified to discover that I didn't like it. How can it be so different, so off? Keeping my mouth shut, my eyes wandered around the table, which had fallen quieter than a church pew.

After an uncomfortable minute, Dave said slowly, "It's kind of . . . a donut."

In other words, it was a flop.

Winemakers use the term donut to describe a wine that has no middle, no substance. This blend had lost much of the vivaciousness of the previous version. "I'm sorry," Peter said, "but I'd never put my name on this and I would never let you guys put your names on this, either."

For a few moments we sat in dejected silence. Then Johannes came up with the best possible next step: "Let's go have lunch."

Back upstairs, the bistro was buzzing with about a dozen tables filled with diners. Dave directed us to a table in the center of the room, long enough to seat all seven of us.

We decided to order about half the items on the menu and pass them around to share. The waiter started us off with a white vegetable lasagna filled with woodland mushrooms and spinach and finished with a garlic cream sauce. I sank my fork into the lasagna and it nearly melted away on both sides.

As we slowly worked through the lasagna, my favorite kind of storm paid a visit. The brilliant blue skies flickered to a blue-gray and then nearly to black. We could see the wall of rain pushing toward us from about a mile away. Diners who had been enjoying the outdoor air hustled inside, carefully moving their plates to safer settings. Lightning, with crisp and singular bolts, arrived first, followed almost immediately by the distinctive song of hard rain. The bistro was silent, with diners enjoying the violent rhythm of the storm.

The waiter broke our concentration when he arrived with the second course: chicken, rapini, and white bean soup. The rapini was enjoying its peak of the season and Deb Whiting was adamant about using local ingredients. As we settled into the soup, Deb emerged from the kitchen to check on the table next to us. When she asked for the diners' assessment of the meal, they stood up. An elderly gentleman began to clap and the other five members of his party burst into applause. Deb, clearly moved but caught off guard, nodded sheepishly and thanked them. *I don't think I've ever seen that before*, I thought.

Johannes launched into his idea for an entirely new blend for the Tierce Red as the waiter showed up with stuffed burritos. We divided our attention between the food and Johannes's proposal as the German gesticulated wildly.

"I've figured something out!" he announced, nearly knocking himself out of his chair. "Blend 4-A is a swimmer. Blend 4-B is a *diver*." He was now mimicking a diving motion to the laughter of his colleagues. "It's a diver because it's deep. You know, it has depth. Deepness."

"Your English has come a long way," Peter said with a grin, and then. "It's a good place to restart."

They could easily have wrapped up the blending hours earlier, but no one in that room was going to waste the best harvest weather in a generation by settling for an inferior wine. A historic vintage does not mean that making great wine will be easy. It means that, with focus, a good wine can become great.

The afternoon blending brought the kinds of disagreements that can sink friendships, let alone professional partnerships. But the winemakers never made their disagreements personal. As the hours passed I was struck by how significantly different the wine would be if even one of the nine parts were changed.

As the hours wore on we grew quieter in evaluating each new iteration. We were tired and intensely focused on unlocking the optimal blend. Eventually someone came back with a new combination that was far different and obviously superior. It was an aromatic lightning bolt, and unlike so many previous blends, it wasn't awkward or clunky. This wine was like velvet sheets.

I kept my head low, trying to conceal my reaction as I glanced around the table. Brandon and Tricia were smiling like they were auditioning for a toothpaste commercial. Dave was looking at Peter, quickly arching his eyebrows in satisfaction.

"Looks like it's time to vote," Peter announced.

One by one, this weary group approved this blend to become Red Tierce. They had saved my vote for last and when I said, "Yes," a cheer rocked the cellar and Johannes pounded a celebratory fist on the table. The sounds of shattering tasting glasses temporarily silenced us.

Johannes shrugged in embarrassment. "Let's say it this way: oops."

The broken glass was a small price to pay for the success we had finally achieved. But Peter was quick to caution against any grand proclamations for the new Tierce.

"This should have a real chance to become the best red wine ever made in the Finger Lakes," Brandon said.

"Too early for that," Peter said with a grimace. "We won't know what we've got for quite some time. It's possible this wine won't be released until 2011. And even then it will need more time to really come together."

"Wow," I said. "What a tease."

Peter laughed. "I used to think women were the ultimate test of patience and willpower. As I get older it's clear to me that that distinction belongs to wine."

Then he added, "But I always say that the best wine comes from a cool climate in a warm year. We had exactly that."

Johannes threw a soft elbow to Peter's ribs. "And we had a little help from our friends, too!"

I couldn't help but think of Johannes's looming immigration disaster. I said nothing—it would have ruined a triumphant moment—but I felt that sense of nausea returning.

* * *

The night before the awards ceremony for the New York State Governor's Cup, Johannes Reinhardt received a phone call. The committee announcing the winner wanted to make sure the team from Anthony Road was there at the Watkins Glen Harbor Hotel to hear the announcement.

Each year, two dozen wine critics from around the world judge more than eight hundred New York State wines. They hand out awards for a long list of categories, but the one that matters most is the Governor's Cup. This goes to the critics' choice for Best Wine of the Year. It's an award that brings prestige—and immediate cash, with the winning wine selling out within days.

I wondered what this kind of honor might do for Johannes's immigration status. If Anthony Road were to win, how could any bureaucrat declare that this German winemaker was simply doing a job that any American could do?

The ballroom was packed for the announcement. Wine writers filled several tables, but most of the room was packed with Finger Lakes winery owners and employees. There was electricity in the air as the master of ceremonies approached the podium.

He thanked everyone for participating and explained that the New York Wine and Grape Foundation, which runs the event, is proud to attract so many high-wattage critics to help decide the awards. "Now, without further ado . . ." he said, drawing a few laughs.

"The Governor's Cup goes to Anthony Road Wine Company for the 2008 Semi-Dry Riesling."

The room simply exploded. Owner John Martini got up first and halfway to the podium he realized that Johannes was still seated, so he pointed to his winemaker and shouted, "Let's go!"

Johannes reluctantly joined his boss on stage as the audience continued its thunderous approval. More than a minute passed, with every table standing and cheering. They were applauding the outstanding wine, and the Anthony Road Wine Company, but I sensed that more than anything they were applauding a man who was desperate for a chance to stay in the Finger Lakes.

Finally John Martini spoke, with Johannes standing over his shoulder. The German did not wear the expression of a man receiving the honor of his career. He looked like a man getting ready for hernia surgery. The notion of a room full of people applauding him was almost more than this painfully humble man could bear.

John did the talking, keeping the remarks terse and focused. He spoke about his son, Peter, who managed the excellent vineyards. And he concluded with a remark about his winemaker: "Credit also goes to Johannes Reinhardt, who has a dedication to this process that few have."

Once again the room burst into applause, with Johannes looking thrilled to get off the stage. Some in the audience had tears in their eyes as they congratulated the Anthony Road family.

When the ceremony was over I asked Johannes if this award would cement his immigration status and allow him to stay. "I thought about that," he said. "But let's be honest. I didn't think we'd still be dealing with this, so I can't predict anything anymore. If it happens, it happens. But Imelda and I have accepted the possibility that we could have to go somewhere else."

For a moment we said nothing. I sensed in him a serenity. He did not seem to be defeated by this process; he seemed to be prepared to accept defeat as part of life.

"This final effort is going to work out for you," I said.

"Maybe. But we have done all that we can. This award is more than I dreamed. If we are not meant to live here and work here and build a family here, we'll find happiness in another country."

Then a faint, wounded smile crossed his lips. "But everything we want is right here."

* * *

So now we wait. Johannes's Labor Department application would take months to process, and his attorney explained that he might not know the final decision until 2011. Contrary to what we've learned from pop music, the waiting is not the hardest part. The hardest part is even having to contemplate what a man would do if forced to tear apart a life he had built through determined, honest work.

In many ways, Johannes Reinhardt embodies the future of the region he has grown to call home. All across the region there are outstanding wine producers that mirror some of Johannes's best attributes. He brought old-world winemaking skills and opened his doors for anyone who wanted to share ideas, calling to mind the warm-hearted family operations making ever-improving wines: the Stamp family at Lakewood Vineyards on Seneca Lake, the Wiltberger family at Keuka Spring on Keuka Lake, the Hunts of Hunt Country, also on Keuka. Johannes carries no pretense to his job, reminding me of the winemakers who are ego-free despite tremendous talent: Rob Thomas at Shalestone on Seneca Lake, Vinny Aliperti of Atwater and Billsboro wineries on Seneca, Aaron Roisen at Hosmer on Cayuga. The German is carving a new path, just as Glenora and Fulkerson had done on Seneca Lake, and just as Lucas had done over on Cayuga. And Johannes is unafraid of using the blunt language that is occasionally necessary to push for higher quality. I see that drive in the wines of Damiani, Hazlitt, Standing Stone, and Lamoreaux Landing on Seneca Lake. It is evident in the wines of Rooster Hill and Keuka Lake Vineyards on Keuka. Imagine Moore Winery shows it on Canandaigua Lake. And perhaps no one shows more determination than Bob Madill of Sheldrake Point on Cayuga Lake.

Johannes Reinhardt's dream is the dream of this region. It's about finding happiness in a land made for growing grapes. It's about sharing that happiness with family and friends.

On an autumn evening, with another frenetic harvest finally concluded, I poured a glass of Anthony Road's 2008 Semi-Dry Riesling. There is a case in my cellar, and I will ration the remaining bottles with care. I plan to open the last bottle with Johannes and Imelda in the distant future, and I hope I won't have to fly to Europe to join them. Something special is happening around these lakes. This story is too good for him to miss the ending.

Epilogue

July 1, 2011
Rochester, NY

When the phone rang, I didn't think anything of it. Not the first time, anyway. I was sitting in court, covering a case in Rochester, New York. My phone, set to vibrate, was easy to ignore.

But then it rang again—and again. My wife was calling, as were members from the Finger Lakes winemaking community. And when the fourth person called in a span of three minutes, I became gripped with a sense of dread. For reasons I couldn't explain, I felt that something must be wrong.

Then a text came in from a friend, with the message, "Evan, Deb Whiting was in a car accident last night!"

No further explanation. But I knew. I was sickened, and scared to confirm what my stomach was telling me. I fired back, "Is she okay?"

The devastating answer: "No."

* * *

If it sounds like hyperbole, it's not far off to say that before Deb Whiting, the Finger Lakes culinary scene was stuck on fast food and faster food. A few higher-end restaurants inevitably sprang up and then shut down. There was no sense of regional purpose or cohesion.

In the 1990s, Deb worked to imbue the region with an appreciation for local produce. When she launched Red Newt Bistro, it was the most localized menu in the area, and she never hesitated to explain why.

"This isn't a trend," she had told me over dinner one night several years ago. "People understand that local food is often better food, and it's better for them, and it's clearly better for the local economy. There's too much going for the local food movement to see it fade away. It's here, and it's only going to get stronger."

She was right, of course, but it required more than just one great restaurant. Deb Whiting became the regional culinary conscience, helping guide other chefs, convincing them to work with local meats and cheeses. She headed the Finger Lakes Culinary Bounty, an organization created to bring attention and support to regional farms and restaurants.

At her memorial service, on the Tuesday after her passing, her friends expected a few hundred people might come out. It should be no surprise that they had underestimated by roughly a thousand.

* * *

Red Newt Cellars and Bistro is set atop a long hill. On the night of Deb's service, the line of cars and people stretched out the door, through the parking lot, and down the road toward the lake. Winemakers joined growers, chefs, customers, politicians, family, and friends. The Whiting family was determined to make this a celebration of Deb's accomplishments, and dozens of industry professionals had volunteered to staff the food and drink. In every corner of the building they poured wine, donated by ten neighboring producers. They served food, prepared by local chefs or brought by guests. They offered dessert or sparkling wine or a hug.

Like so many others, I was overcome with grief and—I confess—a sense of anger. Here was a woman in her undeniable prime, making an impact on a daily basis, improving lives. There is no fairness in death, but in this case, it felt shatteringly unjust.

But in that moment of darkness, the Finger Lakes community demonstrated that the spirit of regional collaboration was not solely a marketing slogan or vague idea. It was real, and it was necessary. It was the only way that Dave Whiting was going to come through this tragedy.

How was he going to run the restaurant, I wondered? The first answer was that Deb's staff was so well trained, so professional, that they could do much of the work already. And during Deb's service, dozens of people volunteered to come to the restaurant and wait tables or clean dishes or work the tasting bar at the winery. Dave would need time away, and the hundreds of people who had come out to pay respects to Deb wanted Dave to know that he would not have to deal with this loss alone.

I found it remarkable that Dave could even stand that night to hug the people who waited in line an hour to offer their sympathy. In a shirt and tie, his face still bruised from the car accident, he looked like a beaten man, but not broken. When Morgan and I finally reached the front of the line, Dave smiled, took our hands, and joined them together. "You two are living the dream," he said. "Embrace it."

This is a loss that will hurt the Finger Lakes for a long time, but the pain does not have to triumph. Already, local chefs are carrying forward the ideals carved out by Deb Whiting and her prolific career. They are welcoming the produce from more regional farms, and they're hosting more events together to educate their customers about the value of eating local food. The sharp pain of loss will eventually evolve into a dull throb. The Finger Lakes region is a better place thanks to Deb Whiting, and grief doesn't have to have the last word.

Late in the evening, Dave Whiting stood on a chair to address the packed dining room. He referred to his wife as a great mother, daughter, lover, and friend. After a few short remarks, he raised a glass. The toast echoed across the bistro, into the winery, and out into the street: "To Deb." That is exactly where the credit for so much of the culinary success of this region goes.

To Deb, indeed.

September 4, 2011
Geneva, NY

When the phone rang, Imelda Reinhardt was startled. Who, she wondered, would be calling at nine o'clock on a Sunday night? She and Johannes had tried to watch a movie, but their minds were elsewhere. Tomorrow was Labor Day, and while most of their friends had the day off, the Reinhardts would be working. After picking up a pizza and a six of beer, they found themselves locked into that familiar Sunday-night routine: Johannes doing dishes, Imelda packing lunches.

Imelda was the first to notice Johannes's phone ringing. She handed it to him and then went back to packing lunch.

From across the room, Imelda felt herself studying her husband's face. Often she could discern who was on the phone from his expressions or the way he talked. This time, he was largely quiet, only occasionally saying, "Uh-huh."

After several minutes she had grown curious enough to walk over to her husband and simply ask whom he was talking to. But before she could, Johannes said, "John, don't joke with me, okay?"

Imelda stopped. She instantly knew what the call was about. John Martini, owner of Anthony Road Wine Company, was calling about Johannes's green card application. What troubled Imelda was the fact that she still could not read her husband. Was he happy or devastated?

The next sixty seconds must have felt like hours to Imelda as she strained to discover some clue from Johannes's face. He was nodding occasionally but still betraying no emotion. She wanted to shout but could only wait.

Then she saw it, and she knew. In the corner of Johannes's eye, a tear had formed. It was, in one drop, the bubbling up of seven years of hope, of rejection, of persistence, of uncertainty. It was coming to the surface because it was all about to be over.

Johannes said quietly into the phone, "We're coming down. We'll be there in twenty minutes." Then he hung up and turned slowly to face his wife.

"So," she said, "did you get it? Is that what happened?"

He exhaled and closed his eyes. "We got it."

For a moment Johannes and Imelda both looked down, not overwhelmed with joy but instead enveloped by a feeling of peace they had longed for.

"Darling, they have sparkling wine ready for us," Johannes said. "Can you drive?"

* * *

What Johannes and Imelda's friends struggled to understand was why they had never seriously pursued plans to move to another country. After all, everyone knew that this application was essentially the last hope. Why not be ready for the next step, as painful as it might be? Johannes and Imelda loved Greece in particular, and they were comfortable traveling the world. It would seem logical that they'd begin to establish options beyond the Finger Lakes.

But the answer is rooted in faith. They often prayed together, and Johannes and Imelda routinely asked for spiritual guidance. They knew there would be no obvious announcement, no overt message from God. But they believed they would both feel a change in direction if they were meant to leave the Finger Lakes. And even with time running out on Johannes's applications, they never had felt right in looking elsewhere; not with seriousness, anyway. If their friends saw it as an obdurate refusal to confront reality, Johannes and Imelda knew it was simply a position of faith.

Before leaving for Anthony Road, Johannes and Imelda stopped to pray together. The car ride that followed was silent, with Johannes occasionally squeezing his wife's hand and looking over at her, smiling.

When they walked into the kitchen, they found five sparkling wine glasses on the counter. John and Ann Martini, who had sponsored Johannes's immigration applications, were smiling broadly. Their son, Peter, the vineyard manager at the winery, had joined them. John passed out the glasses, then said, "Johannes, I really think you got it. Do you want to see the letter?"

Johannes didn't hesitate. "Yes please."

The letter had arrived the day before, but John had been in New York City on business. Johannes read it quickly while Ann kept tugging at him. "Is that it? Is that it, Johannes?"

Finally the German turned to her, his face brightening. "Yes, Ann. That's it."

The short, white-haired woman launched herself at the broad-shouldered winemaker, who laughed. He was their son now, and they had suffered disappointments with him.

It felt like the end, but Johannes knew it was only the beginning. For across the road, a piece of land prepares for his hand. He had waited for the chance to make his own mark on the hills and the vines that cover them, sloping down toward the lakes that protect them. For seven years he didn't know if he would be allowed to create that story. Someone else was always in charge of his fate. Now the doubt had lifted and the future stretched out before him, unwritten.

Index

Acknowledgments

WHEN I FIRST VERBALIZED THE IDEA THAT BECAME THIS BOOK, my wife convinced me it was not preposterous. She told me it could be done despite my joyously erratic work schedule for my employer in Rochester. Without her repeated urgings, this book would have remained an idea.

I could not conceivably list every generous person I met on this journey. This is a book that could have contained many more chapters, considering the talents and compelling stories behind the people who receive only passing mention on these pages. I am grateful for their willingness to meet with me, indulge my questions, and scour their memories—even when they didn't know if it would result in a featured chapter. I have found that people in the wine industry are unfailingly warm and thoughtful, and that is a treasure to be celebrated.

A group of family and friends became essential advisors over the past two years, reading chapters and offering the vital and punishing feedback that made this book stronger. My deepest thanks to Katy Lumb, Colleen Dawson, Rosemary Pennington, Lois Christensen, Darren Mark, Christian Dawson, Amy Cheatle, Joy Morris, Steve Patchett, and George and Vicki Dornberger.

Joanna Purdy is the brilliant designer who created the map for this book.

Lenn Thompson encouraged me to write for the New York Cork Report, which will stand as one of the best decisions of my career. His high standards and good judgment helped me in this book—and continue to help me improve as a writer.

My colleagues at WHAM-TV have demonstrated what real journalism is, and I hope that is reflected here.

Carlo DeVito and the group at Sterling took a significant chance on this project. I have worked tirelessly to reward their decision and I will never forget the professionalism they brought to this effort.

Cheryl and Don Burke told me, when I was eight years old, that I should continue to write no matter what else I do. My brothers Ryan and Drew might not realize that I mine their considerable writing talents in an effort to improve my own. Phil Dawson kept this book focused through his withering and painfully thorough edits. I simultaneously dreaded and loved his phone calls.

Morgan is the conscience of this book. She knows the land and she has grown to know the people. She shared most of these experiences with me, and she ensured they would be faithfully brought to the page. I cannot imagine a more ideal traveling companion.